ARTHUR YOUNG GUIDE TO FINANCING FOR GROWTH

ARTHUR YOUNG GUIDE TO FINANCING FOR GROWTH

Ten Alternatives for Raising Capital

ROBERT R. OWEN
DANIEL R. GARNER
DENNIS S. BUNDER

JOHN WILEY & SONS

New York • Chichester • Brisbane • Toronto • Singapore

This publication is designed to provide accurate and
authoritative information in regard to the subject
matter covered. It is sold with the understanding that
the publisher is not engaged in rendering legal, accounting,
or other professional service. If legal advice or other
expert assistance is required, the services of a competent
professional person should be sought. *From a Declaration
of Principles jointly adopted by a Committee of the
American Bar Association and a Committee of Publishers.*

Library of Congress Cataloging in Publication Data:

Owen, Robert R. (Robert Randolph)
  Arthur Young guide to financing for growth.

  1. Small business—Finance.   2. Business enterprises—Finance.
3. Capital.   I. Garner, Daniel R.   II. Bunder, Dennis S.   III. Title.
HG4027.7.O94 1986   658.1'522   86-1612
ISBN 0-471-81946-8

ISBN 0-471-85007-1 (pbk)

Printed in the United States of America

10 9 8 7 6 5 4 3 2

PREFACE

In the life of an entrepreneur at the helm of a small or midsize company, one of the most interesting and potentially rewarding experiences you will have is raising capital to take advantage of growth opportunities.

Financing for growth, the subject of this book, is also surprising, for nothing in your business life is likely to prepare you for the limitless variety of methods available to fill your capital needs. At some point, your company's survival will require more research and development, new products, product improvements, modern factories, wider markets, or some other manifestation of growth. Financing this growth will then bring you into the world of the financiers—banks, venture capitalists, and investment bankers—who will sell your stock to the public, and government agencies with outright loans and loan guarantees. It also will bring you in close contact with business advisors, such as the accountants and consultants at our firm, Arthur Young, whose contributions to this book are based on their knowledge and experience in helping businesses mesh their capital-raising strategies with their overall business strategies.

Through our work with hundreds of growing companies, we have seen that the suppliers of capital have been nothing if not imaginative in devising techniques to match your requirements, and that they have been equally creative in their expectations of how you will pay them for risking their money.

As methods differ, so do the suppliers. They have different goals and operating styles: some are conservative, while others relish risk in the hope of greater reward. Some will take no hand in the running of your company, while others will move in aggressively as an active participant in management. If government is the lender, the scenario changes further since the principal motivation is often to achieve a social goal and save jobs. Keeping current with this changing picture is literally impossible for anyone whose focus is running the day-to-day affairs of a company and plotting its future. Historically, change has been a major factor behind the raising of money. Periodically, great events have occurred that launched significant bursts of growth and demands for capital. For example, during the Civil War the need for great quantities of supplies gave sudden impetus to mass production, which had more or less languished until then. Similarly, when the economies of many European and Asian nations were in ruins at the close of World War II, this made global operations feasible for American companies.

In recent years, we have seen how high technology companies have created a computer-driven revolution in information handling that is transforming even the smallest of businesses. New products and technological processes created a feverish growth environment and a huge need to raise capital.

Another element also recently entered the picture. It is the distinct turn toward less government regulation in the belief that this will spur competition and encourage more aggressive, imaginative, and better-managed companies to search for new opportunities in the best tradition of old-fashioned entrepreneurship. This, too, has fueled the need for growth capital.

By any measurement, growth financing has become a growth industry of its own. There is more money available from more sources and in a truly amazing variety of instruments and strategies than we could have imagined only a few years ago.

The purpose of this book is to help entrepreneurs and those professionals who advise them get a clear, current picture of this ever-expanding array of financing methods. In drawing upon our own experience, as well as those of our colleagues in Arthur Young's Entrepreneurial Services Group and other areas of our firm, we have sought to provide an array of professional insights. You will read how

the different methods work, learn about the advantages and disadvantages of the various financing techniques and the kind of outside
help from which you might benefit.

Our hope is that you find this book both interesting and useful.
We also hope that you find it a reliable reference for your bookshelf,
readily at hand the next time a growth opportunity begins to take
shape on your company's horizon.

BOB OWEN
DAN GARNER
DENNIS BUNDER

New York, New York
April 1986

ACKNOWLEDGMENTS

The scope of experience reflected in this book is the result of contributions from many professionals at Arthur Young. As accountants and consultants, we advise and help small- and medium-sized companies select and gain the means of financing that appear right for them. We have learned from our vast experience that few business activities are more critical than raising capital; and all of us thought we could make an especially meaningful contribution by sharing our knowledge in this area with growing businesses.

The Arthur Young contributors are:

Jerome Engel, San Francisco
Harry Casari, San Diego
Steve Burrill, San Francisco
George Fink, Houston
Robert Borsch, Dallas
Robert Center, Chicago
John Staley, Chicago
James Needham, New York
Edmund Hubler, Dallas

Diane Blount, Atlanta
Larry Davidson, Providence

Other important contributions were made by a number of Arthur Young professionals, including Jack Sadden, Dallas; Robert Auten, Dallas; Keith Phillips, Providence; Douglas O'Brien, San Francisco; and Karen Shaw, Chicago. Special thanks also go to David Pearson, who provided important technical analysis and review. Ralph Zeuthan helped in the writing and Phyllis Arkwright provided especially valuable help as a writer, an editor, and coordinator of the manuscript.

Finally, we thank Mort Meyerson, Arthur Young's director of communications, who first suggested this book, and then planned and helped us develop it.

R. O.
D. B.
D. G.

CONTENTS

ARTHUR YOUNG GUIDE TO FINANCING FOR GROWTH

1

TRENDS IN FINANCING

Recent developments in raising capital for growth through:

Capital markets can and do tighten quickly. Chief executives and owner managers are, by necessity, becoming more innovative in their approach to securing finance.

Maturing companies are finding they have to use a variety of techniques to obtain the money they need to continue their growth.

New venture financing and public offerings are volatile partially because investors are not realizing anticipated gains. As a result, a new, more complex financing environment exists today.

With tighter markets, companies must seriously consider alternative financing, everything from the traditional to the avant-garde—credit cards with high spending limits, lines of credit from suppliers, and loans or investments from customers. Some even suggest starting up a quick profit company to finance the larger, more important venture.

Leasing, debt financing, joint ventures, research and development partnerships, mergers and acquisitions, tax strategies, and financing from positive cash flow are some of the most promising techniques for raising capital.

The following is a brief insight into many of the trends in financing for growth.

BUSINESS COMBINATIONS

As a source of capital, business combinations include mergers, acquisitions, joint ventures, pooled resource groups, and one of the newest and fastest growing combinations—collaborative ventures between small and large companies. The latter can take various forms such as licensing or selling manufacturing rights, distribution rights, or actual technology, often in conjunction with private equity investments. Structuring and timing are critical to the success of collaborative ventures.

LEASING

Equipment/asset leasing, including the sale and subsequent lease-back of an asset, is the second largest source of capital, especially for companies with sales of less than $2 million. Leasing ranks behind only public offerings as the major source of funds for small to midsized companies. As smaller businesses are reluctant to tie up cash in purchasing equipment, they expand their capital with asset lease arrangements.

Leasing arrangements can take various forms, offering a flexibility in negotiated terms that can affect a company's balance sheet. For instance, certain lease with option to buy arrangements can be deemed, by the IRS, to represent installment payments thereby canceling the lease fee tax deduction. On the plus side, the lessor can agree to pass along the investment tax credit on the leased item for the lessee to claim.

Whether leasing assets or selling current assets and then leasing them back, the cash flow benefits can be greater than purchasing an item with borrowed funds.

RESEARCH AND DEVELOPMENT ARRANGEMENTS

Research and development (R&D) funding arrangements take a number of configurations—pooled funds, partnerships, tax shelter funding, government participation—and have numerous applications for financing growing companies. The importance of R&D funding is reflected in the *INC*. 100 fastest growing small public companies. Among these businesses, an average of 7.5 percent of sales is committed to research and development.

Pooled Funds

The pooled research and development fund is one of the most promising recent developments in R&D financing. The fund, made up of any number of investors and managed by a third party, seeks to diversify their risk among a variety of investments including a wide selection of research projects.

The pooled funds specialize in midsize investments—$2 million to $10 million—and consequently are attracting much *new* capital including the institutional investor.

Tax Shelter Funding

Tax shelter R&D funding is dependent on favorable tax treatment and high after-tax returns to individual investors. Attracting such capital can be significantly affected by one factor: should outside R&D funding be shown on the balance sheet as a liability or as a contract for the sale or performance of services? The decision as to which accounting method to use can have a striking effect on a firm's earnings and debt/equity ratio, both traditional indicators of a company's ability to attract outside funding. Financial Accounting Standards Board (FASB) Statement No. 68 is designed to help guide companies in making this decision.

Government Awards

Small businesses (usually less than 500 employees) can benefit directly from federal government research and development. Under the Small Business Innovation Development Act, each federal agency with an outside R&D budget of $100 million or more is required to set aside up to 1.25 percent of those funds and award them to small businesses (at this time through the Small Business Administration monitored Small Business Innovation Research program). Total funding to small businesses under this program is expected to surpass $360 million by the end of the 1980s. About six percent of all federally funded R&D contracts go to small firms.

Partnerships

The traditional R&D partnership is most effective when applied to bringing a product from the laboratory to the marketplace. When such partnership investments are applied to basic research, with no specific product or defined market, conflict and failure often occur.

VENTURE CAPITAL

In addition to experienced management, good cost control, forecasts, and a solid business plan, what are venture capitalists looking for today?

Size. A venture capital firm will rarely look at a financial deal below $250,000.

Growth. Businesses with a large upside—the ability to grow very large in a short period of time.

Product. A company that will grow by producing more assembly line type products versus growth by adding more people, that is, labor-intensive services or products such as contract software.

Uniqueness. A "niche" business—one with some sort of monopoly on its product or service. An idea that is either unique, proprietary, or special and that is in demand now or is likely to be in the near future.

Market. A company with potential sales that are large but not so large (no less than $25 million nor more than $50 million) that they will attract direct, big corporate competition. A market of $50 million and up will soon attract the big guns.

Availability. Large company investors want start-ups where they can purchase a minority interest (5 or 10 percent) with the thought of buying the company outright at some point. Written into the first equity deal may be an option to acquire within four or five years.

Overseas potential. Foreign investors, intent on marketing U.S. products overseas, are investing in early-stage U.S. companies that have foreign market product potential.

CASH MANAGEMENT AND TAX STRATEGIES

Through creative cash management combined with full use of tax deductions, exemptions, credits, expensing, and so forth, smaller companies can increase their working capital by 10 to 50 percent.

Some of the current most popular methods for creating cash internally include:

Expensing. Taking a tax deduction of up to $5,000, in the first year of life, on the cost of purchased property. There are complicated rules about what kind of property qualifies but, in general, it must normally be subject to depreciation and does not include real estate. Usually, you will want to choose first-year expensing for the property with the shortest recovery period under the accelerated cost recovery (ACRS) depreciation system.

Credits. Deductions reduce taxable income but investment tax credits cut taxes dollar for dollar. Many smaller companies are unaware of all the credits available to them. For instance: (1) Real estate does not qualify but certain components of commercial buildings may—those that are there to serve the business process rather than for the maintenance or operation of the building (e.g., an air conditioner to cool a computer room may qualify). (2) There are rehabilitation credits for substantial renovation of existing properties. Credits range from 15 to 25 percent depending on the age of the building. (3) Research and development credits can help companies recover up to 25 percent of the costs of developing new technology, including wages. Most credits are currently being reviewed and are therefore subject to change or repeal.

Bad Debt Reserve. Establish a reserve account geared to the amount of outstanding indebtedness to your company and then deduct for debts which are *expected* to become bad. Since the deduction is more immediate than with the direct write-off method, the interest-free use of the tax money improves cash flow.

PRIVATE PLACEMENTS

The private sale or placement of exempt (unregistered* but not un-regulated) securities to one or more investors is an excellent prelude or alternative to going public. For smaller companies, private placement is the third largest source of capital after going public and equipment leasing.

Private placements are an especially effective tool for raising second and third round capital. Successful companies can usually raise between $4 and $5 million. As many venture capitalists are concentrating on current portfolio companies, and looking very cautiously at new investments, it may be possible to secure second and third round capital exclusively through the sale of exempt securities to current investors. SEC regulations allow for an unlimited range of offering sizes when combined with time and/or buyer stipulations.

GOVERNMENT FINANCING

Despite some Small Business Administration (SBA) uncertainties, government and quasi-government initiatives abound for smaller companies. Two newer, non-SBA, entries are decided bright spots.

Capital Assistance. The Export-Import Bank (Eximbank) is seeking to assist smaller U.S. exporters, some with a minimum net worth as

---

* Transactions exempt from federal registration requirements may not be exempt from registration under the laws of the state(s) in which the securities are to be offered.

low as $2 million. Eximbank assistance programs include a small business credit program, a working capital loan-guarantee program and a new export credit insurance program.

State Aid Growing.   More and more state governments are furnishing assistance funds for small business development. Capital is being made available for both expansion and start-up.

More than half the states are now participating in venture capital financing, principally through state employee pension funds and public business development corporations. The SBA estimates that states have already spent or committed well over $300 million in equity investments. As an avenue for creating jobs and retaining businesses, state involvement, including the easing of regulatory and tax burdens, can only be expected to grow.

TRADITIONAL FINANCING

Traditional financing includes the standard sources of debt financing—commercial banks, finance companies, investment bankers, insurance companies, pension funds—and the standard instruments—credit lines, mortgage financing, asset-based loans, sale of accounts receivable. Yet there is much that is new.

Asset-Based Bank Loans.   Once available only from commercial finance companies, many commercial banks are now offering asset-based loans—loans secured by accounts receivable and/or inventories. These loans are short-term, intended for working capital, available in amounts up to 55 to 80 percent of receivables, and cost two to seven percentage points above the prime rate.

Delinquent Loan Disclosure.   Both financial statements and loan portfolios should be considered when evaluating a bank's performance. When measuring a bank's delinquent loans against total loans, FDIC figures reveal that past due loans average less than 5 percent of total loans at 80 percent of U.S. banks. Loans 90 days past due (or no longer accruing interest) should be no more than 1 percent of all loans, and loan losses should be no higher than 0.4 to 0.5 percent of total loans.

Sale Accounting for Pledged Receivables. Under revised accounting standards—Financial Accounting Standards Board (FASB) Statement No. 77—companies pledging their accounts receivable to raise capital need not show the transaction as a liability if the transfer of receivables is structured as a sale. Receivables transferred with a guarantee will be considered a sale, not a liability, when the company surrenders economic benefits, makes a reasonable estimate of its obligations, and agrees that the buyer cannot return the receivables except under special provisions.

S&L Commercial Loans. Savings and loan associations have actively entered the commercial market, including loans on commercial real estate. With up to 10 percent (gradually increasing to 30 percent) of their assets authorized for investment in commercial loans, the amount of funds available is significant. S&Ls are becoming an increasingly important source of smaller company financing. Savings and loans are willing to consider nontraditional financing terms, including acceptance of profit participation agreements and stock options.

Domestic Bankers' Acceptances. Domestic companies, selling to entities 25 or more miles away, can now qualify for bankers' acceptances, a financing and cash management tool previously available only for international transactions. When used for financing product purchases: these short-term loans (90 to 120 days) to the seller of goods, are arranged for and guaranteed by the buyer, at below prime rate, with the product sold acting as collateral.

Float Services. Benefits accrue to small companies from services previously offered only to large corporations. Float services, the *daily* reporting of a company's bank account activity, relieves the need to overfund accounts. By maintaining only the minimum amount required to cover each day's transactions, debits plus credits, companies can have continued use of available funds until actually needed.

Flexible Loan Terms. As a result of deregulation and increased competition, skip-payment and other flexible loan terms are becoming more widely used in bank loan agreements. With a skip-payment clause, companies that experience periods of poor cash flow, often seasonally related, can skip principal payments for short periods of time. However, interest payments must still be made.

GOING PUBLIC

Now or Later. If the capital required is available from other sources, at reasonable rates, consider a delay. This alternative source capital, if used to increase the company's growth potential, could increase the value of stock brought out at a later date.

Momentum. Investors and underwriters look for a company with years of strong, steady growth and rising profits. Both indicate management's ability to compete over the long haul.

Market. Even if the economic climate is bad, a company may still go public successfully if it has an experienced management team, a good financial record, and an important product or service.

Pricing. Ideally, the stock should be priced to ensure an early profit for the first shareholders. However, underwriters will sell the shares at a price that is based on how similar offerings have fared and on the current state of the market.

FINANCING FOR GROWTH

How Much Debt Is Too Much?

Some believe that the healthy smaller company has a debt-to-equity ratio of 60/40, others 3 to 1, still others 50/50, and some believe that smaller companies should borrow as much as they can, thinking of money as an investment. One guide may be that several federal agencies consider the 60 percent debt to 40 percent equity ratio as financially sound for companies seeking their financing. However, on one thing almost everyone can agree:

A highly leveraged business allows no room to maneuver against the unexpected, such as falling markets and widely fluctuating interest rates.

And there is no doubt that:

> A disproportionately large number of businesses entering Chapter 11 (protection from creditors for the purpose of reorganization) are highly leveraged. Many borrowed so heavily that the tremendous interest payments overwhelmed them.

With no determining rule-of-thumb and only credit grantors' verdicts for temperance, each CEO must make the final decision on how much debt is too much for the company.

What Follows

Each of the financing categories covered in this chapter:

Going public	Government financing
Private placements	Business combinations
Venture capital	Research and development
Traditional financing	Cash management
Leasing	Tax planning

is the subject of a separate, in-depth discussion in the chapters that follow.

This book is designed to serve *both* as a guide to financial decision making for the *chief executive officer* or *owner manager* and as a working reference for the *chief financial officer*.

2

THE GOING PUBLIC DECISION

If you are thinking about going public, this chapter has been written expressly for you.

It explains the fundamentals of this complicated process, unravels some of its mysteries, and warns about potential pitfalls.

Going public is one of the most interesting and challenging experiences you can have as a top executive: selling stock in your company for the first time, satisfying all the requirements of federal and state regulatory agencies, supervising a thousand and one other tasks and, in the process, giving up some of the control and privacy you have as the proprietor of your own business.

As professional accountants and advisors, we have helped hundreds of companies go public, and know that every company has its own special needs. This chapter should give you a better understanding of what lies ahead and help you reach sound decisions at one of the crucial moments in your company's history.

MAKING THE DECISION

Going public is one of the most important events in a company's life. As a method of raising capital, it has served American business remarkably well. Virtually all large U.S. companies and many smaller, vigorous companies with strong growth momentum have chosen to sell shares to the public.

Once your company makes the decision to sell its shares to the public and sets the process in motion, nothing will ever be quite the same. Every facet of the company's character and operations will feel the effects.

If all goes well, the new capital can dramatically increase the company's potential for growth—supplying funds to finance research, new product development, plant construction and modernization, expansion into new markets and, perhaps, a promising acquisition. On a personal level, going public can bring gratifying financial rewards.

However, going public goes far beyond just raising capital, and even when it is the best thing to do, it is always a mixed blessing. For a start, you will give up the privacy and autonomy you previously enjoyed. Your freedom of action will be curtailed as outside investors hold you accountable, and you will be required to disclose important information to the world, including your competitors.

In addition, many public offerings have fallen below expectations or even failed, for a variety of reasons. Perhaps the offering was made just as the stock market slumped and prices dropped, or the company's profits fell just before the offering, or it was discovered, too late in the process, that the company didn't have the right line-up of advisors.

You need to clearly visualize the company's future direction and ask the right questions *before* you make a decision as important as this one:

What kind of company do you want to become?

How much capital do you need?

For what purposes?

How much will it cost to raise the money?

Is going public the best financing method?

Is the timing right?

What are the specific advantages and disadvantages of going public?

At the very beginning of your deliberations, you will need the best advice you can get, because this once-in-a-lifetime experience will set the company's course for the foreseeable future.

The discussions that follow will help bring the principal factors into perspective.

Advantages to the Company

• *Improved Financial Condition.* The sale by the company of shares to the public brings in money that does not have to be repaid, immediately improving the company's financial condition. This improvement may enable the company to borrow funds at more attractive interest rates. Moreover, if the initial stock offering is successful and a strong "aftermarket" develops, the company may be able to raise more capital by selling additional shares of stock at terms even more favorable than those of the initial offering.

• *Using Stock for Acquisitions.*   Public companies often find they can issue stock (instead of paying cash) to acquire other businesses. Owners of a company you seek to acquire may be more willing to accept your company's stock if it is publicly traded. The liquidity provided by the public market affords them greater flexibility—they can more easily sell their shares when it suits their needs, or use the shares as collateral for loans.

The public market also assists in valuing the company's shares. If your shares are privately held, you have to estimate their value and hope the owners of the other company will agree; if they don't, you will have to negotiate a "fair price." On the other hand, if the shares are publicly traded, the price per share is set every day in the stock market where the shares are traded.

• *Using Stock as an Employee Incentive.*   Companies frequently offer stock incentives, such as stock options, stock appreciation rights, or stock bonuses, to attract and retain key personnel. These arrangements tend to instill a healthy sense of ownership in employees, who also benefit from certain tax breaks and the chance to gain if the value of the stock appreciates.

Stock incentives are generally more attractive to employees of public companies, since the public market independently values the shares and enhances their marketability.

• *Enhancing Company Prestige.*   One of the intangible, but widely recognized, potential benefits of going public is that the company becomes more visible and attains increased prestige.

Through press releases and other public disclosures, and through daily listing in stock market tables, the company becomes known to the business and financial community, investors, the press, and even to the general public.

While both good and bad news must be disseminated to enable investors to make well-informed decisions, a public company that is well-run and compiles a record of success can gain a first-class reputation that can prove an immeasurable benefit in many ways. As a company's name and products or services become better known, not only do investors take notice, but so do customers and suppliers who often prefer to do business with well-known companies.

Disadvantages to the Company

• *Loss of Privacy.*   Of all the changes a company makes when it goes public, perhaps none is more troublesome than its loss of privacy. When a company shifts to public status, it is required to reveal highly sensitive information, such as compensation paid to key executives, special incentives for management, and many of the plans and strategies that underlie the company's operations. While this need not include every detail of the company's operation, information that could significantly affect investors' decisions must be disclosed.

Such information is required at the time of the initial public offering, and it probably will have to be updated on a continuing and timely basis thereafter.

As a result of this loss of privacy, some companies feel that special arrangements with key personnel or other related parties that are normal for a private company, but that might be misconstrued by outsiders, should be discontinued.

• *Limiting Management's Freedom to Act.*   While the management of a privately held company generally is free to act by itself, the management of a public company must obtain the approval of the board of directors on certain major matters, and on special matters must even seek the consent of the shareholders. Thus, as a consequence of going public, management surrenders its right to act with the same degree of freedom that it previously enjoyed. (This need not be a significant problem. The board of directors, if kept informed on a timely basis, can usually be counted on to understand management's needs, offer support, and grant much of the desired flexibility.)

Shareowners generally judge management's performance in terms of profits, dividends, and stock prices, and apply pressure to increase earnings and pay dividends each quarter. This may cause management to emphasize near-term strategies instead of longer-term goals.

• *The High Cost of Going Public.*   The cost of an initial public offering is substantial. The largest single cost will be the underwriters' commission, which can be as much as 10 percent of the offering price. In addition, legal and accounting fees, printing costs, registration fees, and the underwriters' expenses can easily total more than 10 percent of the offering price for small offerings.

Costs depend upon such factors as the complexity of the registration statement, the extent to which legal counsel must be involved, and whether audited financial statements for recent years are available.

Beyond the initial offering, there are the continuing costs of the periodic reports and proxy statements that are filed with regulatory agencies and distributed to shareholders, and the increased professional fees paid to attorneys, accountants, registrars, and transfer agents for additional required services.

The time management will spend preparing the ongoing reports and statements should be considered, since this responsibility will divert its attention from managing operations.

The company may also need to upgrade its management and accounting information systems to enable it to maintain adequate financial records and systems of internal accounting controls, as required by the accounting provisions of the Foreign Corrupt Practices Act. Upgraded systems may also be necessary to report timely financial information.

Advantages to the Owners

• *Obtaining Marketability.* Once your company goes public, you will often find yourself in a new and more favorable position. Instead of holding shares with limited marketability, you will hold shares that can easily be sold in the market (subject to certain restrictions if your shares are unregistered) or used as collateral for loans.

• *Getting a Better Price.* One of the principal benefits of going public is that the value of your stock may increase remarkably, starting with the initial offering.

Shares that are publicly traded generally command higher prices than those that are not. There are at least three reasons why investors seem willing to pay more for public companies: (1) the marketability of the shares, (2) the maturity/sophistication attributed to public companies, and (3) the availability of more information.

• *Settling an Estate.* The marketability of public shares makes it easier to value and settle an estate. Some of the shares can be used, if necessary, to raise funds to satisfy estate tax obligations without having to sell the entire company, as might be required if the company were privately held.

Disadvantages to the Owners

- *Constraints on Activities.* Privately held companies frequently engage in transactions with their owners, management, and directors. Such transactions might involve sales, leases, or joint ventures. Since such transactions might not be advantageous to public investors, you might decide to forego them once your company decides to go public.

  A second constraint relates to your investment in the company after it goes public. As part of management, you have access to important information before it is released to the public. Since this "insider information" could give you an edge over outside investors, the Securities and Exchange Commission (SEC) prohibits you from using it to buy or sell the company's securities. In addition, officers, directors, and persons holding 10 percent or more of the company's stock must give the company any profits they make on sales of the company's stock held less than six months.

  A third constraint results because the securities you own are "restricted securities," unless they have been registered in a public offering. Restricted securities must be held at least two years, and the number of shares you can sell in any three-month period thereafter is limited.

  Underwriters usually limit the number of shares the owners can register in an initial offering in order to avoid the appearance of a "bail out" by existing shareholders and to maximize the proceeds to the company.

- *Potential Loss of Control.* When a company goes public, there is a possibility that if enough shares are issued an investor or a group of investors could wrest control from the present owners. This can happen following the original public offering or subsequent issuances of shares (e.g., in business combinations). If a large block of shares finds its way into the hands of dissidents, they may vote in new management.

  This can happen, and does.

  However, if the stock is widely distributed, management can usually retain control even though it holds less than 50 percent of the shares.

  (An offering can be structured to ensure that the present owners retain voting control. This can be accomplished by issuing a new class of common stock with limited voting rights. However, such stock may have limited appeal to investors, and accordingly, may sell for less than ordinary common stock.)

- *Estate Valuation for Tax Purposes.*   The increased value that generally results from public trading could result in higher inheritance taxes.

Is This the Time?

Let's suppose you have weighed all the pros and cons, and have decided that the best thing for the company is to go public. But when? Timing is crucial, and this raises several questions.

- *Is Now the Best Time to Go Public?*   If needed capital is available from nonpublic sources at reasonable cost, you may want to delay going public. If funds raised from other sources can be used to increase the company's growth potential, the value of your stock may increase if you sell it later. This may mean raising more capital while selling fewer shares, so that you can retain a larger interest in the company.

- *Are Your Plans in Order?*   Once you have successfully made the offering, the stock's price may decline unless the company continues to show good progress and profits. A well-developed strategic business plan (including a multiyear financial plan) can help you minimize adverse surprises by identifying the critical elements for continued success and providing bench marks against which to monitor the company's progress.

- *Is Management Ready?*   Now is the time, before the decision is irreversible, for management to analyze itself. Can you comfortably adjust to the loss of the relative freedom to act as you see fit, and to the loss of your customary privacy? Are you ready to cope with the public's scrutiny of the company's actions? Are you ready to admit outsiders to your decision-making process? Do you have the leadership capability to grow as the company grows? Does management command the necessary credibility in the financial community?

- *Are the Company's Information Systems Adequate?*   As a public company, you will be required to provide timely and reliable financial information to investors. If the company's management and accounting information systems are inadequate, now is the time to get them in first-class working order. There are legal liabilities for reporting false or misleading information, not to mention the loss of investors' confidence if information is not timely or accurate.

- *Does the Company Have Impressive Momentum?*   Investors buy stock with the expectation that its value will go up if the company prospers, and that the past often foreshadows the future.

That's why investors (and underwriters) tend to look for companies with several years of strong, steady growth and rising profits, indicating management's ability to compete over the long haul. If the momentum is not there when you go public, investors will likely turn to more promising opportunities and your offering may fizzle.

There are no hard-and-fast rules, but some underwriters will not consider taking a company public unless it can point to revenues of at least $10 million and annual net income of $1 million, with anticipated growth of 25 to 50 percent a year for the next few years. There are exceptions, of course—new companies in the relatively new glamour industries, for example—so each company must consider its own circumstances, bearing in mind that few elements in the overall picture will impress the investor as much as momentum.

- *Is the Market Right?*   The market for initial offerings has varied dramatically from the depressed levels of the mid-1970s, when fewer than 50 companies a year went public, to the record highs of the early 1980s.

In deciding whether this is the right time to go public, one of the critical questions is whether the mood of the market is right. Is the market strong or slumping? Are prices rising or falling? Is volume up or down? One of the ironies is that, even though your company might more than satisfy every criterion for going public, market conditions might go sour just at the time you are ready to make your offering.

Or, you may catch the market when prices and volume are strong, and investors are eager for new opportunities.

A thousand things influence the market—political developments, interest rates, the rate of inflation, economic forecasts, and sundry matters that seem unrelated to the quality of your stock. The market is admittedly emotional, and investors' moods change from bullish to bearish and back again, to everyone's consternation, even the experts.

Underwriters track these changes, to anticipate when investors are likely to be receptive to new offerings. When the market is favorable, companies often go to the market to obtain funds that they will not need until sometime in the future, thereby eliminating the need to speculate on future market conditions.

Determining whether the market is right for your offering deserves the utmost attention from you and your advisors, for success or failure is at stake.

• *What Are the Risks of Going Public at the Wrong Time?*   The most obvious risk is that your offering will not be completed and the costs that you have incurred will have gone for nothing. This may occur because changes in the market or disappointing financial results cause the underwriter to back out.

Alternatively, you may have to offer more shares at a lower price per share to attract investors.

Further, offerings that sell enthusiastically can crash meteorically in the aftermarket, particularly if subsequent operating results are less than anticipated. A company that loses credibility in the financial community faces a long, difficult process in regaining investors' confidence.

The price you pay for bad timing can be almost beyond calculation.

ASSEMBLING THE REGISTRATION TEAM

Who to Include

After making the decision to go public in the near future, you must assemble the group of specialists needed to guide you through the complex registration process. The team should include members of the company's management, your company's legal counsel, the managing underwriter, the underwriter's counsel, and the independent accountants.

The lawyers and independent accountants you choose have the expertise to work effectively with the (Securities and Exchange Commission (SEC) during the registration process, and to help the company meet its SEC reporting requirements after it has gone public.

Experience with securities filings is so important that it is not unusual for companies to hire new counsel and independent accountants when they go public.

Choosing an Underwriter

In finding an underwriter, you can turn to certain trusted sources for guidance—your legal counsel, independent accountants, or acquaintances in your local investment community—or you can ask companies that have recently gone public, especially those in your own industry. Here are six suggestions in choosing an underwriter:

1. Review the underwriter's performance in other offerings, and its general reputation earned over the years. A helpful source for this kind of information is *Going Public: The IPO Reporter*, which tracks initial public offerings and their performance in the aftermarket.

2. Look for an underwriter who understands the important characteristics of your industry.

3. Check whether the underwriter has experience with offerings of the size you contemplate.

4. Determine the extent of the underwriter's distribution capabilities. If you want the company's stock to be widely distributed, you will want a firm with nationwide facilities. On the other hand, if the company's operations are regional, a regional underwriting firm might be a better choice.

5. Find out whether the underwriter will provide support in the aftermarket once the initial offering is sold. This can take the form of bringing your stock to investors' attention, providing market research, or offering financial advice to your company.

6. Don't be unduly swayed by the highest offering price mentioned when you are interviewing potential underwriters. Reputable underwriters will usually sell the shares at approximately the same price based on how similar offerings have fared and the current state of the market.

Once the registration team has been chosen, the process of going public can begin.

THE GOING PUBLIC PROCESS*

The sale of securities to the public is governed by the Securities Act of 1933, which requires that a registration statement containing specified financial and other information about the company and the proposed offering be filed with the SEC. The 1933 Act provides certain exemptions from the requirement that a registration statement be filed; these exempt offerings are not considered public offerings and are covered separately in Chapter 3 entitled "Private Placements."

The process of going public generally takes from 60 to 180 days, depending upon the complexity of the registration statement and the SEC's backlog of filings in process (registration periods of less than 90 days are unusual). The more significant steps in the registration process include:

- Planning
- The initial meeting of the registration team
- Preparing the initial registration statement
- Filing the initial registration statement and the initial regulatory review
- Amending the registration statement
- Selling the securities
- The closing

A sample timetable for the steps involved in going public is contained in Appendix 2-2.

Planning: Questions to Be Considered

After you have decided to take your company public, you should consider the steps needed to ensure a smooth transition from private

* As you would expect, the process of going public is highly technical and complicated. While we will keep the discussion of this complex process relatively simple, from time to time we will use technical terms. They are described in Appendix 2-1.

company to public company. You may need to do some corporate housekeeping, and you will have to determine whether the necessary information is available and, if not, make plans to assemble it.

• *Corporate Housekeeping.* Corporate housekeeping generally begins during the planning stage and is often not completed until the registration statement is filed. You should consider whether the existing corporate, capital, and management structures are appropriate for a public company and whether transactions with you and the other owners have been documented and recorded properly. The following are typical questions to be considered during this phase:

Should the company's capital structure be changed? You may want to simplify it by exchanging common shares for preferred stock or special classes of common stock.

Should additional shares of stock be authorized? They might be needed for the public offering or for future acquisitions or sales.

Should the stock be split before you go public? Reducing the price of your shares, possibly to $10 to $20 per share, can increase their marketability.

Should affiliated companies be combined? Affiliated companies might provide services to each other, compete with each other, or sell related products and services. The combined entity may well be more attractive to investors, and thus command a higher price in the market.

Should the company's articles of incorporation or bylaws be amended? A private company may have special voting provisions that are inappropriate for a public company, or it might be desirable to establish certain committees of the board of directors, such as an audit committee.

Are the company's stock records accurate and up to date? Accurate shareholder information is a must for a public company. (While reviewing the stock records, be alert for problems with previous issuances of unregistered securities.)

Are the company's transactions or arrangements with the owners and members of management appropriate for a public company, and are they adequately documented? Since related party transactions can be a problem, they should be identified and discussed with the company's counsel early in the process.

Have material contracts and employment agreements been reduced to writing? Do they need to be amended? Should a stock option plan be implemented? Should additional options be granted under existing plans?

Does management possess sufficient depth and experience for a public company? The company may need to supplement or upgrade its financial and/or operating management before it goes public. Changes in the board of directors are often appropriate—for example, adding outside directors.

• *Information Requirements.* The registration statement will require substantial amounts of financial information and disclosures about the company's history and business. Early in the registration process, you should determine whether the required information is available and begin to assemble it. Obtaining the required information about predecessor companies and acquired companies can be especially difficult.

The registration statement must include audited financial statements, usually for the preceding two or three years. If the company's financial statements have not been audited previously, it should be determined whether financial records are adequate and auditable.

The Initial Meeting of the Registration Team

During the initial meeting of the registration team, responsibilities for the various portions of the registration statement are assigned and the proposed terms of the offering are discussed. The registration form to be used should also be decided upon.

Forms S-1 and S-18 are the most commonly used registration statement forms in initial public offerings. Form S-1 imposes no limitation on the amount of funds that can be raised, whereas Form S-18 can be used only for offerings up to $7.5 million.

Some companies prefer to use Form S-18 because it requires less information than Form S-1 (e.g., income statements for two years rather than for three years). In addition, the SEC may process Form

S-18 faster since it can be reviewed at a regional office, rather than at SEC headquarters in Washington.

Following the initial meeting, the offering timetable and a letter of intent between the company and the lead underwriter should be formalized. The timetable should detail the tasks to be performed, the identity of those responsible for each, and when each should be completed. (See Appendix 2-2 for a sample timetable.) The nonbinding letter of intent confirms the intended nature of the underwriting (i.e., "best efforts" or "firm commitment"), the underwriters' compensation, the number of shares expected to be issued, and the anticipated price. A binding underwriting agreement is not signed until the registration statement is about to become effective.

Preparing the Initial Registration Statement

A registration statement usually requires a considerable period of time to prepare. The statement must contain all disclosures, both favorable and unfavorable, necessary to enable investors to make well-informed decisions, and the document must not include any materially misleading statements. The SEC's disclosure requirements are contained in Regulations S-K and S-X. Regulation S-K specifies the requirements for the nonfinancial-statement portion of the document, while Regulation S-X specifies the financial statements to be included and their form and content.

Information Requirements. The registration statement consists of two parts. Part I is also printed in booklet form and initially constitutes the preliminary prospectus or "red herring," which is distributed to prospective investors prior to the effective date of the registration statement. Part II contains information that is not required to be in the prospectus.

Exhibit 2-1 summarizes the information required in a Form S-1 registration statement. (Appendix 2-3 contains a more detailed discussion of the information required in Forms S-1 and S-18.) Item 11, "Information with respect to registrant," is the most time-consuming and difficult item to prepare. Item 11 contains the requirements for disclosures about the company's business, properties, and management; for financial statements and other financial disclosures; and for man-

EXHIBIT 2-1.   FORM S-1 INFORMATION REQUIREMENTS

PART I: INFORMATION REQUIRED IN PROSPECTUS

Item

1. Forepart of registration statement and outside front cover of prospectus
2. Inside front and outside back cover pages of prospectus
3. Summary information, risk factors, and ratio of earnings to fixed charges
4. Use of proceeds
5. Determination of offering price
6. Dilution
7. Selling security holders
8. Plan of distribution
9. Description of securities to be registered
10. Interests of named experts and counsel
11. Information with respect to registrant
12. Disclosure of Commission position on indemnification for Securities Act liabilities

PART II: INFORMATION NOT REQUIRED IN PROSPECTUS

Item

13. Other expenses of issuance and distribution
14. Indemnification of directors and officers
15. Recent sales of unregistered securities
16. Exhibits and financial statement schedules
17. Undertakings

See Appendix 2-3 to this chapter for additional information regarding these requirements.

agement's discussion and analysis of financial condition and results of operations.

The entire registration team ordinarily participates in the initial drafting of the registration statement. The company and its counsel generally prepare the nonfinancial sections (if the company's legal counsel is inexperienced in preparing registration statements, the underwriters' counsel assists). The managing underwriter and underwriters' counsel prepare the description of the underwriting arrangements and, in some cases, the description of the offering. The company prepares the required financial statements and schedules, as well as other financial disclosures. The independent accountant usually advises the company about the financial statements and disclosures.

Financial Statement Requirements. Form S-1 registration statements require audited balance sheets as of the end of the last two years and audited income statements and statements of changes in financial position for each of the three fiscal years preceding the latest audited balance sheet. The SEC recognizes the difficulty in providing audited financial statements immediately after year-end. Thus, for registration statements that become effective within 45 days after year-end, the most recent audited balance sheet may be as of the end of the second preceding year.

Condensed interim financial statements, which may be unaudited, are required unless the date of the latest year-end financial statements presented is within 134 days of the effective date of the registration statement. Exhibit 2-2 shows the latest financial statements required under various circumstances in an initial public offering for a company with a December 31 year-end.

Separate financial statements may also be required for unconsolidated subsidiaries, for entities for which the company's investment is accounted for under the equity method, and for entities that the company has acquired or plans to acquire. (The need for separate financial statements depends on the relative significance of such entities to the registrant.)

Preparation Procedures. After the registration statement has been drafted and circulated to the registration team, the company's management, and possibly to its directors, the members of the registration team meet to review it. The draft is modified as appropriate (several redrafts may be necessary), and the amended copy is sent to the printer for the first proof. The printer's proof goes through the same circulation, comment, and revision process. When the members of the registration team are satisfied with the document, it is distributed to the board of directors for their final review and approval prior to filing with the SEC and the appropriate state agencies.

Preparing a registration statement that is acceptable to all the parties is an extremely difficult task and often involves a series of compromises.

EXHIBIT 2-2. FINANCIAL STATEMENT REQUIREMENTS

Expected effective date	January 1, 19X2 to February 14, 19X2	February 15, 19X2 to May 14, 19X2	May 15, 19X2	July 15, 19X2
The most recent audited financial statements must be as of a date no earlier than[a]	December 31, 19X0[b]	December 31, 19X1	December 31, 19X1	December 31, 19X1
The most recent condensed unaudited interim financial information must be as of a date no earlier than[c]	September 30, 19X1	None	January 31, 19X2	March 31, 19X2

[a] If the annual audited financial statements included in the registration statement are "not recent" (e.g., 9 months old at the effective date), underwriters often require audited interim financial statements as of a more recent date.

[b] Unless later audited financial statements are available.

[c] In addition to the condensed interim financial information, capsule information describing the results of subsequent months may be necessary to prevent the registration statement from being misleading (e.g., if the company incurs operating losses or develops severe liquidity problems).

For example, underwriters' counsel may insist on disclosures about the company that management is initially reluctant to make; however, management may be willing to accept such changes if other disclosures are also included. These discussions, when coupled with severe time pressures and changing market conditions, can result in frazzled nerves and frayed tempers, particularly as the proposed offering date approaches.

Filing the Initial Registration Statement and the Initial Regulatory Review

The SEC and the states have concurrent jurisdiction over securities offerings. The registration statement must be filed with the SEC, with any state in which the securities will be offered, and with the National Association of Securities Dealers (NASD). The review by the SEC is designed to assess compliance with its requirements, including the adequacy of the disclosures about the company, without addressing the merits of the offering. In addition to reviewing the adequacy of the disclosures, some states also consider the merits of the offering under their "blue sky" laws (i.e., whether the offering is "fair, just, and equitable"). The nature and extent of the various states' reviews are not uniform—some states perform in-depth reviews while others perform cursory reviews. The primary purpose of the NASD's review is to determine whether the underwriters' compensation is excessive.

Based on the reviews, the SEC (and sometimes one or more of the states) issues a formal comment letter, generally 20 to 60 days after the initial filing. The SEC's letter describes the ways in which it believes the filing does not comply with its requirements.

The SEC's comment letters often focus on the specified uses of the proceeds (including the adequacy of the proceeds for the designated purposes), management's discussion and analysis of financial condition and results of operations, and the disclosures about the risk factors. Comments on the financial statements may question or seek information about such matters as accounting policies and practices, related party transactions, unusual compensation arrangements, off-balance sheet financing methods, or the relationship among certain components of the financial statements.

Amending the Registration Statement

The registration team should address *all* of the comments in the regulatory review response letters, either by amending the registration statement, or by discussing with the SEC and the state regulators the reasons why revisions are unnecessary, and obtaining concurrence with that conclusion.

A draft of the amended registration statement is distributed to the registration team for review, any necessary changes are made (including updating the financial statements), and the amended registration statement is filed. After all the parties involved are satisfied with the technical and disclosure aspects of the registration statement, the pricing amendment is filed. The pricing amendment discloses the offering price, the underwriters' commission, and the net proceeds to the company.

Although technically there is a 20-day waiting period after the final registration statement is filed before it becomes effective, an "acceleration request" is usually filed concurrently with the pricing amendment. The request asks the SEC to waive the 20-day waiting period and declare the registration statement effective immediately.* Except in unusual cases, the SEC approves acceleration requests.

Selling the Securities

After the registration statement becomes effective, the final prospectus is printed and distributed to everyone who received a copy of the preliminary prospectus (and to others who expressed an interest in purchasing the stock).

Offers to purchase the securities may not be accepted until after the registration statement becomes effective.

The Closing

The registration process culminates with the company issuing the securities to the underwriters and receiving the proceeds (net of the

---

* Acceleration is particularly critical in firm commitment underwritings, since underwriters are generally unwilling to risk deterioration in the market after the offering price has been set.

underwriters' compensation) from the offering. The closing for "firm commitment" underwritings generally occurs five to seven business days after the registration statement has become effective. The closing for "best efforts" underwritings generally is 60 to 120 days after the effective date, provided the underwriters have sold at least the minimum number of shares specified in the registration statement.

Publicity During the Offering Process—Restrictions

The SEC has established guidelines limiting the information that may be released during the "quiet period." This period begins when you reach a preliminary understanding with the managing underwriter and ends 90 days after the effective date of the registration statement.

You are prohibited from "offering" a security prior to the initial filing of the registration statement. The term "offer" has been broadly interpreted by the SEC to include any publicity which "has the effect of conditioning the public mind or arousing public interest in the issuer or in its securities." However, the SEC encourages you to continue publishing the company's normal advertisements and financial information. On the other hand, if you issue new types of publicity, the SEC may delay the effective date of your registration statement. (You should consult your attorneys and underwriters before issuing any publicity releases during the "quiet period.")

After the initial filing, the SEC prohibits you from distributing any written sales literature about the securities, except for the preliminary prospectus which may be distributed to prospective investors.

Oral presentations are permitted, such as the "road show" in which you and your underwriters discuss the offering with prospective members of the underwriting syndicate, financial analysts, and institutional investors. However, sales of the securities cannot be made until after the registration statement has become effective.

Liability Claims and Due Diligence

Material misstatements in, or omissions from, the registration statement can result in liabilities under the Securities Act of 1933. Purchasers of the securities can assert claims against the company, the underwriters, the company's directors, the officers who signed the registration statement, and any experts (such as accountants or attorneys) who "expertized" certain portions of the registration statement.

The company cannot avoid liability as a result of material misstatements or omissions. On the other hand, the other parties may be able to assert the "due diligence defense." That is, they may be able to avoid liability by demonstrating that, with respect to the applicable portions of the registration statement, they had conducted a reasonable investigation and thus had a reasonable basis for belief and did believe that the statements in the registration statement were true and not misleading at the time the document became effective, and that no material facts were omitted from the document.

The members of the registration team begin performing their "due diligence procedures" at the initial meeting, and continue them throughout the registration process. As part of these procedures, underwriters usually require the independent accountants to provide them with letters ("comfort letters") that contain assurances about the unaudited financial data in the registration statement. In addition, the members hold a "due diligence meeting" shortly before the registration statement becomes effective. Representatives of all the firms in the underwriting syndicate usually attend this meeting.

Suggestions for Facilitating the Process of Going Public

Based on our broad experience with many initial public offerings, we have a number of suggestions for facilitating the process of going public. Some suggestions are designed to prevent delays in the registration process, while others address steps to take before or during the registration process. (See also the discussion on "Planning" earlier in this chapter.)

- Begin planning and considering the implications of going public long before you will finalize the decision to go public. For example, develop a well-thought-out strategic business plan, including a multiyear financial plan, which considers alternative means of financing and the effects the decision to go public will have on future operations.

- Establish relationships with an investment banker, and with a law firm and an independent accounting firm experienced with the federal securities laws.

- Establish a program before the offering process begins of providing information about your company to the financial community and potential investors. Unless your company has established a practice of releasing information through the media or through advertising, the company will be prohibited from doing so during the registration process. Public visibility can enhance the initial sales effort, and can maintain the public's interest in your company's stock in the aftermarket.

- Consider engaging an independent accounting firm to observe the taking of the year-end inventories—even though it may be several years before you go public, and your company's financial statements are not being audited currently. Observation of significant physical inventories by the independent accounting firm is usually essential if you are to receive an acceptable audit opinion on prior years' financial statements as required by the SEC.

- Consider whether the company's accounting principles are appropriate, or whether they should be changed to conform with prevalent industry practice.

- Anticipate potential accounting and disclosure problems, such as accounting for noncash and other unusual transactions, and disclosures about legal proceedings and transactions with owners and officers. Be prepared to explain to the SEC why the disclosures or methods of accounting followed in the registration statement are appropriate. In some cases, a prefiling conference with the SEC may be helpful. The early resolution of accounting and disclosure problems can prevent subsequent delays in the registration process.

- Establish a timetable for the registration process and stick to it. An isolated delay may not be significant, but the cumulative effects of several delays can be. Significant delays may force your company to provide more recent interim financial statements, or cause the underwriters to question whether your company is really ready to go public.

- Avoid entering into significant business combinations or disposing of significant amounts of assets during the registration process. Pro forma financial statements and audited financial statements of acquired companies will be required in such cases and for combinations or dispositions that are probable but have not yet occurred. The preparation of these financial statements requires gathering additional information and can significantly delay the registration process.

- Limit the number of revisions that the printer must process since typesetting, reprinting, and recirculating printed drafts can be costly. One member of the registration team should be designated to gather comments from all the parties, make the appropriate changes, and then submit all the approved changes to the printer at one time.
- Make arrangements for the SEC's comments to be delivered by express mail or telephone. This can save one or two days in the registration process.
- Respond promptly and completely to *all* of the SEC's comments. One easy way to assure a complete response and to facilitate the SEC's review of the amended registration statement is to number the comments on a copy of the comment letter which should accompany the amended statement. The statement should be marked to indicate where each comment has been addressed.

Certain of the SEC's comments may be inappropriate because it misinterpreted the information in the statement. You should arrange to discuss these comments with the SEC.

If the SEC suggests insignificant changes, it is usually better to make them than to delay the registration process while resolving them with the SEC.

REPORTING REQUIREMENTS FOR PUBLIC COMPANIES

After the initial public offering under the Securities Act of 1933, your company will have to file certain nonrecurring reports with the SEC, including Form S-R, which describes the securities sold, the proceeds to the company, and the use of the proceeds. Further, your company will have to file an annual report on Form 10-K under the Securities Exchange Act of 1934 in its initial year as a public company. Only those companies registered under the 1934 Act must file a Form 10-K in subsequent years.

Companies that elect to be listed on a national stock exchange* and companies with 500 or more shareholders of a class of equity securities and total assets of more than $3 million must register under

* Companies that elect to list their securities on a national or regional stock exchange must file a listing application with the exchange. Certain exchanges may require additional disclosures that were not included in the registration statement.

the 1934 Act on Form .10 or Form 8-A. (Form 10 is the basic 1934 Act registration statement and requires disclosures similar to those required by Form S-1. Form 8-A is a simplified 1934 Act registration statement that can be used to register securities issued in an initial public offering, provided that the statement becomes effective within one year after the end of the last fiscal year for which audited financial statements were included in a 1933 Act filing.)

Companies registered under the 1934 Act must file the following periodic reports:

- *Form 10-K.* This annual report must be filed within 90 days after the end of the fiscal year. The financial statement requirements and the required nonfinancial disclosures about the registrant are similar to those in Form S-1, except that interim financial statements are not required. (Appendix 2-3 compares Form 10-K with Forms S-1 and S-18.)
- *Form 10-Q.* These quarterly reports must be filed within 45 days after the end of each of the first three quarters of the fiscal year. Comparative financial statements and notes are required, but they may be condensed and need not be audited. In addition, other disclosures relating to the occurrence of certain events during the period are required.
- *Form 8-K.* This form is used to report changes in control, acquisitions or dispositions of significant assets, bankruptcy, changes in independent accountants, and resignations of directors. It must be filed within 15 days after the occurrence of the reportable event. Financial statements of significant acquired businesses must be filed, and certain pro forma information must be provided. An extension of time is available for filing the required financial information about acquired businesses. Form 8-K can also be used to disclose other events that the company believes are important to security holders; when used for this purpose, the 15-day filing requirement does not apply.

A public company is required to disclose all information that is material to investors. Such information cannot be disclosed selectively; it must be disclosed regardless of whether it is favorable or unfavorable, and it must be released simultaneously to all shareholders.

The SEC's integrated disclosure system has standarized the required financial statements and other disclosures in 1933 Act registration statements and 1934 Act annual and quarterly reports. This facilitates the filing of future registration statements. In fact, after a company has been subject to the reporting requirements of the 1934 Act for three years, it is eligible to file "short-form" 1933 Act registration statements, which can incorporate by reference information previously included in annual, quarterly, and current reports. This can expedite significantly the registration process and result in lower accounting, legal, and printing costs.

Registration under the 1934 Act also subjects the company (and certain shareholders and members of management) to a multitude of SEC rules, including those on soliciting proxies, insider trading, and tender offers:

- *Proxy Rules.* These rules require a company that solicits proxies from its shareholders to distribute a proxy statement containing a description of the matters to be voted on. In addition, the rules require that the annual report to shareholders be distributed with, or prior to, the proxy materials for the company's annual meeting. Even if proxies are not solicited, the rules prescribe certain disclosures for the company's annual report (e.g., the financial statements must comply with Regulation S-X, management must discuss and analyze the company's financial condition and results of operations, and the company's business during the past year must be discussed).

- *Insider Trading.* Officers, directors, and persons holding 10 percent or more of a company's stock must file reports on their holdings and changes in their holdings of the company's stock. Changes in security holdings in one month must be reported by the tenth day of the next month. Reporting persons are required to turn over to the company any profits they realize on sales of the company's stock held less than six months. They also are prohibited from selling the company's securities short.

- *Tender Offers.* Persons who tender to become owners of more than 5 percent of a company's stock must make certain disclosures to the company and to the SEC. The tender offer rules also describe the mechanics for making a tender offer and limit a company's activities in resisting a tender offer.

This chapter has introduced the going public process: It does not include all the possible considerations that will affect your unique company. Nothing can take the place of the firsthand advice of experienced professionals—attorneys, independent accountants, and investment bankers. They can consider your special circumstances and tailor their advice to your needs, to help you make the important decisions that will set your company's future course.

APPENDIX 2-1. COMMONLY USED TERMS GLOSSARY

The purpose of this appendix is to provide a reference source for persons unfamiliar with the terminology of the registration process. The descriptions of the terms are not intended to provide precise definitions as much as they are intended to describe how the terms apply when a company goes public.

ACCELERATION REQUEST.   A request to the SEC to waive the statutory 20-day waiting period and to declare the registration statement effective at an earlier date.

BEST EFFORTS UNDERWRITING.   An underwriting arrangement in which the underwriters commit to use their best efforts to sell the shares, but have no obligation to purchase any shares not purchased by the public. Under certain best efforts offerings, the offering is cancelled unless a minimum number of shares is sold.

BLUE SKY LAWS.   State securities laws. The states and the SEC have concurrent jurisdiction over securities transactions. Some states have the authority under their "blue sky laws" to prohibit the offering of securities in their states if the offering is not "fair, just, and equitable."

COMFORT LETTER (LETTER TO UNDERWRITERS).   The letter or letters underwriters require from independent accountants as part of the underwriters' due diligence process. The matters to be covered in these letters are generally specified in the underwriting agreement. Comfort letters generally require the independent accountants to make representations about their independence and the compliance of the financial statements with the requirements of the Securities Act of 1933, and to provide "negative assurance," based on the results of applying certain specified procedures, about the unaudited financial statements and other financial information. Comfort letters are not required by the Securities Act of 1933 and are not filed with the SEC.

COMMENT LETTER.   A letter issued by the SEC describing the ways in which a registration statement does not comply with its requirements or questioning whether additional information should be included or whether disclosures should be changed. The states in which the securities are to be sold may also issue comment letters. Comment letters generally are received 20 to 60 days after the initial filing of the registration statement.

DUE DILIGENCE.   A "reasonable investigation" performed by the underwriters, the directors, the officers who signed the registration statement, and the experts (e.g., independent accountants, attorneys, or engineers) who participated in the securities offering to provide them with a "reasonable ground for belief" that, as of the effective date, the statements contained in the registration statement are true and not misleading, and that no material information has been omitted.

EFFECTIVE DATE.   The date on which the registration statement becomes effective and the securities may be sold to the public.

EXEMPT OFFERING.   A securities transaction for which a registration statement need not be filed due to an exemption available under the Securities Act of 1933. Common exempt offerings are intrastate offerings and Regulation A and Regulation D offerings. See Chapter 3, "Private Placements."

FIRM COMMITMENT UNDERWRITING.   An underwriting arrangement in which the underwriters commit to purchase all the securities being offered, regardless of whether they can resell all of them to the public.

FOREIGN CORRUPT PRACTICES ACT (FCPA).   An amendment of the Securities Exchange Act of 1934 that requires reporting companies to maintain adequate accounting records and systems of internal accounting control.

GOING PUBLIC.   The process by which a private company and/or its shareholders sell securities of the company to the public for the first time in a transaction requiring a registration statement prepared in accordance with the Securities Act of 1933.

GREEN SHOE OPTION.   An option often included in a firm commitment underwriting which allows the underwriters to purchase additional shares from the company or the selling shareholders to cover overallotments.

INITIAL PUBLIC OFFERING (IPO).   The sale of its securities to the public for the first time by a private company (and/or its shareholders).

LETTER OF INTENT.   A nonbinding letter from the underwriter to the company confirming the underwriter's intent to proceed with the offering and describing the probable terms of the offering. A typical letter generally covers the number and type of shares to be sold, the type of underwriting, the anticipated sales price, and the arrangements for compensating the underwriters.

NATIONAL ASSOCIATION OF SECURITIES DEALERS (NASD).   NASD's role in the registration process is to review the offering materials to determine whether the underwriters' compensation is excessive considering the size and type of the offering, the nature of the underwriting commitment, and other relevant factors.

PRO FORMA.   A financial presentation designed to provide investors with information about certain effects of a particular transaction. Historical financial information is adjusted to reflect the effects the transaction might have had if it had been consummated at an earlier date. In registration statements, pro forma combined financial statements are required for significant business combinations, including those that will probably occur.

QUIET PERIOD.   The period between the commencement of the public offering process (which begins when the company reaches a preliminary understanding with the managing underwriter) and 90 days after the registration statement becomes effective. The period is referred to as the "quiet period" because of the SEC's restrictions on publicity about the company or the offering.

RED HERRING.   The preliminary prospectus that is circulated to prospective investors before the registration statement becomes effective. The preliminary prospectus is called "the red herring" because the following legend must be printed on its cover in red ink:

A registration statement relating to these securities has been filed with the Securities and Exchange Commission but has not become effective.

Information contained herein is subject to completion or amendment. These securities may not be sold nor may offers to buy be accepted prior to the time the registration statement becomes effective. This prospectus shall not constitute an offer to sell or the solicitation of an offer to buy nor shall there be any sale of these securities in any State in which such offer, solicitation or sale would be unlawful prior to registration or qualification under the securities laws of any such State.

REGISTRATION STATEMENT.   The document filed with the SEC to register securities for sale to the public. The most common registration statements for initial public offerings are Forms S-1 and S-18.

REGULATION S-K.   Regulation S-K contains the disclosure requirements for the nonfinancial-statement portion of filings with the SEC.

REGULATION S-X.   Regulation S-X specifies the financial statements to be included in filings with the SEC and provides rules and guidance regarding their form and content.

SECONDARY OFFERING.   An offering by the company's shareholders to sell some or all of their stock to the public.

SECURITIES AND EXCHANGE COMMISSION (SEC).   The SEC is the federal agency responsible for regulating sales and trading of securities by administering the federal securities laws, including the 1933 and 1934 Acts.

SECURITIES ACT OF 1933 (1933 ACT).   Under the 1933 Act, a registration statement containing required disclosures must be filed with the SEC before securities can be offered for sale in interstate commerce or through the mail. The 1933 Act also contains antifraud provisions that apply to offerings of securities.

SECURITIES EXCHANGE ACT OF 1934 (1934 ACT).   The 1934 Act requires companies registered under the Act to file annual and periodic reports with the SEC and to disclose certain information to shareholders. Companies with 500 or more shareholders of a class of equity securities and total assets of more than $3 million and companies that elect to be listed on a national stock exchange must file a Form 10 or Form 8-A registration statement to register under the Act.

SHORT-SWING PROFIT RECAPTURE.   The 1934 Act requires officers, directors, and persons holding 10 percent or more of a class of a company's stock to turn over to the company profits they realize on the sale of any shares of the company's stock that they held for less than six months.

STUB-PERIOD FINANCIAL INFORMATION.   Financial information or financial statements for interim periods. Under Forms S-1 and S-18, the most current financial information included in the registration statement must be as of a date that is within 134 days of the effective date of the statement. This requirement is usually met by providing unaudited condensed financial statements for periods of one or more months subsequent to the latest audited financial statements.

UNDERWRITER.   An investment banker or broker-dealer who acts as the middleman between the selling company and the investing public in an offering of securities. (See FIRM COMMITMENT UNDERWRITING and BEST EFFORTS UNDERWRITING.)

UNDERWRITING AGREEMENT.   An agreement between the company and the underwriters that states the terms of the offering, including the nature of the underwriting (i.e., "best efforts" or "firm commitment"), the number of shares to be offered, the price per share and the underwriters' compensation. Usually it is not signed until just prior to the anticipated effective date of the registration statement.

APPENDIX 2-2.   SAMPLE TIMETABLE FOR GOING PUBLIC

The following sample timetable presents a fairly typical registration schedule. Additional time may be required if significant corporate housekeeping is necessary or if the required financial statements for prior years were not previously audited by independent accountants. The waiting time for SEC comments can range from 20 days to 60 days or more, depending on the complexity of the registration statement and the SEC's backlog of filings in process.

Day	Tasks	Responsible
1	Hold an initial meeting of the registration team to discuss the preparation and filing of the registration statement, the assignment of responsibilities, and the proposed timetable; begin preparation of the letter of intent describing the structure of the proposed offering and the underwriting arrangement	All parties
2	Begin the preparation of the registration statement:	
	• Textual information, including the description of the business	Company, Company Counsel
	• Financial statements, schedules and pro forma information	Company, Independent Accountants
	Begin the preparation of the underwriting documents including:	Underwriters' Counsel
	• Agreement among underwriters	
	• Underwriting agreement between the company and the underwriters	
	• Blue-sky (state security laws) survey	
	Complete corporate cleanup, as necessary	Company, Company Counsel
	Commence due diligence procedures	Company Counsel, Underwriters' Counsel
10	Distribute to directors and officers a questionnaire requesting information that may	Company

Day	Tasks	Responsible
	have to be disclosed in the registration statement (e.g., stock ownership, transactions with the company, remuneration, stock options)	
30	Circulate the initial draft registration statement, including the financial statements	Company, Company Counsel
37	Meet to review the comments on the initial draft	All parties
	Discuss the financial statements and the proposed comfort letter procedures	Company, Underwriter, Underwriters' Counsel, and Independent Accountants
40	Send the corrected draft to the printer for the first proof of the registration statement	Company or Company Counsel
43	Circulate the printed proof for review	Company or Company Counsel
47	Meet to review the comments on the first proof of the registration statement	All parties
48	Send the revised proof of the registration statement to the printer	Company or Company Counsel
49	Hold a meeting of the Board of Directors to approve the registration statement	Company
50	Distribute printed proofs of the various underwriting documents	Underwriters' Counsel
	Meet at the printer to review the final proof of the registration statement	All parties

Day	Tasks	Responsible
51	File the registration statement with the SEC, the states, and the NASD	Company Counsel
52	Distribute the preliminary "red herring" prospectus to the proposed underwriters' syndicate	Underwriter
81	Receive comment letters from the SEC, the NASD, and the states	Company
83	Meet to discuss the comments and to prepare Amendment No. 1 to the registration statement. (The amendment should respond to all the comments, include material developments since the previous filing, and include updated financial statements, if necessary.)	All parties
85	Meet at the printer to review Amendment No. 1 to the registration statement	All parties
86	File Amendment No. 1 to the registration statement with the SEC, the states, and the NASD	Company Counsel
	Inform the SEC of the date on which the final pricing amendment will be filed	Company Counsel
88	Hold a due diligence meeting for the members of the proposed underwriting syndicate	All parties
92	Finalize the offering price	Company, Underwriters
	File the pricing amendment and request acceleration of effectiveness	Company Counsel

Day	Tasks	Responsible
	Sign the underwriting agreement and the agreement among the underwriters	Company, Underwriters
93	Deliver the first comfort letter to the underwriters	Independent Accountants
	Receive notification from the SEC that the registration statement is effective	Company
	Issue a press release	Company
	Begin the public offering	Underwriters
100	Deliver the final comfort letter to the underwriters	Independent Accountants
	Close, receive the proceeds from the underwriters, and issue the stock	Company, Underwriters

APPENDIX 2-3. COMPARISON OF REGISTRATION FORMS S-1, S-18, AND ANNUAL REPORT 10-K INFORMATION REQUIREMENTS

	Form S-1	Form S-18	Form 10-K
Purpose	Registration of securities with the SEC under the 1933 Act	Registration of securities with the SEC under the 1933 Act	Annual report under the 1934 Act
Dollar limit			
• Registrant	No limit	$7.5 million	Not applicable
• Secondary offering	No limit	$1.5 million	Not applicable
Eligibility for use	No restrictions	Companies not previously subject to the 1934 Act are eligible; this form is not available to insurance companies, investment companies and certain majority-owned subsidiaries	No restrictions
Significant required disclosures	Summary information, risk factors, and ratio of earnings to fixed charges (S-K Item 503)	Same as S-1, except the ratios need to be presented	Not applicable

	Form S-1	Form S-18	Form 10-K
Significant required disclosures: (cont'd.)	Use of proceeds; determination of offering price; dilution; selling security holders; plan of distribution; description of securities to be registered; interests of named experts and counsel (S-K Items 504–509 and Item 202)	Same as S-1	Not applicable
	Information with respect to the registrant:	Information with respect to the registrant:	Information with respect to the registrant:
	Description of the business (S-K Item 101)	Less extensive than S-1	Less extensive than S-1
	Description of property (S-K Item 102)	Less extensive S-1	Same as S-1
	Legal proceedings (S-K Item 103)	Same as S-1	Same as S-1
	Market and dividend data (S-K Item 201)	Less extensive than S-1	Same as S-1
	Financial statements must comply with Regulation S-X; additional financial statements are required for significant unconsolidated subsidiaries and equity investees[a] and for significant acquired or to-be-acquired companies[b]	Financial statements need not comply with Regulation S-X; additional financial statements are required for significant acquired or to-be-acquired companies[b]	Financial statements must comply with Regulation S-X[c]; additional financial statements are required for significant unconsolidated subsidiaries and equity investees[a]
	• Two years' audited balance sheets, updated by a condensed interim balance sheet as required	One year's audited balance sheet, updated by a condensed interim balance sheet as required	Two years' audited balance sheets[c]
	• Three years' audited statements of income and changes in financial position, and reconciliations of other stockholders' equity accounts, updated by comparative condensed interim statements as required	Two years' audited statements of income and changes in financial position, and reconciliations of other stockholders' equity accounts, updated by comparative condensed interim statements as required	Three years' audited statements of income and changes in financial position, and reconciliations of other stockholders' equity accounts[c]
	• Financial statement schedules required by S-X	No schedules	Same as S-1[c]

	Form S-1	Form S-18	Form 10-K
Significant required disclosures: (cont'd.)	Selected financial data; supplementary financial information; management's discussion and analysis of financial condition and results of operations; and disagreements with accountants on financial and disclosure matters (S-K Items 301-304)	Not required	Same as S-1
	Information about directors and executive officers (S-K Item 401)	Same as S-1	Same as S-1
	Executive compensation and transactions with management (S-K Items 402 and 404)	Similar to S-1	Same as S-1
	Ownership of securities by certain beneficial owners and management (S-K Item 403)	Same as S-1	Same as S-1

[a] Financial statements need not be audited for those years in which the significance test in rule 3-09 of Regulation S-X is not met; interim financial statements are required in a Form S-1.

[b] The number of years for which financial statements are required is determined by the significance tests in rule 3-05 of Regulation S-X; interim financial statements are required.

[c] After using a Form S-18, the Regulation S-X requirements and the number of years for which financial information is to be presented are phased in.

3

PRIVATE PLACEMENTS
(EXEMPT OFFERINGS OF SECURITIES)

It is safe to say that most entrepreneurs at the head of a small but growing company dream of taking their companies public as a means of raising capital for growth, not to mention two other enticing advantages—the prestige of being a public company, and the considerable financial gain that present investors often realize. But what if this is not the time?

Perhaps a limited amount of capital is needed, but at least three factors seem to be saying, "Don't do it." (1) Your company does not yet have the financial strength or reputation to attract enough investors for a public offering. (2) You cannot afford the expense of going through the public offering process. (3) You need the money now and cannot wait for the lengthy process to run its course. Going public will be feasible eventually, but what now?

The answer may be an exempt offering, commonly called a private placement.

A private placement is an exempt offering of stock in your company because you do not have to file a registration statement with the Securities and Exchange Commission (SEC), an enormous advantage since it cuts down paperwork and saves precious time. It is called a private placement because you can offer the stock to a few private investors instead of the public at large, thus saving the cost and time of going through all the procedures involved in a public offering.

Saving time and money for small companies in need of growth capital was exactly what Congress had in mind when it spelled out these exemptions in the Securities Act of 1933.

While "exemptions" is the key word, you do not have a completely free hand—far from it.

For one thing, while your private placement may be exempt from federal registration, it may not be exempt from registration under state laws. Some states require registration, some do not.

Keep this in mind, too. Private placements are not exempt from antifraud provisions of the securities laws. This means that you must give potential investors the necessary information about your company to make a well-informed decision, and exercise meticulous care that you do not omit or misstate the facts or give them a rosier hue than they deserve.

There are other restrictions that apply, as your attorney or independent accountant will tell you. But they are not difficult and generally conform to the spirit of Congress when it decided to include the exempt offerings section of the 1933 Act. The aim was to simplify things and make it easier for companies to raise capital so they could seize a growth opportunity when it came along. The Small Business Investment Incentive Act of 1980 expanded exempt offering opportunities, and the resulting changes in SEC regulations have made private placements an increasingly popular method of raising capital.

This chapter discusses why you might undertake a private placement, who the potential investors might be, and the types of exempt offerings that you should understand before you decide to proceed.

WHEN TO CONSIDER A PRIVATE PLACEMENT

In most cases, the purpose of a private placement is to raise a limited amount of capital in a relatively short time, at a relatively low cost.

Your company does not yet have the financial track record or reputation to draw the general investing public to your stock, so a public offering is out. You have considered a traditional bank loan, government assistance or any number of other sources. For one reason or another, they do not quite fit your needs. Some would turn you down. Others are too costly or take more time than you can afford.

But a private placement appears to meet your needs on four basic considerations: it may be the cheapest way to get the capital you need, the fastest way, it is money you do not have to pay back, and there is little danger that you will lose control of your company to outside investors.

If your analysis is correct so far, the next question is: Where will I find the investors?

WHO WILL BUY YOUR STOCK?

Compared with a public offering, your private placement will probably involve only a few investors. They might be relatives, friends, neighbors, business acquaintances, anybody. If you know enough of such people and feel comfortable laying your proposition before them, fine. But more likely you will place the job of finding investors in the hands of a broker who makes a business of keeping track of investors who are willing to take risks with small companies.

In addition, there are at least three more or less homogeneous groups that might have a special interest in your situation:

1. Let us say you manufacture a product and sell it to dealers, franchisees, or wholesalers. These are the people who know and respect your company. Moreover, they depend on you to supply the product they sell. They might consider it to be in their own self-interest to buy your stock if they believe it will help assure continuation of product supply, and perhaps give them a favored treatment if you bring out a new product or product improvement. One problem here is this: If one dealer invests and another does not, can you treat both fairly in the future? Another problem is that a customer who invests might ask for exclusive rights to market your product in a particular geographical area, and you might find it hard to refuse.

   Still, these are people who know you and your operation and, therefore, you would not have to spend time and money to prepare an elaborate presentation. You could sell stock to them directly and save yourself the cost of an investment banker (as much as 10 percent of the value of the issue). And, finally, your customers are a diverse group and there is little likelihood they would get together and demand a voice in your management.

2. A second group of prospective buyers for your stock are those professional investors who are always on the lookout to buy into a good, small company in its formative years, and ride it to success. Very often, these sophisticated investors choose an industry they believe will become "hot" and then focus 99 percent of their attention on the calibre of the management. If your management, or some one key individual, has earned a reputation as a star in management, or technology, or marketing, these risk-minded investors tend to flock to them. (The high-tech industry is an obvious example.) Whether your operation meets their tests for stardom in a hot field may determine whether they find your private placement a risk to their liking.

3. There are other investors searching for opportunities to buy shares of small growth companies in the expectation that, in the foreseeable future, the company will go public and as share-

holders they will benefit as new investors bid the price up, as often happens. For such investors, news of a private placement is a tip-off that a company is on the move and worth investigating, always with their eye on the possibility of it going public. These investors usually have no interest in taking a hand in running the company, so you have no fear of losing control or suffering their interference.

4. But private placements often attract another group, called venture capitalists, who hope to benefit when the company goes public. To help assure that happy development, these investors get intimately involved in running the firm, applying their expertise (often invaluable) in production, marketing, management or any other phase of the operation where their skill and experience can help the company reach its potential.

PRIVATE PLACEMENT AFTER GOING PUBLIC

Sometimes a company goes public and then, for any number of reasons that add up to bad luck, the high expectations that attracted investors in the first place turn sour. Your financial picture worsens; there is a cash crisis; down goes the price of your stock in the public marketplace.

You find that you need new funds to work your way out of the difficulties, but public investors are disillusioned and not likely to cooperate if you bring out a new issue.

Still, there are other investors who are sophisticated enough to see beyond today's problems; they know the company's fundamentals are sound. While the public has turned its back on you, these investors may well be receptive if you offer a private placement to tide you over. In such circumstances, a wide variety of securities can be used to the benefit of both the company and the investors (e.g., common stock, convertible preferred stock, convertible debentures, etc.).

TYPES OF EXEMPT OFFERINGS

There are several types of exempt offerings. They are usually described by reference to the securities regulation that applies to them.

Regulation D

Regulation D is the result of the first cooperative effort by the SEC and the state securities associations to develop a uniform exemption from registration for small issuers. The SEC hoped most states would adopt the Regulation with little change. Unfortunately, there has been little indication that this will happen.

Although Regulation D outlines procedures for exempt offerings, there is a requirement to file certain information (Form D) with the Securities and Exchange Commission. Form D (see Appendix 3-1) is a relatively short form that asks for certain general information about the issuer and the securities being issued, as well as some specific data about the expenses of the offering and the intended use of the proceeds.

Regulation D provides exemptions from registration when securities are being sold in certain circumstances. The various circumstances are commonly referred to by the applicable Regulation D rule number. The rules and application are as follows:

Rule 504. Issuers that are not subject to the reporting obligations of the Securities Exchange Act of 1934 (nonpublic companies) and that are not investment companies may sell up to $500,000 of securities over a 12-month period to an unlimited number of investors.

Rule 505. Issuers that are not investment companies may sell up to $5 million of securities over a 12-month period to no more than 35 nonaccredited purchasers, and to an unlimited number of "accredited" purchasers (defined in Exhibit 3-1). Such issuers may be eligible for this exemption even though they are public companies (subject to the reporting requirements of the 1934 Act).

Rule 506. Issuers may sell an unlimited amount of securities to no more than 35 nonaccredited but "sophisticated" purchasers (defined under "Requirements and Restrictions" following), and to an unlimited number of "accredited" purchasers. Public companies may be eligible for this exemption.

Regulation D—Requirements and Restrictions

The Small Business Exemption (Rule 504). Rule 504 is an attempt to establish a clear and workable exemption for small offerings (up to

$500,000) that are not regulated at the federal level and left to the states to oversee. Although the federal antifraud and civil liability provisions are still applicable, the company is not required to register at the federal level. The exemption is not available to issuers that are subject to the reporting obligations of the Securities Exchange Act of 1934 (public companies). There is a ban on general solicitation of investors as well as restrictions on resales (see Exhibit 3-4); however, if such offerings are registered at the state level, requiring the delivery of a disclosure document, the ban on general solicitations and resale of the securities does not apply.

The $5,000,000 Exemption (Rule 505). Only 35 investors that are *not* "accredited" may participate in an exempt offering under Rule 505, while an unlimited number of "accredited" investors may participate under this rule, which allows up to $5,000,000 in securities to be sold. (See Exhibit 3-1 for a definition of "accredited.")

EXHIBIT 3-1. ACCREDITED PURCHASER DEFINITION AS DEFINED BY REGULATION D

In order to determine whether the exemptions in Rules 505 and 506 apply, one must understand the term "accredited" purchaser or investor. Regulation D enumerates eight categories of "accredited investors":

1. Institutional investors (banks and insurance companies, for example), including ERISA plans, with total assets in excess of $5,000,000.
2. Private business development companies (defined in the Investment Advisors Act of 1940) which offer "significant material assistance."
3. Tax exempt organizations that are defined in Section 501(c)(3) of the Internal Revenue Code, with total assets in excess of $5,000,000.
4. Certain insiders of the issuer, such as directors, executive officers, and general partners (these persons need not meet the financial criteria set forth in items 5 through 7 below).
5. An investor who purchases at least $150,000 of the securities, if the purchase price does not exceed 20 percent of the investor's net worth (as defined).
6. Any person whose net worth at the time of purchase is $1,000,000 or more.
7. A person who has an income in excess of $200,000 in each of the last two years and who reasonably expects an income in excess of $200,000 in the current year.
8. An entity in which all the equity owners are accredited investors.

Even though a company is exempt from registration under Rule 505, proof that all accredited investors are indeed accredited requires a substantial legal and paperwork process.

Furthermore, if any nonaccredited investors (limited to 35) purchase the securities, Regulation D specifies that minimum disclosures, about your company and the offering, must be made to *all* investors. These disclosures include the information required by Part I of SEC public registration Form S-18 (see Exhibit 3-2). In addition, the disclosures include two years' financial statements, with one year having been audited. Thus, the process of undertaking an exempt offering under Rule 505, as well as meeting any state regulatory requirements, can involve substantial legal and financial costs.

The Unlimited Exemption (Rule 506).   Disclosure requirements for sales to nonaccredited investors under Rule 506 are similar to those

EXHIBIT 3-2.   FORM S-18, PART I DISCLOSURE INFORMATION REQUIREMENTS

Item
1. Forepart of the registration statement and outside front cover page of the prospectus
2. Inside front and outside back cover page of the prospectus
3. Summary information and risk factors
4. Use of proceeds
5. Determination of offering price
6. Dilution
7. Selling security holders
8. Plan of distribution
9. Legal proceedings
10. Directors and executive officers
11. Security ownership of certain beneficial owners and management
12. Description of securities to be registered
13. Interests of named experts and counsel
14. Statement as to indemnification
15. Organization within past five years
16. Description of business
17. Description of property
18. Interest of management and others in certain transactions
19. Certain market information
20. Executive compensation
21. Financial statements

of Rule 505 (see Exhibit 3-3). Rule 506 adds one further stipulation for the maximum of 35 nonaccredited investors who may purchase securities in this unlimited offering—the "sophisticated" investor. All nonaccredited investors in a Rule 506 offering must be "sophisticated" which is defined as follows:

> Each purchaser who is not an accredited investor either alone or with his purchaser representative must have such knowledge and experience in financial and business matters that he is capable of evaluating the merits and risks of the prospective investment.

Like Rule 505, an unlimited number of accredited investors may participate under Rule 506.

In order to determine whether potential investors qualify as either accredited or sophisticated, you should, with the aid of counsel, draw up a questionnaire to be completed by the prospective investor. These questionnaires should be retained by the seller as evidence of compliance with Regulation D.

Regulation D does not require that any particular information be furnished to investors if they are all accredited; however, the presence of *just one nonaccredited investor* means that all the information specified in Rules 505 and 506 must be furnished to *all* investors.

For an overall comparison of the requirements and restrictions for Regulation D exempt offerings, see Exhibit 3-3.

Intrastate Offerings

In order to qualify for this exemption, *all* the securities must be offered and sold to persons living within the state in which the company is incorporated and does a significant portion of its business, and the securities must remain in the state. Difficulties in monitoring and controlling trading limit the use of this exemption.

Regulation A

The Regulation A exemption is available for sales of less than $1.5 million of securities. Although sales under Regulation A are labeled as "exempt offerings," Regulation A requires the filing of an Offering Circular that includes the types of disclosures required in registration

EXHIBIT 3-3. COMPARATIVE CHART OF REGULATION D EXEMPT OFFERINGS

Restrictions and Requirements	Small Business Exemption (Rule 504)	$5 Million Exemption (Rule 505)	Unlimited Exemption (Rule 506)
Maximum dollar amount	$500,000 (12 months)	$5,000,000 (12 mos.)	Unlimited
Number of investors	Unlimited	Unlimited	Unlimited
Types of investors	Anyone	Accredited (35 may be nonaccredited)	Accredited (35 may be nonaccredited, but must be "sophisticated")
Offering solicitation restrictions	General solicitation is not allowed unless state registration requires delivery of a disclosure document.	General solicitation is not allowed.	General solicitation is not allowed.
Security resale restrictions	Restricted unless state registration requires delivery of a disclosure document (see Exhibit 3-4).	Restricted (see Exhibit 3-4)	Restricted (see Exhibit 3-4)
Who can issue	Any company other than investment companies or public companies.	Any company other than investment companies or issuers disqualified under Regulation A	Any company
SEC Notification	Required as a condition of exemption. Form D must be filed with the SEC within 15 days after the first sale, every six months after the first sale, and 30 days after the last sale.	Form D must be filed with the SEC within 15 days after the first sale, and 30 days after the last sale.	
Disclosure requirements	None specified, but enough should be disclosed to insure compliance with antifraud provisions.	None specified if investors are all accredited purchasers, but enough should be disclosed to insure compliance with antifraud provisions	

If investors include nonaccredited purchasers:

Nonpublic companies (those not registered under the Securities Act of 1934) must furnish:

Information in Part I of Form S-18 including two years financials with one year audited, except if furnishing such financials results in an unreasonable effort, issuer (other than a limited partnership) may furnish an audited balance sheet only as of 120 days before the offering; if the issuer is a limited partnership and furnishing such financials is unreasonable, it may use tax basis financials.

Same requirements as Rule 505, except the information required is that equivalent to Part I of the public registration statement form the issuer would be entitled to use. Either Form S-1 (see Chapter 2 "Going Public"), Form S-18, Form 10, or Form 8-A.

Public companies must furnish:

Rule 14a-3 annual report to shareholders, definitive proxy statement and Form 10-K, if requested, plus subsequent reports and other updating information *or* information in most recent Form S-1 or Form 10 or Form 10-K plus subsequent reports and other updating information.

Issuers must make available prior to sale:

i. Exhibits.
ii. Written information given to accredited investors.
iii. Opportunity to ask questions and receive answers.

EXHIBIT 3-4.   RESTRICTED RESALE OF EXEMPT STOCKS

Restricted Stock: Securities whose resale or transfer is restricted because it was issued in an exempt transaction (see Rule 144).

Rule 144: The Regulation D rule that requires restricted securities to be held for two or more years prior to resale or transfer (and also limits the number of shares of restricted stocks that can be sold by an affiliate of the issuer).

Rule 144 Exception: The resale and transfer restrictions under Rule 144 do *not* apply to offerings made under Regulation D Rule 504, "The Small Business Exemption," *if* such offerings are registered at the state level and the state requires delivery of a disclosure document to all investors. In this case, all resale restrictions are lifted.

Resale Disclaimer: A statement to be included in a disclosure document and/ or on the securities, which states the applicable resale restrictions. Examples include:

- The securities in this offering must be held for two or more years before resale or transfer can take place under the regulations of the Securities Act of 1933, as amended.

- Resale of the securities discussed in this disclosure may not be made unless the securities are registered under the Securities Act of 1933, as amended or unless the resale is exempt from the registration requirements of the Securities Act of 1933, as amended.

---

statements. However, the required financial statements need not be audited, although state security laws or the underwriters may require them to be audited. Regulation A is used infrequently because of the small amounts of capital that can be raised, the extensive disclosure requirements, and the apparent reluctance of underwriters to permit issuers to use it.

STATE SECURITIES REGULATION

Each of the states has rules for private placements, and while there are some similarities, there are many and wide differences as well. While three quarters of the states have adopted The Uniform Securities Act to reduce such differences, subsequent amendments and other changes to the laws mean that whatever uniformity was achieved initially has not been maintained. Therefore, whenever a security is sold in a state, the state's regulations as well as Regulation D must be complied with. The extensive differences among the states may make it necessary to retain local counsel in each state in which a security is offered, sold or purchased.

State securities laws are known as "blue sky laws." The term originated from legislative and judicial actions to prevent the sale of securities for endeavors that had as much substance as the blue sky. State securities laws predate the federal securities law by a couple of decades, and these laws are often different and more confining than federal securities regulations. The purpose of the federal securities acts is the "full disclosure" of relevant data. This allows the sales of very poor quality or high risk securities as long as full disclosure is made to the investing public. Many state securities laws, while calling for full disclosure, go much further. In many states, the administrators of securities laws are also responsible for the protection of the citizens in that state against bad or risky investments. Thus, a security cannot be traded in certain states if it is not "fair, just, or equitable." The interpretation of this term is generally the responsibility of the administrator of the state's securities laws.

Another significant difference between the federal and state laws is that federal regulations govern the initial distribution—the first sale of a security—not its subsequent resale. State regulations, however, may govern the sale each time a security is sold.

While it may appear easy to determine whether a state's blue sky laws apply to a particular situation, such may not be the case. Two potentially troublesome questions must be answered. First, it must be determined that a "security" is involved. There is no uniformity of opinion as to the meaning of the term "security"; it has been broadly interpreted to include such disparate items as stock, bonds, commitment letters, profit sharing certificates, etc. Second, there must be an offer, purchase or sale of the security "in this state" for state laws to apply. Yet there is a conflict among state laws as to how "in this state" should be applied to the many different and complicated transactions which can be involved. As indicated above, one should use legal counsel to determine whether a state's blue sky laws must be observed.

PROCEED WITH CARE—COMMON PITFALLS

Although exempt offerings are much less onerous than federal registration of securities, they still require some care and, usually, professional assistance. Violations of the exempt offering regulations can cause you to lose your exemption from registration and make you vulnerable to litigation brought by disgruntled investors.

Always follow the regulations and *document* your compliance with each. Be aware of these common pitfalls:

1. Do not advertise or solicit large numbers of potential investors. This could be construed as a "public" not a private offering.

2. Do not exaggerate or present information only in the most favorable light—be candid with your information, even pointing out the risks attendant to the investment.

3. Furnish all information required by the regulations, and if specific disclosures are not required, furnish enough information so the potential investor can make an informed decision.

4. Where qualification of investors is required, be sure you have documentation that proves your investors meet the qualifications.

5. Be sure investors understand the restrictions on resales of the securities. The securities themselves should bear a legend disclosing the resales restriction (see Exhibit 3-4).

6. If you are thinking of your second exempt offering, or are planning an exempt offering before or after registering securities, make sure there is sufficient time delay so that the two offerings will not be considered as one issue. There must be at least six months between offerings. Likewise, beware of having sold some shares to a few investors prior to or immediately following an exempt offering. These sales might be construed as part of the exempt offering, subject to its requirements.

PRIVATE PLACEMENT MEMORANDUM

To best present your company information to potential investors, you will want to prepare a Private Placement Memorandum. If nothing else, it should include enough disclosure information to ensure compliance with antifraud provisions—enough information for investors to make a well-informed decision, with no omissions, misstatements or enhancements of the facts. A more elaborate presentation may be required if you engage a broker to solicit investors. A review of our business plan outline, presented in the Appendix at the end of this book, will help you decide what to include based on who you want to approach and the circumstances and purposes of your offering. For example, the start-up of a new venture or the launching of a new product would probably require the most detailed memorandum. The raising of second and third round capital may require only such information as funds required and their uses, historical and projected financial data, and a description of your company and its history.

Most private placement memorandums should also include certain disclaimers regarding the type of securities being offered, the confidentiality of information, and the accuracy of projections, and so forth. Examples of private placement disclaimers are included in the business plan outline mentioned above.

APPENDIX 3-1.

Appendix 3-1, Form D, Notice of Sales of Securities, is represented on the following pages.

FORM D

UMB Approval
OMB 3235-0076
Expires December 31, 1984

SEC USE ONLY

NOTICE OF SALES OF SECURITIES
PURSUANT TO REGULATION D OR SECTION 4(6)

SEC USE ONLY

SERIAL

21- ___ - ___ ◄

Nature of this filing with respect to this offering.

INSTRUCTION Please check the box(es) corresponding to the exemptive provision applicable to this offering.

Rule 504 ☐   Rule 505 ☐   Rule 506 ☐   Section 4(6) ☐

INSTRUCTION Circle "N" for a new filing or "A" for an amended filing.

ORIGINAL 1 $_A^N$ COMBINED ORIGINAL AND FINAL 2 $_A^N$ SIX-MONTH UPDATE 3 $_A^N$ FINAL 4 $_A^N$

INSTRUCTIONS   The issuer shall file with the Commission five copies of this notice at the following times   (a) no later than 15 days after the first sale of securities in an offering under Regulation D or Section 4(6); (b) every six months after the first sale of securities in an offering under Regulation D or Section 4(6), unless a final notice has been filed; and (c) no later than 30 days after the last sale of securities in an offering under Regulation D or Section 4(6), *except that if the offering is completed within the 15-day period described in "(a)" above, and if the notice is filed no later than the end of that period but after the completion of the offering, then only one notice need be filed*. If more than one notice for an offering is required to be filed, notices after the first notice need only report the issuer's name, information in response to Part C and any material changes from the facts previously reported in Parts A and B. This notice shall be deemed to be filed with the Commission for purposes of the rule as of the date on which the notice is received by the Commission, or if delivered to the Commission after the date on which it is due, as of the date on which it is mailed by means of United States registered or certified mail to the Office of Small Business Policy, Division of Corporation Finance, U.S. Securities and Exchange Commission, Washington, D.C. 20549.

A. Basic Identification of Issuer.

INSTRUCTION. State the address of the issuer's executive offices and, if different, the address at which the issuer's principal business operations are conducted or proposed to be conducted.

NAME			
ADDRESS OF EXECUTIVE OFFICES			
CITY		STATE	ZIP
AREA CODE	TELEPHONE NUMBER		
ADDRESS OF PRINCIPAL BUSINESS OPERATIONS			
CITY		STATE	ZIP
AREA CODE	TELEPHONE NUMBER		

INSTRUCTION: Please list the full name and address of the following persons: each promoter of the issuer involved in the offering of securities as to which sales pursuant to Regulation D or Section 4(6) are reported on this notice, the issuer's chief executive officer, and each of the issuer's affiliates. Indicate the status of each person named by placing an "X" in the applicable box(es) opposite such person's name. The term "promoter" includes . . .

(a)   Any person who, acting alone or in conjunction with one or more other persons, directly or indirectly takes the initiative in founding and organizing the business or enterprise of an issuer; or

(b)   Any person who, in connection with the founding or organizing of the business or enterprise of an issuer, directly or indirectly receives in consideration of services or property, or both services and property, 10 percent or more of any class of securities of the issuer or 10 percent or more of the proceeds from the sale of any class of securities. However, a person who receives such securities or proceeds either solely as brokerage commissions or solely in consideration of property shall not be deemed a promoter within the meaning of this paragraph if such person does not otherwise take part in founding and organizing the enterprise.

SEC 1972 (3-82)

	CEO	Aff	Pro
NAME			

| ADDRESS | CITY | STATE | ZIP |

	CEO	Aff	Pro
NAME			

| ADDRESS | CITY | STATE | ZIP |

1. Has the issuer filed any periodic reports pursuant to Section 13 or 15(d) of the Securities Exchange Act of 1934?   YES ☐   NO ☐

   If yes, please indicate the file number of the docket in which the periodic reports are filed _____

2. Please indicate the issuer's IRS employer identification number.   If an application for such number is pending, please enter "00-0000000."

3. Please briefly describe the issuer's business

   _____
   _____
   _____

4. Please indicate the issuer's type of business organization.
   a. corporation   b. partnership   c. business trust   d. other, *please specify* _____

5. Please indicate the issuer's Standard Industrial Classification (SIC) at the 3 or 4 digit level. If the issuer has more than one SIC, please enter the issuer's primary SIC. If a 3 digit SIC is given, enter "X" in the left-most box.

6. In what year was the issuer incorporated or organized?

7. In what state is the issuer incorporated or organized? Please enter the standard two letter U.S. Postal Service abbreviation. Enter "CN" if the issuer is incorporated or organized in Canada, "FN" if the issuer is incorporated or organized in another foreign jurisdiction

8. Has the issuer been assigned a CUSIP number for its securities?   YES ☐   NO ☐

   If yes, please specify the first six (6) digits. If no, please enter "000000."

9. Please check the appropriate box for each exchange or market, if any, where the issuer's securities are traded.

   American Stock Exchange . . . . a ☐
   New York Stock Exchange . . . . b ☐
   Other National Securities Exchanges . . . . c ☐
   Over-the-Counter (including
      National Association of Securities Dealers Automated Quotations System) . . d ☐
   Other   *Please Specify* . . . . e ☐

   SEC USE ONLY

   _____
   _____

   None. . . . . f. ☐

NOTICE OF SALES OF SECURITIES
PURSUANT TO REGULATION D OR SECTION 4(6)

B. Statistical Information About the Issuer

INSTRUCTION   Please enter the letter for the appropriate response to each item in Part B in the box
indicated   If the issuer's first fiscal year has not yet ended, furnish the requested
information as of a date or as to a period ending on a date, no more than 90 days
prior to the first sale of securities in this offering.

1   What were the issuer's gross revenues for its most recently ended fiscal year?   ☐

    a. $500,000 or less   b $500,001 – $1,000,000   c. $1,000,001 – $3,000,000
    d $3,000,001 – $5,000,000   e. $5,000,001 – $25,000,000   f. $25,000,001 – $100,000,000
    g Over $100,000,000

2   What were the issuer's total consolidated assets as of the end of its latest fiscal year?   ☐

    a $500,000 or less   b. $500,001 – $1,000,000   c. $1,000,001 – $3,000,000
    d $3,000,001 – $5,000,000   e. $5,000,001 – $25,000,000   f. $25,000,001 – $100,000,000
    g Over $100,000,000

3   What was the issuer's net income, or income before partners' compensation, for its most recently ended   ☐
fiscal year?

    a None or net loss   b. $1 – $50,000   c. $50,001 – $250,000   d. $250,001 – $1,000,000
    e $1,000,001 – $5,000,000   f. Over $5,000,000

4   What was the issuer's shareholders' or partners' equity at the end of its latest fiscal year?   ☐

    a. Negative   b. $1 – $50,000   c. $50,001 – $250,000   d. $250,001 – $1,000,000
    e. $1,000,001 – $3,000,000   f. $3,000,001 – $10,000,000   g. Over $10,000,000

5   How many shareholders or partners did the issuer have at the end of its latest fiscal year?   ☐

    a. 0 – 4   b. 5 – 9   c. 10 – 24   d 25 – 99   e. 100 – 299
    f. 300 – 499   g. 500 or more

6   What percentage of shares outstanding were held by non-affiliated shareholders at the end   ☐
of the issuer's latest fiscal year? [1]

    a None   b. Less than 5.0%   c. 5.0% – 9.9%   d. 10.0% – 24.9%
    e. 25.0% – 49.9%   f. 50.0% – 74.9%   g. 75.0% or more   h. Not applicable

7   How many shares were outstanding at the end of the issuer's latest fiscal year?   ☐

    a. 500,000 or less   b. 500,001 – 1,500,000   c. 1,500,001 – 2,500,000
    d. 2,500,001 – 3,500,000   e. 3,500,001 – 5,000,000   f. Over 5,000,000   g. Not applicable

8   How many full-time equivalent employees did the issuer have at the end of its latest fiscal year? [2]   ☐

    a None   b. 1 – 5   c. 6 – 10   d. 11 – 20   e. 21 – 50   f. 51 – 100
    g. 101 – 500   h. 500 or more

---

[1]   *A non-affiliated person is defined to be anyone other than a person that directly or indirectly, through one or
more intermediaries, controls or is controlled by the issuer or is under common control with such person.*

[2]   *Full-time equivalent employees is defined to equal the sum of the number of full-time employees plus the
number of part-time employees working 25 or more hours per typical work week.*

C. Section 3(b) or 4(6) Sales Limit and Other Information About the Offering

INSTRUCTION: If a response to any item is "none" or "zero," please enter zero ("0") in the corresponding space.

1. Type and aggregate offering price of securities intended to be sold pursuant to Regulation D or Section 4(6) in this offering.

    a. Debt . . . . $ _____

    b. Equity . . . . $ _____

    c. Convertible . . . . $ _____

2. Number of accredited and non-accredited investors who have purchased securities in this offering in reliance on Rules 505 or 506 and aggregate dollar amounts of their purchases to date. For sales in reliance on Rule 504 or Section 4(6), please enter the number of persons who have purchased securities and aggregate dollar amounts of their purchases to date on the accredited investor lines.

	Number of Investors (A)	Aggregate Dollar Amount (B)
Accredited investors	_____	$ _____
Non-accredited investors	_____	_____
Total	_____	$ _____

3. If this offering is being made pursuant to Rule 504 or 505, report by exemption and type of security (i.e., debt, equity, convertible) the dollar amount of all Section 3(b) sales of securities (other than sales reported in Item C.2 above) occurring from twelve (12) months prior to the first sale of securities in this offering to date.

	Type (A)	Dollar Amount (B)
Rule 505	_____	$ _____
Regulation A	_____	_____
Rule 504	_____	_____
Total		$ _____

4. Please list the full name and address of each person who has been or will be paid or given directly or indirectly any commission or similar remuneration for solicitation of purchasers in connection with sales of securities in this offering pursuant to Regulation D or Section 4(6). If a person to be listed is an associated person of a broker or dealer registered with the Commission and/or with a state or states, then please also list the name of that broker or dealer. If more than five (5) persons to be listed are associated persons of a broker or dealer registered with the Commission and/or a state or states, then the issuer may list the name and address of only such broker or dealer. Please also list, using the standard two-letter Postal Service abbreviation the state or states in which each person, or if an associated broker or dealer is listed, each such broker or dealer, intends to or is offering securities in this offering; if all states, enter "all."

NAME			
ADDRESS	CITY	STATE	ZIP
NAME OF ASSOCIATED BROKER OR DEALER			
STATES			

SEC USE ONLY
8 - | | | | | |

NAME			
ADDRESS	CITY	STATE	ZIP
NAME OF ASSOCIATED BROKER OR DEALER			
STATES			

SEC USE ONLY
8 - | | | | | |

5. a. Aggregate offering price of securities, from C.1 above $ ☐ _____ .

     b. Furnish a reasonably itemized statement of all expenses in connection with the issuance and distribution of the securities being offered in this offering. Please exclude any amounts relating solely to the organizational expenses of the issuer. Insofar as practicable, give amounts for the categories listed below. The information may be given as subject to future contingencies. If the expenditure in any category is not known, furnish an estimate and place an "X" in the box to the left of the amount given.

         a. Blue Sky Fees and Expenses $ ☐ _____ .
         b. Transfer Agents' Fees   ☐ _____ .
         c. Printing and Engraving Costs   ☐ _____ .
         d. Legal Fees   ☐ _____ .
         e. Accounting Fees   ☐ _____ .
         f. Engineering Fees   ☐ _____ .
         g. Sales Commissions *(including Finders' Fees)*   ☐ _____ .
         h. Other Expenses *(Identify)*

         _____   ☐ _____ .
         _____   ☐ _____ .

         Total $ ☐ _____ .

     c. Enter the difference between the aggregate offering price in 5.a. and total costs in 5.b. This difference is the "adjusted gross proceeds to the issuer." $ ☐ _____ .

6. Indicate below the amount of the adjusted gross proceeds to the issuer *(other than amounts specified in Item 5.b. above)* proposed to be used or used for each of the purposes listed below. If the amount to be used for any purpose is not known, furnish an estimate and place an "X" in the box to the left of the amount given.

	Payments to officers, directors and affiliates (A)	Payments to others (B)
a. Salaries and fees	$ ☐ _____ .	$ ☐ _____
b. Purchase of real estate	☐ _____	☐ _____
c. Purchase, rental or leasing and installation of machinery and equipment	☐ _____ .	☐ _____
d. Construction or leasing of plant building and facilities	☐ _____	☐ _____
e. Development expense *(product development, research, patent costs, etc.)*	☐ _____	☐ _____
f. Purchase of raw materials, inventories, supplies, etc.	☐ _____	☐ _____
g. Selling, advertising, and other sales promotion	☐ _____ .	☐ _____
h. Acquisition of other businesses *(including the value of securities involved in this offering which may be used in exchange for the assets or securities of another issuer pursuant to a merger)*	☐ _____	☐ _____
i. Repayment of loans	☐ _____	☐ _____
Other – *please specify*		
j. _____	☐ _____	☐ _____
k. _____	☐ _____	☐ _____
l. _____	☐ _____ .	☐ _____
m. _____	☐ _____	☐ _____
Total	$ ☐ _____ .	$ ☐ _____

D. Undertaking by issuers filing pursuant to Rule 505.

The undersigned issuer hereby undertakes to furnish to the Securities and Exchange Commission, upon the written request of its staff, the information furnished by the issuer to any non-accredited person pursuant to paragraph (b)(2) of Rule 502.

ISSUER _____

SIGNATURE _____

NAME _____

TITLE _____

E. The issuer has duly caused this notice to be signed on its behalf by the undersigned duly authorized person.

DATE OF NOTICE

ISSUER _____

_____

SIGNATURE _____

NAME _____

TITLE _____

INSTRUCTION Print the name and title of the signing representative under his signature. One copy of every notice on Form D shall be manually signed. Any copies not manually signed shall bear typed or printed signatures.

---------ATTENTION---------

Intentional misstatements or omissions of fact constitute Federal Criminal Violations (See 18 U.S.C. 1001).

FORM D Continuation Sheet

NOTICE OF SALES OF SECURITIES PURSUANT TO REGULATION D OR SECTION 4(6)

Page 7

Item of Form
(identify)

Answer

Note: Page 8 of Form D, which is identical to this page, is not represented here.

4

VENTURE CAPITAL

One of the most interesting and fastest-growing ways to raise capital for growth is also one of the oldest. Venture capital—its modern name—dates as far back as business itself. The first time a person with a promising business idea asked an uncle, a friend, a neighbor

71

to help get a business going by putting in some money, and offered to share future profits, we saw the beginning of venture capital as a basic business concept.

To understand venture capital, start with the word itself: "venture" means risk. If your company has a promising but unproven idea (the risk factor) and needs money to take the next big step, yours is the kind of situation that attracts the venture capitalist. He has the money you need and will supply it—by buying stock in your company, by lending it to you, or by some other method. With this ownership stake, he shares your risk. If you fail, he fails. If you succeed, he shares your profits. Because it is a touch-and-go situation, and the risks are high, he will usually be interested only if he sees a chance for a high return on his investment—30 percent a year is not uncommon. By comparison, common stock investors, with greatly reduced risks, will receive only an average yearly return of 10 to 15 percent, and while banks may lend you money, they will only participate if the risk is minimal and so their return will be far less than the venture capitalist expects. The logic is very simple: the more the risk, the higher the expected return. Nothing could be more aptly named than venture capital.

In the last decade or so, venture capital has been something of a growth industry itself. There have always been a few wealthy people ready to invest in young, developing companies—at best, a minor factor in the world of business financing. By the mid-1980s, the picture had changed dramatically. With the flowering of high technology and the sophistication of marketing, new industries came into existence and companies of all sizes discovered new opportunities.

This combination of circumstances led entrepreneurs to search for growth capital, and venture capitalists to multiply both in numbers and in the amount of capital they were willing to risk. There are still wealthy individuals. But now there are more than 600 venture capital firms in the United States. And many states, seeing a chance to help local firms and create new jobs, have marched into the ranks of venture capitalists. In 1984, the aggregate investment of all of these sources of risk capital ran close to $4.5 billion, hardly a minor factor anymore.

As you might imagine, venture capitalists on that scale have become far more than mere suppliers of money. To protect their large investments and realize the high return they expect, venture capitalists tend to concentrate on industries with which they are thoroughly familiar. They concentrate on industries they know because they expect to have a voice in the management of your company, in order to minimize the risks and maximize the profits. What they have to offer—valuable contacts, market expertise, sound strategy thinking, a practical understanding of what you are trying to accomplish with your company—may well turn out to be just as important or more so than their money.

The relationship between entrepreneur and venture capitalist is an intimate one, certainly more intimate than with a bank which normally has little say in your operation. Therefore, before embarking on this arrangement, the venture capitalist will examine your company in detail, particularly the quality of your management and your track record (possibly more important than your skills as an originator). And you will examine him, to satisfy yourself that he understands your kind of business, that your objectives are compatible, and that he might bring expertise that can significantly add to your chances of making a success of this venture. Both parties might bring in outsiders to evaluate each other, such as lawyers, accountants, or other experts who can train an objective eye on the facts that matter. This mutual evaluation is essential since the "marriage" is an important one and any subsequent divorce might be fatal to your company.

Venture capital, with its unique risk-sharing nature, may or may not be the best way for you to raise growth capital. But it is well worth your time to see what it is, how it works, the advantages and disadvantages, how to prepare for negotiations, and factors that enter into a well-reasoned decision, all the subject of discussion in this chapter.

SOURCES OF VENTURE CAPITAL

The demand for venture capital in recent years has not only caused sources of this kind of financing to proliferate, but the sources can be classified in at least seven distinctly different types. First, we will list them, then describe the principal characteristics of each. The list:

1. Private venture capital partnerships (family money, pension funds, large individual investors, etc.)

2. Public venture capital funds
3. Large industrial venture capital pools
4. Investment banking firms' directed venture capital
5. Small business investment companies (SBIC) and minority enterprise small business investment companies (MESBIC)
6. Private investors
7. Some state governments

Private Venture Capital Partnerships

This grouping has the largest number of venture capitalists and is, in the aggregate, the largest source of funds.

Originally, this type of firm was organized by individuals who had been eminently successful in building enterprises of their own. They invested some of their profits in other young companies still struggling for success. They saw opportunities that might be realized with an infusion of capital and perhaps the use of their own expertise and experience. They could afford the risk, and expected a handsome return.

Later, these adventurous entrepreneurs combined their money and formed partnerships. They invested in special situations where they believed they could apply their own experience, contacts, and managerial skills to enhance a growing company's ability to profit and thus bring a high return. This was the forerunner of today's highly sophisticated partnerships.

Historically, low-risk investments such as money market instruments and bonds returned 5 to 10 percent a year, and riskier but still relatively secure equities brought 8 to 12 percent. The early venture capitalists showed that by carefully investing in companies whose business they understood, and by getting personally involved in the management, they were able to achieve much higher returns, equal to the risk. As a result, the venture capital industry as a whole now expects to generate a return on investment of approximately 30 percent a year. Since this 30 percent average includes successful and unsuccessful investments, many ventures will need to yield much more than 30 percent per year in order to meet the industry average. As you might expect, such results have brought many people and businesses into the venture capital field.

Among the family groups that became major factors in venture capital were Rockefeller, Phipps, and Whitney, and many others followed. In addition, firms were created by pooling funds. With very large capital bases—ranging up to $500 million—under management, these private venture capital firms usually have a large number of investments in companies at various stages of their growth. As private venture capital firms have succeeded, they have been able to attract funds from banks, insurance companies, pension funds and other sources. By any measurement, they are a powerful force in the world of risk capital.

Public Venture Capital Funds

As the business of venture capital matures, and the venture capitalists themselves need more capital, some raise funds by selling their stock in the public equity markets. The operation of these public firms is generally the same as private firms with one exception: they must disclose much more detail about their activities because they must conform to disclosure regulations imposed by the Securities and Exchange Commission.

Industrial Venture Capital Community

More than 50 large industrial companies have formed investment pools of their own which they manage themselves. They invest in developing businesses. Some do so in the hope that their investment will help a needy company succeed and then become a choice acquisition target for the firm that supplied the capital. Others offer venture funds as a diversification move, hoping the investment will prove profitable. Many industrial companies view their venture capital investments as a type of research and development—a window on technology—a way of supporting and gaining access to new technology that could prove profitable to their company's operations in the future.

Investment Banking Firms' Venture Capital Funds

The investment banking business has long been a major factor in helping companies raise growth capital, and now it has entered the venture capital field.

Traditionally, they have provided expansion capital and later-stage financing by selling the stock of growing companies in the public and private equity markets.

To provide more service to clients, some have formed their own venture capital firms. In this way, they can provide not only later-stage but also early-stage financing. Thus, while their objective is to serve their clients better, these firms are realizing the same high returns as other types of venture capital firms.

The SBICs and MESBICs

The small business investment companies (SBICs) and minority enterprise small business investment companies (MESBICs) are privately capitalized venture capital firms, licensed and regulated by the Small Business Administration (SBA). These firms receive loans from the SBA (a U.S. government agency) to augment capital that they raise privately. Because of this special status, they are regulated to some degree, which means there are some restrictions. Restrictions include the level of private equity capital required for each funding (SBICs $500,000 to $10 million and MESBICs a minimum of $1 million) to the type of enterprise funded (real estate transactions are usually excluded, see also Exhibit 4-1).

Individual Investors

While venture capital firms play a major role in raising funds for growth, there is still room for the individual investor, and individuals are a considerable force. They were the first venture capitalists when everything was on a much smaller scale—the uncle, the friend, the neighbor. The world probably overlooks them when thinking about the august universe of venture capitalism, but their contribution, if it could be measured, would undoubtedly surprise everybody. Individual investors are usually the source of funds for the true start-up company—the person with an idea or product, but no track record—they often provide the seed capital.

State Governments

In a growing number of states (25 or more), state governments have entered the field of venture capital. True, they operate on a small

EXHIBIT 4-1. SBIC AND MESBIC INVESTMENT RESTRICTIONS

As recipients of government loans, small business investment companies (SBICs) and minority enterprise small business investment companies (MESBICs) are restricted from providing venture capital to the following types of businesses:

1. Nonmanufacturing companies with a net worth in excess of $6 million.
2. Nonmanufacturing companies with an average net income after taxes for the preceding two years in excess of $2 million.
3. Manufacturing companies with more than 250 employees, unless they meet the net worth and net income tests of 1 and 2 above.
4. Investment companies.
5. Lending institutions.

scale compared with the big venture capital firms, with modest investments ranging from less than $100,000 to $500,000. They hope to make a profit if possible, but their primary goal is to aid an ailing company that might have difficulty raising capital elsewhere, and thus save this entity in the local economy and the jobs that might otherwise be lost.

TYPES OF VENTURE CAPITAL FIRMS

Just like your own company, venture capital firms pick out a certain niche in their industry and concentrate their activities there.

Some confine themselves to a certain geographic region. They study the investment opportunities in this region carefully, and believe that being a home-grown operation gives them an edge. Others operate nationwide. And some consider the entire world to be their arena. It is important for you to understand these differences and to match the scope of your operation to theirs.

Venture capital firms differ in another way. Some specialize in early-stage financing, others favor expansion financing for more mature companies, others supply funds for acquisitions and buy-outs. Let us examine these differences in some detail, so you can see clearly how important it is to match your circumstances to theirs.

Early-Stage Financing

Some venture capitalists specialize in putting money into a company in its earliest stages. That is the point at which the risk is highest and, therefore, so is the chance for high rewards if the enterprise succeeds.

Let us say you have started a company. Right now, it consists mainly of an idea—for a new product, a product improvement, or something else for which you are convinced there is a waiting market. Now the first preliminary steps must be taken, and that requires capital.

After considering other sources, you turn to the venture capital field and find a firm* that specializes in your kind of situation. You state your case: you need funds to finance preliminary research and development, to prepare a business plan, and to provide a modest amount of working capital. The firm, impressed by your idea, your knowledge of the market, your objectives and, not least, by your own level-headed intelligence, decides that your goals are compatible with their own, and the deal is made. They supply the necessary seed money.

When that phase of your operation is completed, you take the next tentative step. This is the start-up phase. It takes additional capital, of course, to carry the research and development far enough to develop a prototype product and whatever else is necessary to show that your business has a solid chance to succeed. (If you happen to be in the high technology field, you know how essential the R&D work can be.) Again, this is an early-stage opportunity that some venture capital firms relish. They examine your product, your business plan, your objectives, and satisfy themselves that you have good people in key managerial positions, and agree to supply the capital.

Early-stage financing might also include a third phase in which more funds are raised by the venture capital method to carry your business to the stage of manufacturing and marketing your product. These three early-stage phases may appear to be separate and distinct, and in some cases they are, but in other cases they tend to blend into one early-stage phase where the capital is supplied by a single venture capital firm. Obviously, the needs differ from one industry to another, and from one company to another.

Second-Stage Financing

Just as the term suggests, additional capital may be needed to assist your company through its second stage—the initial scale-up for man-

* See section on "How to Find a Venture Capitalist."

ufacturing and marketing, building the necessary facilities, establishing a working capital base to support inventory, receivables, and other costs in moving the company into the commercial stage. The risk is still high and therefore appealing to venture capitalists who specialize in your kind of business, especially in these formative years of your development (see Exhibit 4-2).

As time goes on and your business matures, you will probably need new infusions of capital to take advantage of opportunities to grow. But now your company is established and has proven itself, so the risk is less. When the risk diminishes and the chance for high returns moderates, the venture capitalist usually turns elsewhere. His place is taken by the more conventional lenders and investors, including the public who may now be willing to buy stock in your company with a comparatively modest return on their investment for the modest risk they see in a seasoned company.

There are times when these conventional capital markets are tight— that is, when borrowing rates are high, or when the stock market is in a slump and investors wary of even the best companies—and, in such situations, you might turn to the venture capitalist again to supply the funds you need to capitalize on an exceptional opportunity that will not wait. As a rule, however, venture capital is not a major factor in the later stages of a mature company's growth.

Acquisition and Buyout Financing

Venture capitalists use their money in many ways. As specialists in certain industries, they keep up-to-date on the affairs of individual companies, even divisions within those companies. If they spot what they believe is an unusual opportunity, they might form a pool of investors and buy a division of a large public company, or buy out a small private company. Then they establish their new possession as a new company with its own management and capital base.

They do this because they believe this new company can be made profitable and will give them the high return they expect in any high-risk situation.

WHEN VENTURE CAPITAL IS WITHDRAWN

When you arrange to bring venture capital into your company, one of the most important things for you to take into account is the basic

EXHIBIT 4-2.   THE VENTURE CAPITAL FUNDING PROCESS

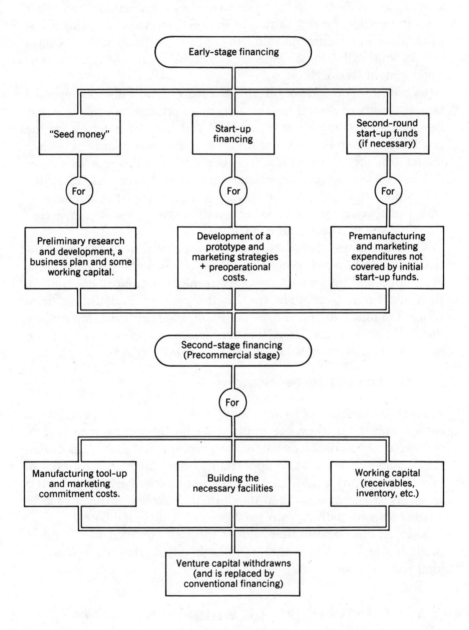

nature of this relationship. At some point in the future, the firm that supplied the funds will want to cash in on their investment. The firm takes its risk, expects to be handsomely rewarded, then, as the company matures and the risk-reward quotient moderates, moves on to invest in another high-risk opportunity elsewhere.

You must prepare your company for this eventuality so it can be done without hindering your momentum or placing an unbearable stress on the operation.

At the very outset, it is wise for you to reach an understanding with the venture capitalist. Exactly what are his investment objectives? What are his liquidity needs likely to be? Making certain that your needs and his are compatible instead of conflicting is probably the most critical step in the entire process of arriving at your decision.

Many venture capitalist pools are partnerships with an expected life of seven to ten years. Their strategy is to invest their funds, then at some point convert them back to cash or securities of your company if the value of these securities has risen high enough to provide a satisfactory reward for the risk they took when you needed their help.

Every venture capitalist's goals differ somewhat from all the others, just as your own company is unique. That is why it is crucially important to understand objectives, and especially the liquidity intentions, in no uncertain terms at the very outset of your talks.

HOW TO FIND A VENTURE CAPITALIST

With well over 1000 individuals and firms in the business of supplying venture capital—many of them specializing in certain industries, some nationwide while others concentrate on smaller geographic areas, some interested in early-stage financing and others in growth and expansion—finding a few that fit your needs may sound like a formidable task. But it need not be; there is good help available.

A good way to begin is to consult a directory. Many are published by industry groups such as the National Venture Capitalists Association, 1655 North Fort Meyer Drive, Suite 700, Arlington, Virginia. Some directories are national, some regional. A well-regarded directory is "Pratt's Guide to Venture Capital Sources," produced by Venture Economics Inc., Wellesley Hills, Massachusetts. Directories usually give the names, addresses, phone numbers of firms, list their officers, and specify the types of investments they are generally interested in—for example, the size and stage of financing, the industries they specialize in, whether they prefer to deal with national or regional companies.

Even when the directories have helped narrow the field, it is advisable to get further guidance from your attorney or accountant, or other consultant who can shed light on the current mood of the venture capital community and help you assess your choices.

The picture is not always what it seems in the cold facts of the directories. Take a venture capital firm that strikes you as likely to fill your needs. You check with your accountant. This advisor happens to know that the firm is in the process of raising money for its own investment pool, has no money to invest at this moment and, therefore, it would be a waste of time for you to meet with the firm. On the other hand, the accountant may know other firms that are well prepared to invest and are searching for opportunities.

It all comes down to a matter of avoiding pointless contacts and concentrating your time, effort and the expense of preparing a presentation on firms that you know are ready to talk seriously.

If your state government is active in the venture capital field, a telephone call to your state office of economic development or state office of commerce should tell you how to set up a meeting. If you have problems making contact, are unsure whether your state has a venture capital program, or just feel you need counsel before or during state negotiations, your accountants, bankers, or business advisors may be able to provide some important assistance.

THE BUSINESS PLAN

In your exploratory meetings with a venture capitalist, you will describe in detail the state of your company, and he will indicate whether he sees an opportunity for his firm to reap a sufficient reward for the risk he would take if he supplies the capital you need.

What Do Venture Capitalists Expect?

Venture capitalists expect you to present a detailed and meticulously accurate account—in writing. This is usually done by preparing a business plan. The business plan will spell out such basics as these:

1. A succinct history of your company
2. The opportunity
3. Your estimate of how much capital is needed
4. The state of the market, as you see it today and in the near future
5. Your assessment of present and potential competitors
6. New technologies and products that might affect the competitive environment
7. Your management team
8. Financial calculations, including cash flow for a number of years, expected profits, expected capital requirements and how this money would be used and any other relevant facts
9. Your short-term and long-term goals

Obviously this list would change somewhat from one company to another, but it illustrates the kind of information needed. Committing all this to writing serves two good purposes: it helps you think things through in a careful, orderly manner, and it helps the venture capitalist evaluate your competence and weigh the risks that underlie his decision.

As you would expect, your business plan, no matter how thorough, is bound to raise questions in the give-and-take of discussions, and this means you would go back to supply further facts, address new problems that came to light in your meeting, and recast the plan. There is a good chance that the venture capitalist will use the help of outsiders more expert than he is in judging certain aspects of the plan. Thus the process of getting to know each other goes on, often stretching into weeks and even months before an investment is structured that meets the objectives of both parties. These negotiations frequently involve attorneys and accountants for both sides to supply objective expertise in this delicate effort to create a relationship that will be fair and effective.

Major Concentration Points

A few features of the business plan deserve emphasis.

Many venture capitalists believe the most important ingredient is your management. Accordingly, they carefully scrutinize the backgrounds of your key managers for assurance that these people have the intelligence, experience and temperament to carry the business through the crucial years ahead when their money is on the line.

They look for entrepreneurial skills, technical training, sophistication in research and development, production, distribution, marketing, finance and administration, plus any other qualifications that pertain to your type of business. And they expect to find enthusiasm and competitive spirit.

All too often the basic business plan tends to dwell overwhelmingly on technical matters and neglects the human factor. This is always a mistake.

In creating the plan, another point of emphasis should be the size and attractiveness of the market. How big is the market? Is it completely saturated or can it be expanded? How do you rate your competitors? Have many new competitors entered the market recently and successfully gained a foothold? No matter how good your product may be, success will depend largely on how well you understand the dynamics of your market, so the venture capitalist looks for signs that you are thoroughly and realistically up-to-date on the state of the market.

A third issue your plan must address: exactly how is this venture unique? Do you have a unique product advantage? A unique packaging advantage? A unique method of distribution? A unique marketing edge? The venture capitalist expects you to define that element of uniqueness that sets you apart from your competitors and gives you the jump on the field. Winners usually have it and it deserves to be a major feature of your business plan.

There is much to consider when preparing a business plan. Some types of information will be applicable to your situation and some will not. Which is which will become more apparent when you review our detailed "New Venture Business Plan Outline" in the Appendix at the end of this book.

WHO GETS CONTROL OF YOUR COMPANY?

Nothing could be more natural than for you, as manager of the business, and maybe as founder and principal owner, to feel uneasy that control of the company might well pass to the venture capitalist. Pangs of worry may come and go as negotiations drag on, but it is important, for the good of the company and your own peace of mind, that you do not let these feelings become stumbling blocks.

One of the realities of running an expanding business is that, bit by bit, larger and larger portions of ownership pass from the original owners to investors as growth opportunities demand that you bring in outside capital.

It is not uncommon that first-round and second-round capital might take 40 to 60 percent of the equity shares, and succeeding rounds of financing, including public offerings, may leave the original owners with as little as 5 to 20 percent of the stock.

The point to keep clearly in mind is that growth depends on this outside capital—without it, the company might fall behind the competition, lose its place in the market, even go out of business. Another reassuring reality is that, though outside investors may own a majority of your stock and demand a voice in managing the company, they are not likely to wrest control away from you if your record proves that you are doing a good job and bringing them the returns they expect.

5

TRADITIONAL FINANCING

As manager of a business, it is easy for you to picture yourself in this position: your company is enjoying a good run of success. The problem now is to sustain that success, build on the momentum, and grow through plant modernization or expansion, new products, new markets, maybe an acquisition, or whatever opportunities beckon you into a promising future. At some point early in your planning, you will turn your mind to financing this growth, and a bank loan may be the first possibility that occurs to you.

Chances are the banks have been thinking about you as well. Their business is making loans. To do this successfully, banks keep a watchful eye on companies that have a look of success about them. Such companies make choice borrowers for a bank because: (1) success breeds growth, (2) growth requires capital, and (3) successful companies are good risks to repay loans on time and in full.

It seems like a match made in heaven.

But it is not a cut-and-dried proposition. Like all companies, yours is somewhat different. Your needs must be thought of individually, and a loan must be tailor-made. Nobody knows this better than the banks themselves (and other finance companies who make business loans).

Accordingly, two things happen when you open discussions. You and the bank begin an intensive examination of each other—you to see whether the bank is your best choice for raising the needed capital and the bank to satisfy itself that you meet its standards for a safe borrower. And then you tackle the question of what kind of loan the bank can offer. Perhaps nothing will surprise you so much as the wide choice of loan instruments the bank has devised. In the fierce competition for your business as a borrower, banks and other lenders have been remarkably imaginative in creating a vast array of instruments to match your special needs.

A good starting point is to list the reasons you might want to borrow. Experience tells us there are four major reasons why companies borrow money:

- To limit the amount of equity investment required of company owners and investors
- To provide working capital
- To obtain the capital to finance an expansion
- To raise the funds to finance the acquisition of another business

This chapter tells how banks and finance companies operate, advantages and disadvantages of debt over equity, the best uses for borrowed funds, the many kinds of loans, how you and a bank should evaluate each other, and how to carry out the negotiations for a loan.

DEBT VS. EQUITY: ADVANTAGES AND DISADVANTAGES

Often, as the owner of a business, you face a dilemma. You wish to expand your business but cannot do so without additional financial resources. You may be unwilling or unable to provide the additional equity investment yourself. The owner has two alternatives for raising the additional money needed—debt or equity. Equity investors receive ownership, a share of control, in the business with their share of stock. Debt, on the other hand, is a way of financing growth without giving up ownership and control.

Advantages of Debt Over Equity

- A debtor has no direct claim on the future earnings of the company. No matter how successful your company becomes, the lender is only entitled to the repayment of the principal and the agreed-upon interest changes.
- Interest on debt can be deducted on the company's tax returns. This, in effect, lowers the real cost to the borrower.
- Debt does not dilute the owner's interest since the lender has no claim to the equity of the business.
- Interest and principal payments are, for the most part, a known amount. Therefore, they can be forecast and you can plan for them. Recent trends toward variable rate loans may eliminate some of this advantage since the interest payment will change as interest rates change.

Disadvantages of Debt Over Equity

- Interest is a fixed cost and therefore raises a company's break-even point. High interest costs during a financial crisis or merely a financially unstable period can increase the risk of insolvency. Companies that become too highly leveraged (that is, having large amounts of debt relative to equity) often find it impossible to remain profitable enough to grow and prosper because of the high costs of debt service.
- Cash flow is required for both principal and interest payments and must be planned for. Repayment of principal is not tax deductible.
- Debt is not permanent capital with an unlimited life; at some point is must be repaid.

- Debt instruments may include restrictive covenants, which limit management's future actions with regard to financing and managing the company.
- A business is limited as to the amount of debt it can carry. The larger the company's debt-to-equity ratio, the more risky the company is considered, and the less a creditor will be willing to lend.

Obviously, the way a company is financed can significantly affect its future financial performance and its options with regard to growth and profitability. The following outlines how a company's financial performance can be affected by different levels of debt and equity financing:

Debt/Equity Example

In 19XX, the Acme Co. had earnings of $10,000 before interest and taxes (EBIT). Its average tax rate was 15 percent and it paid an average of 14 percent interest on any debt outstanding. How would the company's financial performance have varied if its debt-to-equity ratio changed?

COMPANY'S FINANCIAL PERFORMANCE ASSUMING THAT:

	No Debt	Some Debt	More Debt
Equity invested	$100,000	$ 60,000	$ 20,000
Debt	—	40,000	80,000
Total debt and equity	$100,000	$100,000	$100,000
EBIT	$ 10,000	$ 10,000	$ 10,000
Interest expense	—	5,600	11,200
Earnings before taxes	10,000	4,400	(1,200)
Tax expense	1,500	660	—
Net earnings	$ 8,500	$ 3,740	$ (1,200)
Return on equity	8.5%	6.2%	(0.1%)

As you can see, the net earnings and return on equity are significantly affected by changes in the debt/equity mix.

TYPES OF DEBT FINANCING

Borrowing Working Capital

Working capital is defined as the excess of current assets over current liabilities, sometimes referred to as general operating funds. Not having an adequate level of working capital can hamper the ability of your company to grow since the amount of inventory you are able to buy or the number of sales you can make on credit are limited by your level of working capital. Working capital loans are often used to provide the necessary funds to finance inventories and receivables. Working capital loans are particularly useful in helping your company smooth the effect of seasonable business fluctuations when you may need to build inventory for sales in later periods. They can also help weather the effects of troughs in business cycles.

Working capital loans are usually short-term (less than one year) and can be secured or unsecured. Borrowers with strong operating histories and cash-flow positions can generally borrow without a collateral requirement. With young companies where repayment is less certain, banks may require a pledge of assets as collateral. Where the businesses' assets are insufficient, the bank will require personal assets pledged individually by the principals of the company. Lenders generally will make short-term loans to a company only if company principals have a substantial amount of equity invested in the business. These loans are unlikely sources of start-up capital unless the principals can pledge the necessary collateral from personal assets to assure repayment. Even then, banks are reluctant to make loans to businesses without an operating history.

There are three main types of working capital loans:

1. Secured Accounts Receivable Financing, including Factoring
2. Secured Inventory Financing
3. Unsecured Revolving Line of Credit

Accounts Receivable Financing. If your receivables are of good quality with regard to age and collectibility, a bank or finance company may be willing to lend against those assets. Funds are advanced as goods are shipped on the basis of a predefined proportion of the eligible accounts receivable.

In return for pledging your receivables as collateral, banks are normally willing to lend you up to 80 percent of their value. Customers are usually not notified that their accounts have been used as collateral and they pay your company directly, not the financing institution. Typically, the financing agreement calls for the bank to get a copy of all invoices for receivables that are being pledged, along with a form of assignment which gives the bank the right to the money owed by customers. With each new sale, your collateral increases, allowing you to borrow more money, up to the agreed-upon proportion of the collateral. When the receivable is collected, a payment is made to the bank.

In some cases receivables are assigned to the bank and the bank collects payment from the customer in full (either directly or without notice). If the customer fails to pay or the proceeds are insufficient to cover the debt, the borrower is liable for any deficiency. The loan is therefore said to be "with recourse."

Receivable financing loans are flexible and provide a continuous source of funds. However, this form of borrowing can be costly for the borrower and lender to supervise because of the record keeping involved with tracking the collateral. Thus, the rate of interest is usually high, and sometimes there are additional service charges on the loans. Both commercial banks and finance companies provide receivable financing.

Accounts Receivable Financing with Factoring. Factoring is an alternative form of receivables financing, but typically more costly. The extra cost arises because the lender assumes the credit risk of the borrower's customers, and administers collection of the receivables. Factoring involves a continuing agreement under which a financing institution *purchases* your receivables as they arise, assumes the risk of default on any of these accounts, and is responsible for collections. They also perform credit checks on new customers.

Factoring can be valuable to smaller and medium-sized companies by allowing you to take advantage of some of the economies provided by full-scale, professional credit management (the lender's) normally associated only with larger firms. Such arrangements allow smaller companies to avoid establishing a credit department until credit sales are large enough to justify the cost.

There are two general types of factoring. In one type of factoring agreement, the financing institution (the factor) does not perform a typical lending function. You and the factor agree on credit limits for each of your customers and establish an average collection period. Thereafter, you send a copy of each sales invoice directly to the factor and the factor pays you, on the basis of the agreed average collection period, regardless of whether your customer has paid the factor yet or not. For example, if at the end of a normal 30-day collection period, a customer has paid only $5000 on an outstanding invoice of $10,000, the factor must remit the entire $10,000 to you (less whatever fee has been agreed upon). The factor's commission normally amounts to 1 or 2 percent of the value of the invoice. This type of factoring arrangement is called *maturity factoring* and mainly provides assistance with collection and insurance against bad debts.

In another form of factoring, called *old-line* factoring, the factor will perform a lending function by making payment in advance of collection. This makes funds available close to the time of sale, instead of upon anticipated collection. Factors will usually advance 70 to 80 percent of the value of an invoice at an interest cost of 2 to 3 percent above the prime rate.

Factoring arrangements can either be "with recourse" (you are liable for any deficiencies, as described previously) or "without recourse," as is the case when the factor has full responsibility for collection of the receivables with no recourse to the borrower.

Through the use of a factor, a company can usually:

- Increase the turnover of its working capital, reducing other financing requirements.
- Limit credit and collection expenses to a definite percentage of its credit sales, which is the percentage commission on those credit sales it pays to the factor.
- Protect itself against bad debts.

Factoring is an expensive way to finance receivables and is not commonly accepted in many industries. It can be especially costly when invoices are numerous and relatively small in dollar amount. At one time, factoring was considered an indication of a company's unsound financial position. This is no longer true and today many healthy firms engage in this form of financing.

Inventory Financing. Banks and finance companies also lend on the security of inventory, but are selective about the inventory they will accept. For example, hard commodities and nonperishable goods are best because they can be sold if a customer defaults on its payments. Finished goods can also be used for collateral depending on their liquidation value. Since inventory is less liquid than other current assets, a bank will seldom lend more than 50 percent of the value of the inventory.

There are several forms of inventory financing. Two of the most commonly used are described below. Procedures for financing depend on who controls the inventory, either the borrower (Floor Planning) or the lender (Warehouse Financing).

1. *Floor Planning Arrangement.* Under a floor planning or trust receipt arrangement, the lender buys the inventory and you, the borrower, hold the goods in trust for the lender in an area under your direct control, either at a public warehouse or on your premises. A trust receipt is issued by the bank—and signed by you, the borrower— that identifies the assets being used as security. When the assets are sold, the proceeds are used to redeem the trust receipt. The lender makes periodic inspections of the inventory to ensure that the collateral is being properly maintained. Automobile dealers commonly finance their inventories in this manner.

2. *Warehouse Financing.* Warehouse financing is similar to floor planning, except that the goods being used as collateral are stored at a public warehouse with the receipt held by the lender. If that is not practical, a public "field" warehouse can be established on the borrower's premises.

When the goods are stored in a public warehouse, the warehouse company issues a warehouse receipt and will release the goods only upon the authorization of the holder of the receipt. Because the holder of the receipt controls the inventory, the receipt can be used as collateral for lending purposes. Lenders require that the goods be stored under bond in sealed storage, and must not be moved or the seal broken until the loan is repaid. The warehouse receipt serves as a guarantee that the material will remain secure, and it is turned over to the lender for the term of the loan.

If you are unable to store your inventory in a large public warehouse, a field warehouse can be established. With this type of arrangement, a warehouse company leases space on the borrower's premises and is responsible for controlling and managing that space. They will secure the goods and release them only at the request of the holder of the warehouse receipt, in this case the lender. The warehouse company usually puts up signs stating that a field warehouse is being operated.

The costs of establishing a field warehouse are relatively high which makes them somewhat impractical for small companies.

However, this form of financing does have several advantages. The amount of funds available is tied to the growth in inventories which means the availability of funds automatically grows as your financing needs increase. A field warehousing arrangement also increases the acceptability of some inventory items as loan collateral. As a side benefit, the use of specialists in warehousing can often result in improved warehouse practices and procedures.

Revolving Line of Credit.   If your company has a continuous or re-curring need for short-term capital you may be able to obtain an unsecured line of credit. This arrangement allows your company to borrow up to a preestablished limit at any time. Funds are drawn as needed and interest is paid on the outstanding balance only, not the total commitment. The principal must be completely paid off period-ically, typically once a year.

Generally, only the most creditworthy companies can take advantage of this financing arrangement. A revolving line of credit extends for a finite period of time, and is reviewed by the bank's credit committee before it is renewed. You may be able to convert a revolving line of credit loan into a longer running term loan (discussed later in this chapter) at the end of the period. Lines of credit can also be secured with accounts receivable.

There are two major costs frequently associated with this form of financing. One is an interest cost that is normally tied to the prime rate or the bank's cost of funds. The other is a compensating balance, usually about 10 percent of the outstanding balance or the total committed credit line, which is held by the bank in a noninterest-bearing account. The compensating balance requirement may not be a burden or cost to the company if your day-to-day operations require similar amounts to be kept in the company's operating accounts. A fee may be substituted for the compensating balance.

Financing Business Expansion

Expansion generally means an investment in additional plant and equipment and an increase in the overall amount of working capital required in the business. Companies borrowing to finance expansion have capital needs that differ greatly from those borrowing to supply basic working capital. When borrowing to finance an expansion, a company will find that it needs:

- A large amount of long-term financing compared to typical working capital needs.
- Longer repayment terms, since investments do not usually become productive and generate cash flow until several months after the initial expenditure.

Major Types of Plant and Equipment Financing. The two most important types of financing for capital expansion are term loans and leases.

1. *Term Loans.* The principal form of long-term bank debt is generically referred to as a term or installment loan. Most of these loans require regular equal payments of principal and interest, unlike short-term loans that are usually repayable at any time in part or in one lump sum.

Term loans permit repayment over a longer period of time than revolving lines of credit or other forms of short-term debt instruments, usually greater than one year and shorter than seven years. In some cases, the payment period can be even longer, especially if the loan is used to finance capital assets.

Banks have more stringent credit policies and are more cautious about extending this type of credit because of the higher credit risk associated with the uncertainty about the future. Thus, term loans are often subject to additional compensating bank account balance requirements and restrictive covenants.

The interest rate on term loans is generally tied to the prime rate and fluctuates with it. Thus, if the interest rate is "prime plus three," the borrower would pay 13 percent when the prime is 10 percent, 14 percent when it is 11 percent, and so on.

Larger than normal working capital requirements can also be financed through the use of term loans. For this type of financing the bank looks to the ability of the borrower to generate sufficient cash flow to repay the loan within the stipulated period. For more on term loans see section entitled "Long-Term Debt," following.

2. *Leasing.*   Some companies choose to lease capital equipment rather than acquire it outright. Leasing may be a preferred method of financing in some situations:

- Cancellation options are available. These are especially desirable when the asset being financed is associated with a technology that is advancing rapidly and unpredictably. A cancelable lease passes the risk of premature obsolescence to the lessor.
- Maintenance and other services are provided.
- 100 percent of the asset cost, often including installation, can be financed.
- The terms may be longer and more flexible than under other types of financing.
- The tax deduction for the lease payment may be greater than the depreciation deduction that would apply if the asset was purchased. Or the lessor's company may not be able to use their depreciation deduction and, therefore, are willing to make the leasing arrangements financially advantageous to your company. (These concepts are discussed in more detail in Chapter 6, "Leasing.")

For a detailed comparison of the key terms and conditions of the varying types of debt financing instruments just discussed, see Exhibit 5-1.

Other Forms of Expansion Financing.   Industrial revenue bonds are available through many states and can be used to finance the construction and acquisition of new plant and equipment. (See Chapter 7,

"Government Financing"). In addition, as a business grows and matures, it may choose to expand by acquiring another company. Both commercial banks and commercial finance companies provide financing for this purpose, usually through term loans.

SOURCES OF CAPITAL FOR GROWING BUSINESSES

The traditional sources of debt capital for growing businesses have been banks and finance companies. Under rules passed by Congress in 1982, Savings and Loans and other thrift institutions have begun to participate in the lending activities to such companies. In general, the forms of financing offered by these institutions to small businesses are very similar to those traditionally offered by banks. Banks and S&Ls compete most directly, the latter limited by law as to the proportion of their loan portfolio permitted to be in business loans. Finance companies offer similar forms of financing, but are typically willing to assume more risk.

Banks: Traditional and Conservative

Commercial banks have long been a popular source of debt financing for business. Since banks generally require a business to present an operating history that demonstrates an ability to meet its loan obligations, securing this form of financing can sometimes be difficult for younger, start-up businesses. For businesses that qualify, a bank can provide financing in several different forms. While some aspects of these lending arrangements have been discussed previously, additional information follows.

Long-Term Debt

1. *Fixed Asset Acquisition.* Capital assets are generally high-cost items of long-term utility that are difficult to finance internally through regular cash flow. They include assets that enable your business to expand its productive capacity and to serve more customers more efficiently. In short, they are necessary for a young, growing business to continue expanding.

Banks often make capital loans—a specialized form of term loan—
to finance the purchase of these types of assets. The loan is usually
secured by a mortgage on the asset being purchased, although more
established bank customers are sometimes able to rely on their general
earning power and strong credit history with respect to prior loans
and, hence, are able to obtain unsecured loans. The repayment period
for a capital loan is generally greater than 10 years. If the loan is
secured by a specific asset, the bank has the right to repossess the
asset if you do not meet your obligations.

Insurance companies, mortgage companies, and pension funds also
provide long-term financing for capital assets. Generally speaking,
the longer the term the less likely a bank will be interested in the
loan and the more likely these other financing institutions will be the
primary source of funds.

2. *Term Loans.* The principal form of medium-term financing
is the term loan. Term loans are distinguished from capital loans in
that they are generally used for intermediate-term credit needs—that
is, loans that can be repaid over a shorter period of time, usually one
to seven years. They are commonly used to either increase working
capital, to finance a major expansion of capital facilities, or acquire
another business.

Compared to short-term loans, these long-term loans are more risky
mainly because the longer term period involved decreases the certainty
of repayment. Thus, these loans normally carry a higher interest rate
and contain several nonprice factors (to be discussed later in this
chapter). Interest rates are usually based on the prime rate ("prime
plus two," for example), and for the most part are variable.

3. *Leases.* As an alternative to buying equipment, businesses
sometimes lease. Almost any capital asset can be leased, its acquisition
effectively financed in a way similar to that of using a capital loan.
Banks are the second largest source of lease financing, after major
equipment manufacturers.* Chapter 6, "Leasing," provides more detail
on the various types of leasing arrangements.

Short-Term Debt. The objectives of short-term financing differ from
that of long-term borrowing. Long-term financing is designed to help

* Source: Brealy and Meyers.

a business handle large, sometimes irregular growth in capital needs that are planned for in advance. Short-term debt, on the other hand, is generally used to make up for the unplanned cash needs that long-term financing does not cover—weekly and monthly fluctuations that arise from unexpected shortfalls in sales or unforeseen increases in expenses—that are nearly impossible to plan for in advance. The major forms of short-term debt were discussed in detail in the prior section of this chapter. In summary, they include:

- Revolving lines of credit for working capital
- Accounts receivable financing
- Inventory financing

Included on the following page is a detailed reference chart (Exhibit 5-1) which compares the key differences between the varying types of both long- and short-term debt instruments.

Finance Companies: Willing to Take on More Risk

Asset-Based Financing (Secured Loans). Many small and medium-sized businesses have found that asset-based financing, the type of funding offered by commercial finance companies, provides an important source of funds that is not widely available through traditional commercial banking channels. An asset-based loan is secured with collateral provided by the borrower, such as accounts receivable, inventory, or plant and equipment. Annually, commercial finance companies provide billions of dollars in loans for asset acquisitions, general working capital, inventory build-up, leveraged buy-outs and acquisitions. Borrowers generally fall within the $5 million to $50 million annual sales volume range.

Finance companies offer many of the same forms of financing as banks. They fund leasing and equipment financing, for example, and lend short-term as well as long-term. The major differences between banks and finance companies are the criteria by which borrowers are evaluated and the level of risk that the institutions are willing to assume. However, the competitiveness of financial institutions for business is increasing and some banks are beginning to be more competitive in their risk assessments.

EXHIBIT 5-1. COMPARATIVE CHART OF SHORT-TERM & LONG-TERM INSTRUMENTS

Key Terms/ Conditions	Short-Term Instruments			Long-Term Instruments		
	Accounts Receivable Financing	Inventory Financing	Revolving Line of Credit	Capital Loans	Term Loans	Leases[a]
Uses	Provide working capital	Provide working capital	Provide working capital	Finance capital equipment	Finance expansion, finance large W.C. needs	Finance capital equipment
Secured	Yes	Yes	No	Yes	No	Yes
Compensating Balance[b]	Usually no	Usually no	Yes, usually up to 10% of line	Usually no	Varies	No
Repayment Period	Changes with receivable balance	Changes with inventory balance	Less than one year	Approximately ten years	Approximately one to seven years	Varies
Points[b]	1–2%	1–2%	1–2%	1–2%	1–2%	1–2%
Commitment Fee[b]	½–1%	½–1%	½–1%	½–1%	½–1%	½–1%
Prepayment Penalty	Usually none	Usually none	Usually none	Varies	Varies	Varies
Admin/Legal Fees[b]	1–2%	1–2%	1–2%	1–2%	1–2%	1–2%
Other	Often can borrow up to 80% of A/R value	Usually can borrow up to 50% of inventory value	Interest cost that is tied to the prime rate		Interest cost that is tied to the prime rate	

[a] Refer to chapter on leasing.
[b] Many loans contain a combination, but usually not all of these terms and conditions.

In general, bankers are more concerned with your company's financial statements and look carefully at key financial ratios, as well as historical financial performance, as indicators of your firm's health. In contrast, finance companies, in granting secured loans, rely more on the strength of your company's collateral than on its operating record, profit potential, and ability to generate sufficient cash flow. A borrower's financial condition must still be basically sound, but firms do not have to meet the same requirements of conventional banks.

The typical finance company customer is a profitable company whose growth has outstripped its net worth and working capital, and is unable to increase its bank borrowings. In many cases, asset-based lending is the sole source of working capital for these companies.

Finance companies charge higher interest rates than commercial banks. This results from three factors: the increased level of risk associated with undercapitalized borrowers, the greater amount of administration required to monitor collateral, and a higher cost of funds (finance companies obtain some of their funds from commercial banks). However, the true cost differential is sometimes less than would appear on the surface since finance companies do not require compensating balances and interest is charged only on the funds actually used.

Savings and Loans

A relative late comer to the small business lending market is the thrift industry. Under banking rules passed by Congress in 1982, Savings and Loans (S&Ls) are now able to invest up to 10 percent of their assets in business loans, an area that used to be exclusively in the domain of the commercial banks. Additionally, federally chartered S&Ls can commit up to 30 percent of their assets to inventory financing, 40 percent to commercial real estate lending, and 10 percent to equipment financing.* Some state-chartered institutions have been given even broader lending authority. Thrifts are similar to commercial banks in the types of lending arrangements available. These institutions should be considered when evaluating sources for financing.

* Source: *Inc.*, July 1983, p. 99.

Current Developments in Small Business Lending

Traditionally, smaller businesses have borrowed from small and medium-sized banks. In the early 1980s, a Federal Reserve Board study found that small and medium-sized banks (those with assets under $1 billion) lent significantly more to small business, as a percentage of assets than the largest banks and had a higher loan approval rate:

	Asset Size	Percent Loaned to Small Business	Approval Rate (Percent)
Small	Under $100 million	14	52
Medium	$100 million to $1 billion	16	34
Large	Over $1 billion	6	33

Apparently smaller banks have focused more on developing close relationships with their local clients, while larger institutions focus on large, national and multinational companies. Large banks have the reputation, whether it is deserved or not, of being impersonal and bureaucratic, and therefore not as sensitive to the individual client.

In past years, the larger banks have not aggressively gone after the so-called middle market (generally businesses under $100 million in annual sales) because of the higher credit risks and greater amounts of time involved in servicing these accounts. The primary providers of debt financing to smaller businesses have traditionally been banks with under $100 million in assets. Recently, however, the larger banks have begun to realize that this market can indeed be extremely profitable, especially in the long run, and have begun to more aggressively market their services to small business. Statistics show how well-run small and medium-sized banks, which now account for as much as 75 percent of loans to businesses with sales of less than $2.5 million, have consistently realized a larger percent return on equity than their larger competitors.*

* Source: *Inc.*, May 1984, pp. 112–126.

Large Bank Lenders. In recent years, most of the country's top 15 or 20 banks have been establishing loan production offices (LPO) throughout the country at an unusually fast rate. The purpose of the LPO is to generate loans in cities beyond the bank's traditional boundaries. Larger regional commercial banks with strong reputations for responsively serving middle-market clients are joining the largest banks by opening LPOs in major metropolitan areas throughout the country. Do not be surprised when a representative from one of these institutions comes knocking on your door (if they have not already) trying to take your business from your current banker.

In short, the larger banks have caught the entrepreneurial fever that has been spreading across the country in the last few years. Like many other businesses, they have begun to recognize the short and long-term profit potential that smaller clients represent. Not only do higher rates of interest result in higher short-term profits, but the banks bring in new sources of business with the hope that the successful firms will grow and stay with the same institution to serve its expanding banking needs.

Commercial banks, as compared to finance companies and thrifts, provide the lion's share of small business's debt financing, accounting for 90 percent of their short-term needs and 70 percent of long-term. According to recent surveys, though, it appears that a small business market will migrate to whomever can most satisfactorily provide the most nonprice, relationship-oriented services.

In a recent survey of small business owners, the interest rate charged on a loan was the third most important characteristic in a banking relationship, ranking behind "knows you and your business" and "reliable source of credit." The qualities ranked least important were "provides helpful business suggestions" and "comes to you with ideas for improving bank services."* This suggests that the consulting aspect of a banking relationship is less important than the continuing availability of credit. These nonprice components do not come free, though; you can be sure that they are factored into the cost of your loans.

Bankers' Acceptances. A Bankers' Acceptance is a draft, requesting payment for merchandise, drawn by the vendor on the customer's bank. Bankers' Acceptances are used when the customer's credit with

* Source: *The Bankers Magazine.*

the vendor is not adequate. The customer's bank releases the funds to the vendor, in effect loaning the money to the customer. Terms of repayment are usually 90 to 120 days. Acceptances can be secured by the merchandise purchased, other collateral, or can be unsecured based on the business's crerditworthiness as assessed by the bank.

Bankers' Acceptances are an efficient way to overcome suppliers' credit concerns. Historically, they have been available only for international transactions, but are now available to U.S. companies selling to customers 25 or more miles away.

"Selling" Accounts Receivable.   One additional development involves the pledging of accounts receivable. Under new accounting standards, accounts receivable may be pledged to raise capital and yet the transaction need not be reflected on financial statements as a liability. This may occur if the transaction is structured as a sale. That is, receivables transferred to a "lender" with a guarantee will be considered a sale, not a borrowing/liability, when: (1) your company surrenders all economic benefits from the receivables pledged, (2) you give a reasonable estimate of any obligations you may have concerning the pledged receivables, and (3) you agree that the "buyer" cannot return the receivables except under special prestipulated conditions. This ruling is detailed in Financial Accounting Standards Board Statement No. 77.

EVALUATING POTENTIAL LENDERS

As mentioned previously, when selecting a lender, you will probably evaluate them on more than just the interest rate they want to charge you. You will also look at the nonprice components like compensating balances (see following discussion on cost considerations) and a variety of other "relationship factors."

Lender Characteristics

In 1982, the National Federation of Independent Business surveyed their membership on how entrepreneurs evaluate lenders after developing a list of desirable characteristics in a banking relationship, which included:

- Knows you and your business
- Provides helpful business suggestions
- Offers the cheapest money
- One person handles credit needs
- Convenient location
- Easy access to loan officer
- Provides a reliable source of credit
- Knows your industry
- Presents ideas to improve bank services
- Knows your financial needs
- Offers a wide range of banking services.

These characteristics were ranked from "very important" to "not important." All of these characteristics have some level of importance, but the following four were found to be the most important to the entrepreneurs themselves:

1. *Knows You and Your Business.* Stories abound throughout the banking industry about lending officers from smaller banks that land small business accounts from their larger competitors as a result of the more personalized service that they were able to provide. Ideally, your banker should think of you as a partner, not a customer. Services should be tailored to a business's individual needs, and banks should be as responsible to the needs of a small business as those of a larger one.

2. *Reliable Source of Credit.* Does your bank stand behind you if you encounter temporary problems meeting your loan's current obligations? Is your bank willing to support your expansion plans with the capital you need? The survey found reliability of credit to be the second most desired characteristic of a bank. The continued success and growth of your business depends on you being able to depend on your bank to provide a sufficient amount of debt financing in a timely manner.

3. *Offers the Cheapest Money.* The cost of a loan, while not the highest ranking consideration, is still an important one. Borrowers should be aware of so-called hidden costs like com-

pensating balances and take them into account when comparing the relative costs of borrowing.

4. **Easy Access to Loan Officer.** Can you see your loan officer on short notice? Is your officer easily reachable on the telephone? Does your loan officer have few enough accounts that he or she has time to see you other than when you need to discuss a new loan? If the answer to all three of these questions is *not* yes, perhaps you should reevaluate your current banking relationship. If you are in the process of selecting a banker, you will want to investigate these questions.

In general, factors relating to the consulting aspect of the banking relationship were viewed as less important than the continuity and availability of credit. However, you may want to keep them in mind while searching for a new banker or evaluating the one you currently use.

Cost Considerations—The True Cost of a Loan

The true cost of a loan to your business is going to be much more than the quoted interest rate. The ultimate cost is based on a number of factors which can be grouped into two categories: first, those that reduce the amount of capital available and, second, those that raise the overall cost.

Factors That Reduce Available Capital

1. **Compensating Balance Requirements.** Banks will frequently require you to leave a certain amount of funds on deposit, often in a noninterest-bearing or low-interest rate account. The amount of interest you lose by maintaining this account should be added to the cost of your loan. Sometimes you can use your normal "float"—the difference between book and bank balances reflecting uncleared checks—if that float maintains a fairly consistent level, and apply it to your compensating balance requirement, thereby reducing or even possibly eliminating it.

2. **Discounted Interest (In Advance).** Here the lender collects all interest and finance charges in advance thereby effectively reducing the amount of money left for the company to use.

3. *Lags in Check Clearances.* With this arrangement, the bank or finance company will take longer to credit your account for checks received from customers, in effect, slowing the turnover of your receivables and increasing your cost of capital.

Factors That Increase Overall Cost

1. *Points or Fees.* Points or fees are costs usually quoted as a percentage of the total loan which are charged at the closing of the financing and should be amortized over the life of the loan in order to derive the effective interest rate.

2. *Commitment Fee.* Commitment fees are charges for maintaining a committed line of credit. In other words, a charge for agreeing to have the credit available to you for a specified period of time, whether you use it or not.

3. *Prepayment Penalties.* With a good loan at an attractive interest rate, banks are making money. Early repayment of such a loan reduces bank profits and, therefore, the bank may charge a prepayment penalty—a fee for repaying the loan before it is due.

Calculating the Cost. Once you determine what the various cost components are, you will want to be able to compare the costs of different loan proposals. Following are two examples comparing the effect of various factors on the total effective interest rate that you will pay to the lender.

Example 5A. CALCULATING THE COST OF TWO DIFFERENT REVOLVING LINES OF CREDIT

Given: For both loans, loan amount is $100,000, stated interest rate is 15%.

Variable Terms	Loan A	Loan B
Compensating balance	none	10%
Commitment fee	0.5 % on unused balance	1% on total loan
Discounted interest (paid up front)	$ 15,000	—
Loan processing fee	none	1%

Interest Calculation	Loan A	Loan B
Loan amount	$100,000	$100,000
Compensating balance	—	10,000
Discounted interest	15,000	—
Available capital	$ 85,000	$ 90,000
Amount of line actually drawn down	$ 35,000	$ 90,000
Unused balance	50,000	—
Interest—15%	5,250	$ 13,500
Commitment fee	250	1,000
Loan processing fee	—	1,000
Effective interest rate	15.7%	17.2%

Example 5B.   CALCULATING THE COST OF A TERM LOAN WITH VARYING TERMS

Given: Loan amount is $100,000, length of term is 15 years, stated interest rate is 15% fixed.

Variable Terms	Loan A	Loan B
Commitment fee	1.5% prepaid	—
Administrative fee	0.5 % prepaid	—
Compensating balance	5% of loan	10% of loan
Interest Calculation		
Loan amount	$100,000	$100,000
Compensating balance	5,000	10,000
Prepaid fees	2,000	—
Available capital	$ 93,000	$ 90,000
Interest due	$ 15,000	$ 15,000
Effective rate	16.1%	16.7%

WHAT DOES A BANK LOOK FOR?

Your Ability to Repay

Before the bank will agree to your loan request, your banker will analyze your overall financial health and assess your ability to repay the loan. Your banker will evaluate not only your current ability to service the debt but also your future ability to meet the terms of the loan agreement. The banker will examine many sources of information to gain an accurate picture of your firm and how it compares to the industry. The banker's intuitive assessment of the management team's experience, ability, and character is also taken into consideration.

Following are some of the specific factors that will be evaluated.

Financial Statements.   First, the banker will evaluate your firm's financial statements which provide a descriptive picture of your business. They detail how your company has operated over the past few years and project your future financial results. The key ones include:

- Historical and projected cash flow statements.
- Historical and projected balance sheets
- Historical and projected income statements

Your cash flow projections are very important to the banker. They will indicate your ability to generate sufficient funds to pay both the accrued interest and outstanding principal. They will also indicate any ability to prepay some of the principal or forecast the need for additional borrowings.

The balance sheet captures your business at a specific point in time. It details your business's assets, liabilities, and net worth. Because balance sheets are based on the historical cost of the asset and liabilities, the banker may require an additional assessment of the current market value of certain balance sheet components. The balance in these accounts will serve as a guideline for the amount of funds the banker will lend, in general, and for the amount of funds available for receivables financing and inventory financing, in particular.

The income statement presents your revenue and expenses over a period of time. This historical assessment will provide the banker with an evaluation of past performance from which he can extract profitability trends. Based on your projections, the banker will then project your ability to operate profitably in the future and to generate the revenue necessary to repay the loan.

When applying for a loan, you should usually have financial statements for the past two to three years and projected operating results for the next two to three years. The historical statements should be prepared by an independent accountant who could clarify any questions the bank may have and would provide credibility to the numbers. The type and source of accounting services you obtain is evaluated by the banker and is a qualitative component of the loan decision.

Financial Ratios. The banker will calculate certain ratios based on your financial statements. The results of these ratios influence his loan decision. These ratios, by themselves, do not provide the banker with much information, but by analyzing them over a period of time, the banker can chart trends in your business. In addition, the banker compares your ratios with industry standards or other companies in the same business as yours.

Some of the more important ratios include:

- *Receivable Turnover: Net Sales/Average Accounts Receivable.* This ratio is used to appraise the actual value of your accounts receivable. A high ratio is indicative of an effective collection policy. A low ratio suggests slower collections and possible cash flow and collection problems.

- *Inventory Turnover: Costs of Goods Sold/Average Inventory.* The inventory turnover represents the number of times your inventory was sold and replaced throughout the year. Generally, inventory turnover gives some indication of the marketability of the products and the amount of inventory held in stock. If too much inventory is accumulated, this ratio will fall, indicating that your cash flow is being reduced because it is tied up in inventory that is not generating sales.

- *Current Ratio: Current Assets/Current Liabilities.* Sometimes referred to as the working capital ratio, the current ratio measures the extent to which the claims of short-term creditors are covered by assets that are expected to be converted to cash in a period roughly corresponding to the maturity of the claims. To a banker, it indicates the amount of current assets that would be available, in an emergency, to repay the bank loan once your current obligations have been met.

- *Quick Ratio: (Cash + Marketable Securities + Accounts Receivable)/ Current Liabilities.* Similar to the current ratio, the quick, or "acid-test" ratio measures liquidity. It assumes that inventory is a relatively illiquid current asset and that you would not have it available to meet short-term obligations. This ratio indicates your ability to meet your short-term obligations without the proceeds available from the sale of inventory.

- *Percent of Inventory to Cover Deficit in Quick Ratio.* This measure indicates the percent of inventory that must be sold in order to cover the current debt obligations in the event of an emergency. If you are borrowing against inventory, your bankers will limit the amount of financing they will make available by the amount of inventory needed to cover current liabilities.

- *Debt-to-Equity Ratio: (Current Liabilities + Long-Term Liabilities)/ Total Equity.* The debt/equity ratio indicates the extent to which your total funds have been provided by creditors. Lenders use this ratio as a rule of thumb for determining whether or not a company can afford to increase its borrowings.

- *Interest Coverage Ratio: Earnings Before Income Taxes/Interest Expense.* This ratio measures your company's ability to meet its interest charges on a regular basis. Bankers will reduce the amount of funds loaned if this ratio is *not* high enough to meet their credit criteria.

- *Profit Margins.* The banker will be interested to know that your profit margins remain stable over time or, even better, improve over the life of the loan. A solid margin gives the banker the confidence that you will be able to continue regular payments on any loan you have outstanding.

Other Measures. The banker will also evaluate other quantitative and qualitative measures to gain an overall understanding of your business, your position in the industry, and your company's ability to repay its debt. A discussion of the major factors follows.

- *Company Age.* Companies with an established operating history are likely to be viewed as less risky for lending purposes than a new start-up company. In general, new companies will not be able to negotiate as low an interest rate as a company with a proven track record, and will be subject to a much more stringent evaluation in order to qualify for a loan.

- **Term of Present Management.** In general, a banker will believe that the longer a management team has been with the company, the more likely they will be to continue the company's future success. Furthermore, a low rate of employee turnover implies a well-run company and a greater commitment to the organization's future success.

- **Years of Continuing Increases in Profits.** A history of increasing profits is indicative of a strong operating history. Companies that have been profitable in the past are more likely to be profitable in the future, and are more likely to repay their debts on time.

- **Trade Reports.** Bankers will read trade reports to evaluate the industry and answer questions like these for themselves—Is there a significant demand for this product or service? How does this company stack up against the competition? Is the product priced competitively? How long can this company continue to effectively deliver its product or service?

- **Z-Score.** The Z-score, developed by Prof. Edward Altman of New York University, is sometimes used by bankers to predict a company's future financial strength. It has been proven to be a valid indicator of potential insolvency for up to two years before bankruptcy. The public company formula for the Z-score is:

  (1.2 × Working Capital/Total Assets) + (1.4 × Retained Earnings/ Total Assets) + (3.3 × Earnings Before Interest and Taxes/Total Assets) + (0.6 × Market Value of Equity/Total Liabilities) + (1.0 × Sales/Total Assets)

  Companies with a score of 1.81 or less are likely to become illiquid within the next two years. Those with a score of 2.68 or above are likely to remain financially healthy, at least for the near future. A score between 1.81 and 2.68 is considered to be a "gray area" and requires further qualitative evaluation.

  For privately held companies, the formula changes slightly:

  (0.7 × Working Capital/Total Assets) + (0.8 × Retained Earnings/ Total Assets) + (3.1 × Earnings Before Interest and Taxes/Total Assets) + (0.4 × Book Value of Equity/Total Liabilities) + (1.0 × Sales/Total Assets)

  For privately held companies, Altman concluded that a score of 1.23 or less indicates potential for bankruptcy and a score of 2.90

or more indicates continued operations. Again, the middle "gray" area would require more detailed analysis and qualitative evaluation.

General Business Analysis—Your Future Plans

The banker will to a lesser degree assess your overall business strategy to make sure that the company's plans are realistic and well thought out. The banker will evaluate your plans for your business, including your marketing strategy, financial control system, management reporting system, and your personnel utilization. Particularly for young companies, a banker will want answers to such questions as:

- Planning:

    Have specific objectives and courses of actions to achieve those objectives been clearly identified?

- Marketing:

    Has the business clearly defined its marketing objectives and strategy?

    What market need does this product or service meet?

    Has the specific market been identified and analyzed?

    (Many financing proposals are rejected because marketing issues have not been adequately addressed.)*

- Finance:

    Why is the company proposing to finance its growth with debt as opposed to equity?

    Has the company identified opportunities to improve the performance of its assets—improving the receivables collection period and increasing the inventory, or disposing of unneeded fixed assets, for example?

    Have the merits of leasing versus buying been evaluated?

- Systems:

    Have the proper financial and inventory controls been instituted?

* Additional insights into the complexities of marketing and market analysis, as well as other general business considerations, are presented in our "New Venture Business Plan Outline," the Appendix at the end of this book.

(A timely reporting structure will help safeguard the assets and assure proper recording of sales and purchases. Further, the results of operations should be analyzed periodically and variances with budgets should be explained.)

- Human Resources:

  How does the company identify and retain qualified personnel?

  Are current compensation and incentive plans appropriate and adequate?

  Are key personnel leaving the company?

  Are personnel being used productively?

Ongoing Business Analysis—Signs of Trouble

On an ongoing basis, the bank will monitor your company's operations to make sure it is in compliance with any covenants included in the loan agreement and to look for warning signals of possible trouble in the business. A number of signals may indicate the potential for failure to meet the loan terms and the need for bank intervention:

- *Hesitation in Providing Financial Exhibits.* Being late with providing your financial statements may indicate that you have something to hide. The banker's reaction will be to investigate the material thoroughly and to carefully question any ambiguities or irregularities.

- *Shrinking Bank Deposits.* If the amount of cash you hold on deposit at the bank drops, the banker will question whether cash will be available to service the debt. If the cash is deposited at another bank, the lender will question the firm's commitment to the lending bank and will evaluate further loan requests more skeptically.

- *Overdrafts and/or Returned Checks.* Overdrafts and/or returned checks indicate an inability to manage cash effectively. The banker will then question the company's continued ability to meet its loan obligations.

- *Failure to Meet Other Obligations.* If your firm fails to meet other obligations, including the personal debts of the principals, the banker will question the company's ability to meet its business loan obligations.

- *High Inventory Levels.* High inventory levels indicate either weak purchasing controls or slower than expected sales levels. Having too much cash tied up in inventory could limit the firm's ability to repay its loan.

- **Delinquent Loan Payments.** The bank will investigate any delinquent loan payments to determine whether they are one-time events or are likely to recur.

- **Reluctance in Arranging for Plant Inspections or Meetings with Top Management.** Again, any action that suggests that the company has something to hide will be carefully scrutinized.

- **Legal Actions Against the Company.** Legal actions taken against the company have the potential of resulting in cash flow problems and difficulty in meeting its loan obligations.

- **Growing Accounts Payable and/or Accruals.** Increase in accounts payable and/or accruals may suggest an inability to generate the cash necessary to meet your obligations. On the other hand, it could imply that improved purchasing agreements are permitting the company to hold onto its cash longer. The cause of the payables increase should be explained to the banker before he questions your ability to service the debt.

- **Slowing Turnover of Receivables.** Inadequate collection procedures reduce cash flow and increase the chance of the company defaulting on a loan payment.

- **Increasing Fixed Assets.** If the company is purchasing new assets, the banker will want to make sure that all assets are being used effectively and efficiently. The banker may conclude that a better use of cash would be to repay the loan rather than to buy new assets.

- **Expansion Through Merger or Acquisition.** In a merger or acquisition, the company must have the ability to fund the purchase and to assume the increase in liabilities and expenses. In addition, the personnel must have the ability to assume the increase in responsibilities. The banker must be convinced that this expansion will not overburden the company and that all obligations will be met on time.

- **Increasing Debt and Debt-to-Equity Ratio.** If the debt has been increasing, the cash needed to service that debt also increases. The company's cash flow must be able to meet these growing demands.

- **Management Changes.** High rates of turnover in key management positions may signify a lack of faith in the future of the firm.

Continuing communication is essential between your company and the bank. Bankers do not like to be surprised. They want to understand the issues affecting your company and want to be kept well informed. Maintaining good relations with your bankers increases their desire to accommodate your requests, whether they include extending the loan term, removing any covenants attached to the loan agreement, making the terms of deposit more favorable, or agreeing to future loan requests quickly and easily. For a summary of what banks look for, see Exhibit 5-2.

NEGOTIATING WITH A LENDER

You should approach the negotiating process with a bank or other lending institution just as you approach negotiating any business transaction.

You prepare for negotiating before meeting with a potential supplier, before agreeing on price and terms with a new customer, before meeting with labor unions, and so on. In each case, you have probably decided ahead of time what you hope to accomplish during the negotiations. It is advantageous if you have determined ahead of time those points on which you are willing to make concessions and those on which you are not. It is even better if you have estimated the cost, both in dollars and in convenience, of any concession you may be required to make.

The same principles apply when meeting with a potential lender. Be prepared to negotiate the best possible deal for you and your company. To give yourself the best possible chance of accomplishing this goal we suggest that you:

- Prepare a loan package which details your borrowing needs and objectives.
- Identify ahead of time those terms and conditions which you believe are most critical to obtaining a workable loan agreement.
- Make full use of your business advisors, such as your lawyer and accountant. They can review any agreements you enter into and help you to understand the implications of any conditions to which you agree.

EXHIBIT 5-2.   IN SUMMARY: WHAT DOES A BANK LOOK FOR?

Your Ability to Repay
Financial statements
    Historical and projected cash flow
    Historical and projected balance sheets
    Historical and projected income statements

Financial ratios (calculated by lender) including:
    Receivable turnover
    Inventory turnover
    Current ratio (working capital)
    Quick ratio (liquidity)
    Percent of inventory to cover debt
    Debt-to-equity
    Interest coverage
    Profit margins

Other considerations
    Company age
    Term of present management
    Years of continuing increase in profits
    Trade reports
    Z-score

Your Future Plans
    Marketing strategy
    Financial control system
    Management reporting system
    Personnel utilization

Signs of Trouble (Ongoing analysis)
    Hesitation in providing financial exhibits
    Shrinking bank deposits
    Overdrafts and/or returned checks
    Failure to meet other obligations
    High inventory levels
    Delinquent loan payments
    Reluctance in arranging for plant inspections or meetings with top
    management
    Legal actions against the company
    Growing accounts payable and/or accruals
    Slowing turnover of receivables
    Increasing fixed assets
    Expansion through merger or acquisition
    Increasing debt and debt-to-equity ratio
    Management changes

The Loan Package

Earlier we discussed the type and amount of information that a banker
will usually want to see when approving a loan application. The banker
will certainly want to see historical financial statements, but your
banker will also want to see information which relates much more
directly to the loan application itself. For example, if you are applying
for a term loan to purchase a new piece of machinery or equipment,
the banker will want to see the analysis which you performed to cost
justify the purchase. If it is machinery which will save man hours,
your banker will want to know how many and when. Typically, you
might want to calculate the internal rate of return or do a pay-back
analysis on the project you want financed.

Specific Negotiating Points

Outlined below are some of the specific negotiable items you will
likely be able to address with your future banker. With any of these
points, once you have agreed there is no going back, make sure you
understand and are happy with the implications of any and all terms
and conditions.

Interest Rates.   The interest rate is one of the obvious key factors of
any loan agreement. Usually there is not a lot of leeway in negotiating
the rate of interest; however, small concessions on the part of the
bank can make a big difference to you over time.

When negotiating a variable rate loan you may want to try to get
the bank to agree to a "ceiling" above which the rate will not go. To
get such a ceiling you may have to agree to a "floor" below which
the rate will not fall no matter how far the prime rate drops. If you
believe interest is not likely to drop over the life of your loan, agreeing
to such a condition may be very attractive to you.

Collateral Agreements.   Make every attempt to minimize the amount
of collateral which you are pledging against the loan. If too many of
your available assets are tied up with one loan, it will greatly limit
your ability to borrow in the future. Lenders tend to request all the
collateral they can get.

In addition to the amount of collateral pledged, also consider the type and nature. Keep in mind industry practices. If it is unusual to pledge inventory or receivables and agreeing to do so could limit your competitive edge, make the lender aware of this and try not to agree to such provisions.

When pledging personal assets against a business loan, try to set a reasonable limit and exempt certain assets rather than signing a general personal guarantee pledging everything you own. If you pledge your stock in the company, take a close look at the default provisions. You may find that the banker can, in effect, take control of your company.

Ask for collateral release provisions as you pay down term loans to avoid significant over collateralizing loans as they mature.

Use of Capital and Payments Terms.   Borrow all you can when you can for as long as you can is an adage subscribed to by many business owners. While it is an overstatement, having access to funds when you need them is vital. Seek repayment terms that you know you can live with. For example, sometimes you can delay repayment of principal for a specified period of time, such as one to two years while keeping interest payments current.

Attempt to negotiate the ability to prepay all or any part of the loan. This will allow you to take advantage of a drop in interest rates should they occur or to refinance all of your loan agreements should that be advantageous.

Future Borrowing Constraints.   Any covenants with regard to future borrowings should not be too restrictive. You do not want to be in a position where the bank can significantly curtail your future operating options. Bear in mind that opportunities to grow and expand may arise in the future, and you will want to be able to take advantage of them. Likewise, try to avoid severely limiting your ability to make major capital expenditures in the future.

Ratio Requirements.   Lending institutions may insist that your company maintain certain minimum levels of some of the ratios discussed previously. They know that if certain ratios prevail, they have a very safe loan. Carefully review the implications of any ratio requirements to which you agree. What may not seem burdensome now could become so in the future. Be sure you have time to correct a ratio imbalance before the loan can be declared in default. Your accountant or other financial advisor can be particularly helpful in this regard.

Other More General Guidelines

As you can see, negotiating a loan agreement is no simple matter. Nonetheless, business owners and senior management should actively participate in the process. Not only will it illustrate to the lender that you carefully evaluate all aspects of your business but through the negotiation process you will make clear all of your needs to the lender.

Since lenders view their relationships with customers as long-term ones, the negotiating process can serve as the first and sometimes most useful step in developing this relationship, and the relationship *is* important. Historically, many bank loans have been made without the presentation of all the detailed financial and other matters described in this chapter being performed by the borrower or required by the banker. Relationships between the banker and the businessperson have been the key ingredient to many bank loans. Because of loan failures and the general increase in business and banking sophistication in recent years, most bankers are now requiring the thorough analysis depicted in this chapter.

While the relationship is still important, the better prepared you are to present your loan requirements, the more likely you will not only get the loan, but do so on favorable terms.

No matter what you ultimately agree to as a final loan contract, always remember:

- Voice all of your objections. Once you sign you have no negotiation position.
- Evaluate how the loan agreement will affect you and your business in the long run. You, not your banker, should be running your business.
- Get everything in writing. No matter how friendly you are with your banker, you are really dealing with an institution, not an individual.

6

LEASING

The concept of leasing as a method of raising capital is probably as old as business itself, and probably more widely used today than ever.

One reason for its popularity is that a lease can be so simple and clean. The basic concept is that one party offers to rent a piece of property—land, a building, equipment, anything—to a second party.

The first party thus gains income in the form of rental payments; the second party gains use of the property at minimal cost, avoids a large outlay that purchasing the property would have required and thus saves cash for other financing needs.

Imaginative people in business have been refining the simple lease for generations. The feature of simplicity remains, but experts have discovered that the lease can be surprisingly flexible. New advantages for both parties are constantly being created to help enterpreneurs like yourself manage your funds wisely as you pursue a growth opportunity.

The versatility of leasing may surprise you in many ways. And it might well play a part in financing your company's growth. The discussion that follows defines leasing, spells out responsibilities and advantages, and gives you an easy-to-grasp short course in how leasing might fit into your financing plans.

TRADITIONAL LEASES

A lease is an agreement between the owner (the lessor) and the renter (the lessee) whereby the owner allows the renter to use his property in exchange for periodic payments of rent. Thus, you as the renter, are able to use the property with a limited outlay of your own funds. In a traditional lease, the owner maintains the rights (and risks) of ownership and allows others to use the property in return for rents.

Characteristics

The traditional lease has been around for a long time—businesses have been renting real property for office space, production facilities, farm lands, et cetera. This form of financing has the following characteristics:

- The lessor owns the property and is responsible for maintaining it and paying the costs associated with it (e.g., property taxes, insurance, etc.).

- The lessee has use of the property for a specific term and a fixed obligation to pay for its use.

- As owner of the property, the lessor benefits by any capital appreciation to the property during the lease term and likewise stands the risk of any depreciation in value.
- The owner typically enjoys the tax benefits associated with owning property (such as deductions for depreciation and cash expenditures including interest, property taxes, etc., as well as tax credits for investment or rehabilitation property).

Advantages

With a traditional lease you, as the lessee, are offered some significant advantages not available under other types of financing. These advantages include:

- Your short-term equipment or space needs can be met without significant capital investment. Businesses have met short-term needs through leases for such items as temporary (or long-term) space requirements, phone systems, office equipment, and automobiles. Virtually any nondepletable and nonspecialized/noncustomized asset can be used for a period of time and returned under a traditional lease arrangement.
- Traditional lease arrangements may not be subject to restrictions applied by lenders or other financing parties, allowing traditional leases to be executed simply and without loss of time. Some traditional leases can be arranged using a standard form supplied by the vendor. Because the obligations under the lease are both clear and measurable, you can often execute a lease without the need to consult your professional advisors and without the fear of assuming great risks.
- Traditional lease arrangements leave the risks (and rewards) of ownership with the lessor, thereby insulating you from the risks of obsolescence or changes in needs.
- Traditional leases are treated as executory contracts—no assets are recorded and no liabilities are shown, except payments as they become due—in financial statements thus reflecting lower liabilities and lower expenses for your firm, especially in the first, low cost years of the lease. This generally presents a more favorable view of your financial condition and results of operations. (See following section, "Accounting for Leases on the Financial Statements.")

MODIFIED LEASES—COLLATERALIZED LOANS

Modifications

In recent years, lenders have come to realize that the form of the traditional lease can be modified in any number of ways so as to resemble a collateralized loan. These modifications might include the following:

- You become responsible for payment of insurance, property taxes, and other executory costs.
- The term of the lease may be set for an extended period of time (or to the end of the economic life of the property) or option periods may be added which guarantee you the right to use the asset for as long as you wish.
- Purchase options may be added so that you are entitled to purchase the asset at the end of the lease (or prior to its term) for either fair market value, an agreed-upon stipulated price, or one dollar.
- Provisions can be added that *require* you to purchase the property at the end of the lease term for a fixed amount, or fair market value or, alternatively, pay the difference between the fair market and a stipulated amount based on the end of the lease term.
- The rental payments may be set as a percentage of the underlying cost of the property. The property, on which the percentage is based, need not be identified in the lease terms, thereby allowing even more flexibility.
- The rental payments may be variable based upon certain volume factors (such as sales or production) or upon interest rates (creating a floating rate interest lease).
- The rental payments may be increased over the term to reflect inflation or they can be reduced dramatically to provide you with a significant cash-flow increase.

As a result of the number of modifications and combinations that can be made to a traditional lease, the two parties can sign what is called "a lease" but which is, in substance, a collateralized loan.

Advantages

The fact that a traditional lease can be modified into an arrangement that resembles a collateralized loan has made it a very attractive vehicle for providing financing. It offers the following advantages over the collateralized loan:

- Lease arrangements can be very flexible offering you and the lessor the ability to make a deal that meets each one's objectives.
- Lease arrangements can be structured so that either the lessor or you are treated as the owner. Generally if you are treated as the "owner" and cannot take full advantage of the tax benefits (because of the rate structure or limitations), transferring those benefits to the lessor will allow the lessor to lower his costs and pass a portion of those benefits back to you in the form of reduced rental payments.
- Leases can often be written for longer terms and usually provide for a lower down payment (often just two months rent) than an equivalent collateralized loan.
- Since the lessor maintains title to the leased property, it is easier for the lessor to obtain the rights to the property in the event of default.
- Leases provide a certain flexibility in the pricing of the arrangement related to the value of the property at the end of the lease term (see following section, "Pricing a Lease"). This value, often referred to as the "residual value," is estimated at the beginning of the lease and may be assigned to the lessor, to you, or split in some fashion. Since the estimate of the residual value impacts each party's cash flow, and thus the pricing of the lease, the estimate of its value is a very important feature in leasing and can cause flexibility in the pricing of a lease. "Shopping" for a price may be productive. (See Exhibit 6-1.)

ACCOUNTING FOR LEASES ON THE FINANCIAL STATEMENTS

The inherent advantage of leasing (i.e., almost total flexibility in structure) has lead to the development of a total range of lease products

EXHIBIT 6-1. BASIC MODIFIED LEASE CONSIDERATIONS

Modified Lease Agreement

Determination of Rental Payment Basis	Determination of Estimated Residual Value	Appropriate Length of Term	Allocation of Associated Costs Payment	Determination of Ownership	Options to Purchase
Variable Payment Possibilities	Assignment of Residual Value	Inclusion of Option Periods		Allocation of Tax Benefits	Required Purchase Stipulations
Escalating or Deescalating Payment Options	Estimated Value Risk Protection and Guarantees	Amount of Down Payment			Determination of Purchase Price

that can meet almost any need. Likewise, the almost endless combinations and permutations of modifications to lease agreements have left accountants constantly debating over the last several decades as to "when is a lease, a lease, and when is it not a lease." While the answer to this question has been elusive, the standards setters have reached agreement (perhaps only temporarily) as to some basic guidelines. They have categorized leases into two basic types—the operating lease and the capital lease. At one extreme is the operating lease, which can be equated to the traditional lease; the payment of rent for temporary use of the owner's property. At the other extreme is the capital lease, whereby you, the lessee, have obtained all the rights and risks of ownership. Most leases fall somewhere in between.

Defining a Lease

For practical purposes, the standards setters have developed tests, each of which must be met to qualify as an operating (traditional) lease. In general, a lease will *fail* to meet the operating lease tests if, at the origination of the lease, (1) the property subject to the lease will likely be transferred to you, the lessee, at the end of the term; or (2) the lease term is for a significant portion of the economic life of the asset; or (3) the rental payments are equal to at least 90 percent of the value of the property (plus interest).

Financial Statement Presentation

The characterization of a lease as either operating or capital becomes important because they are treated differently in the presentation on financial statements. Operating (traditional) leases are treated as executory contracts—no assets are recorded and no liabilities are set up (except to record the payments as they become due) and the expense is measured by the amount of rent actually paid (or payable).

On the other hand, if a lease is defined as a capital lease it is recorded, on financial statements, as: (1) the purchase of assets, and (2) the incurring of liabilities (both at the present value of the total future payments). The expense is then measured as both depreciation on the property and interest on the obligation. While, by the end of the lease term, both the balance sheet and the income statement will be the same for both an operating lease and a capital lease, during the lease term the capital lease will serve to increase assets and liabilities (generally as the lease progresses, the asset will diminish faster than the liability resulting in a greater liability than asset) and will generate larger expenses at the beginning and smaller expenses at the end of the lease. Thus, the capitalization of a lease will appear to make your company's balance sheet look weaker and its income appear lower. (See the accompanying illustration.) This is the same result that would have occurred had the property been purchased with a mortgage.

Comparative Balance Sheet Illustration.   The following is an illustration showing the approximate effects on your financial statement, of leasing land and building under an operating lease versus a capital lease:

	Operating Lease	Capital Lease
Summarized Balance Sheet—Initially:		
Current assets	$700,000	$ 700,000
Land and building	—	1,000,000
Total assets	$700,000	$1,700,000
Liabilities	$375,000	$ 375,000
Capitalized lease obligation	—	1,000,000
Total liabilities	375,000	1,375,000
Stockholder's equity	325,000	325,000
	$700,000	$1,700,000
Income statement—Year 1:		
Revenues	$1,000,000	$1,000,000
Expenses before rent, depreciation and interest	850,000	850,000
Rent	110,000	—
Depreciation	—	100,000
Interest	—	15,000
Income before tax	$ 40,000	$ 35,000

Balance sheet—End of Year 1:

Current assets	$ 740,000	$ 740,000
Land and building (net of $100,000 depreciation)	—	900,000
Total assets	$ 740,000	$1,640,000
Liabilities	$ 375,000	$ 375,000
Capitalized lease obligation	—	905,000
Total liabilities	375,000	1,280,000
Stockholder's equity	365,000	360,000
	$ 740,000	$1,640,000

Observations

- Although the equity is the same at the beginning of the lease, for both types of lease, the debt/equity ratio is 1.15 to 1 under the operating lease as compared to 4.23 to 1 under the capital lease.
- At the end of year one, the debt/equity ratios are 1.02 to 1 and 3.55 to 1 under the operating and capital lease, respectively.
- Additionally, although not as significant, the income statement shows $5000 greater income under the operating lease than the capital lease reflecting the difference between operating rentals and the sum of interest and depreciation. This excess will reverse itself sometime after halfway through the lease term; the debt/equity ratios will become equal at the end of the lease term.

TAX REPORTING

The tax authorities are just as interested in proper reporting of leases as your accountants are. A capital lease tends to lower the reported income on your books just as its tax equivalent, the conditional sales contract, lowers your net taxable income. As the term conditional sales contract implies, the tax rules generally attempt to determine whether the agreement to lease is actually an agreement to sell by the lessor. If yes, the IRS considers it a conditional sales contract. If not, it is a "true lease," the tax equivalent of an operating lease.

Determining a "True Lease"

To determine whether an equipment lease qualifies as a true lease, the lease must pass four tests that can be summarized as follows.

1. *Minimum Investment.* The lessor must maintain an investment of at least 20 percent of the cost of the property at all times during the lease. At the end of the lease, the property must also have a useful life of the longer of one year or 25 percent of its useful life.

2. *Purchase and Sale Rights.* The lessee may not have the right nor can he be required to purchase the property from the lessor at a price less than fair market value.

3. *Lessee Investment, Loan or Guarantee.* The lessee can not fund (either through purchase, loan or guarantee) any part of the cost of the property or improvements which are an integral part of the property.

4. *Profit Requirement.* The lessor must demonstrate that it expects to receive a profit on the transaction exclusive of the tax benefits.

These same types of considerations must be evaluated in determining if real property leases are leases or sales.

While these rules are similar to the financial accounting rules, they are not precisely the same and thus some leases will qualify as conditional sales contracts for tax purposes but will be treated as operating leases for accounting purposes and vice versa.

Minimizing Personal Taxes

Leasing may also be used to minimize personal taxes and transfer cash from a corporation to the individuals who run the corporation. Instead of your corporation acquiring the asset, you, the business owner, may acquire the asset personally and lease it to your corporation. In this way, depreciation deductions shelter your personal rental income and provide you with up-front cash. Even if you finance the leased property with a personal loan, with the rental payments used to repay that debt, in most situations your depreciation deductions, in early years, will be greater than the principal loan repayments thus, still providing you with extra personal cash flow due to tax savings.

In addition, there are rate differentials between corporations and individuals. Individuals in top tax brackets benefit from depreciation deductions at a 50 percent marginal federal tax rate, while the maximum federal rate for corporations is 46 percent. Further, when the property is sold, the top corporate tax rate for capital gains is 28 percent, while it is 20 percent for individuals. In addition, upon sale, 20 percent of any straight line depreciation taken by a corporation will be subject to recapture and treated as ordinary income while no recapture is required for individuals.

Individuals who wish to avail themselves of these benefits must structure the lease properly in order to receive investment tax credit and to avoid investment interest limitations. You should not undertake such transactions without competent professional assistance.

PRICING A LEASE

The cost of a lease to you is a direct result of the cost of that lease to the lessor. The lessor views the lease as a cash outflow to acquire the property and a stream of cash inflows represented by the rental payments and the residual value (the estimated value of the property at termination of the lease). The rate the lessor is willing to accept is a function of his costs, primarily his cost of capital (usually a combination of borrowed funds and equity) and his overhead costs and the risks associated with the lease. These risks can generally be divided into two portions—the risk that the user will default on his payments (the credit risk) and the risk that the estimated residual value will not be realized. The credit risk is generally evaluated the same in a lease transaction as it is in a collateralized debt arrangement. The residual value risk, however, is often viewed quite differently by different lessors.

Residual Value Determination

The lease agreement, for example, may provide for a guaranteed residual value by you, the lessee. Thus, the residual value risk becomes an extension of the credit risk. In other arrangements, such as an operating lease, the residual value may be the largest item of cash inflow and estimation of the amount of the inflow is critical to the pricing. In these situations, the nature of the property, its marketability and alternative uses, cost of refurbishing and relocation and the historical price movements of similar property come to bear. In the case of real estate, the lessor will likely estimate a high residual value in pricing the lease and accept lower current rents as a result. In the case of computer equipment, the lessor will usually have a low estimate of residual value and price the lease accordingly. Alternatively, the lessor may request that you guarantee a specified residual value, eliminating his downside risk (but retaining his upside potential) and thus lower the pricing to you. If the lessor is affiliated (by ownership or by contract) with the equipment manufacturer, he is more likely to accept a higher risk and higher estimate of the residual value than other lessors.

Tax Advantages

Another key consideration in the pricing will be the tax advantages. If you, the lessee, cannot use the tax deductions or credits associated with owning property, then the lease should be structured so that the tax deductions and credits go to the lessor. The lessor will be willing to pass these deductions back to you in the form of lower lease payments—but only if the lessor can use the tax benefits. Leasing companies that have a limited appetite for tax benefits, often structure deals that either pass the benefits to you or become involved in brokering the lease by selling it to third parties. On the other hand, some lessors can readily use the related tax benefits and therefore may price the lease very competitively.

LEVERAGED LEASES

One particularly interesting *third-party sale* is the so-called leveraged lease. A leveraged lease provides you with the equipment under a capital lease, while the property is "owned" by a third-party investor (who can use the tax advantages afforded by the property) who has purchased the equipment using funds borrowed from the leasing company. The "owner's" investment generally becomes negative in the early portion of the lease (taxes saved become less than his cash outlay) with most of the cash flow going to pay the debt. Thus, the total cash return on such an investment is small. Because the cost of structuring a leverage lease can be quite high and because the owner of the property has a small percentage investment in the property, the total value of the property generally needs to be quite large for the transaction to be attractive. As a result, typically only high value purchases, such as commercial airplanes, are subject to such leases.

CONCLUSION

Leasing can be used to fill a variety of needs in a variety of circumstances and, thus, will probably be useful to some degree in financing your business.

7

GOVERNMENT FINANCING

It comes as a surprise to many business people that the government, often cast in an antibusiness light, meddlesome, slow-moving, awash in regulations and red tape, turns out to be one of the principal benefactors of business in need of capital. The astonishing truth is this: through a variety of federal, state, and local programs, government is the largest single source of funds available to business for growth and expansion.

This being the case, it is important that you, as an entrepreneur, understand the range of programs and services government provides, what government's aims are, and whether government financing is the right or wrong source for you to tap for new capital. Understanding government programs is rarely easy for the business executive, for the picture is often bewilderingly complex. Moreover, these government programs, and the philosophies behind them, frequently change as the leadership in government changes and as old programs are phased out and new ones make their appearance.

Given this ever-changing scene, keeping up to date is a heavy burden on management trying to run a business. To keep abreast, it is essential for you to stay in touch with the people who administer these programs in your area, and to get help from your banker, accountant, attorney, and any other specialists who make a business of tracking the twists and turns of these programs in all their variety.

Getting money from the government is not likely to be anyone's first choice as a means of raising capital. The government will usually impose the same conditions as a bank or other lending organizations, but with political provisos added. In many cases, the government will lend you money only after a bank or private source has turned you down—a last resort. Sometimes, when a bank will not make you a loan on your own, the government will guarantee the repayment of most of your loan and thus make it safe for the bank to go ahead.

And, whatever the nature of your transaction with the government, you can count on one invariable fact: it will be a long, paper-ridden, cumbersome, time-consuming procedure, and more than once you will wonder whether it is worth the bother. In short, it takes a heap of patience.

But it may pay you handsomely to take the trouble to understand why the government acts as it does.

This chapter describes the major government lending programs, presents them in understandable terms, shows how they apply to small and mid-sized companies, and clears away the confusions that often obscure the real meaning in a practical sense for the business executive.

To begin, let us examine three basic reasons why government offers financial help to private businesses.

1. *Supporting the Economy.* The first reason government lends money to business is to help make the economy strong and give companies like yours a better chance to realize their ambitions. The entire political, social, and economic structure of this country rests on the exciting expectation that private business will prosper, innovate, and expand, and this concept underlies government's commitment to hold out a helping hand. One of the clearest examples is the Small Business Administration (SBA) created by Congress in 1953.

Most Americans believe the government has a legitimate role in making certain the private sector remains independent and vigorous. One way to do this is to offer loans and other financial assistance, as we shall see as this chapter unfolds.

2. *Creating Jobs.* A second reason government lends money to private business is that growth and expansion usually lead to more jobs, and that goal is dear to the hearts of government leaders. Nothing is more fundamental.

Moreover, in a private enterprise system like ours, it is usually more sensible for the government to help the private sector create jobs than to try to absorb the unemployed into government work projects that might be inefficient and temporary.

There are also humanitarian motives. The government often uses its support to encourage business to create jobs where the need is especially urgent—in specific communities, for example, and among certain ethnic groups.

One example of this job-related support is the Urban Development Action Grant, administered by the U.S. Department of Housing and Urban Development (HUD). In such programs, the underlying goal is to preserve jobs and income patterns and hire people who are unemployed.

3. *Supporting Special Situations.* The third reason for government involvement is to supply funds for projects of great importance that private lenders might find too risky. For example, certain government loan programs encourage investment in research and development for critical technologies in defense, science, and agriculture. Some of these programs will be explored in detail as we proceed through this chapter.

IDENTIFYING GOVERNMENT FINANCING TOOLS

Governments at all levels—federal, state, and local—provide financial assistance to businesses. Most resources are provided by the federal government; some of these funds may be "passed through" and made available by a local or state organization. Before reviewing these federal financing tools, local and state financing mechanisms should be briefly discussed.

Local Governments as Lenders

Many cities and counties have established industrial development authorities to issue tax-exempt bonds—Industrial Revenue Bonds— to promote new and expanded business. Some communities have also established downtown development authorities which are responsible for tax-exempt notes to be used for commercial revitalization. Business people seeking financial resources should contact their city and county governments to see if such organizations are in place and may be able to provide assistance.

Some areas have established locally operated revolving loan pools which are controlled by city or county governments. At times, funds may be available through one of these sources. Although this tool is not available in most places, if your business is operating where such a lending institution is functioning, it would be worth investigating. Often such pools of money are the result of federal grants or pass-throughs, but they may be locally controlled.

The use of tax-exempt financing through local development authorities has been controversial in recent years. Under consideration is legislation that would phase out such authority to grant tax-exempt financing by the end of this decade. As a result, it may be only a few years until many local governments are completely out of the business of providing financing. Recent legislation puts a ceiling on the amount of bonds that each state can issue.

State Governments as Lenders

Just as local policies and resources vary widely from place to place, different states have diverse resources to offer in the area of financing. Some states have committed money to a state-wide business development corporation with money to lend to healthy enterprises. Other states are utilizing Community Development Block Grant (CDBG) funds from the Department of Housing and Urban Development to promote economic development and business investment. Many of these programs are aimed at creating jobs for low and moderate income individuals and, therefore, have a great many restrictions on how the money is used for business growth.

In looking for these potential lending resources, information may be obtained by contacting your state office of economic development, or state office of commerce. Once again, your banker, accountant, or business analyst may be able to bring you up to date on state programs.

The Federal Government as Lender

Since most government loans and loan guarantees come from federal agencies, this chapter will go into detail on the variety of these programs and their requirements. As noted earlier, there are many federal organizations involved in lending activities, all for slightly different reasons. It would be false to assume that one agency on the federal level is aware of what all, or even most, of the other agencies, also involved in making business loans, are doing. Do not expect coordination or cooperation among the agencies. In addition, there will be some important requirements, noted in detail, about limits on the use of federal funds from different sources.

WHAT TO EXPECT FROM A GOVERNMENT LENDER

The basic approach to a government entity with a loan request is similar to approaching a private lender. There are also important differences. A lending officer for a bank or similar financial institution is concerned primarily about the loan he or she is about to make, and asks, "How does this look in the bank's portfolio? Will the loan be good? Can we collect? Is the collateral sufficient? Is this a creditworthy client?" The government lender may ask some of these same questions, but another concern will be: "Are all the forms complete and filled out properly? Do we have all the information required by law and regulation?" It is this additional set of questions that leaves many business people shaking their heads after an encounter with the government as lender.

Your banker may be able to make a loan based heavily on one of the "Three Cs"—character, collateral, and credit. Some bankers place special importance on the character of the client. Most government loan organizations do not have that option. They will depend almost entirely on what is presented to them in the loan application—and all the *correctly and completely filled-out* forms.

With that in mind, the entrepreneur should always ask the question, "Is it worth my investment of time to secure this government financing?" Although not all public sector loan programs require a great deal of time, many contain a complex set of steps which are not present with other lending institutions. The business executive should be prepared to invest time and energy in dealing with a government lender.

Government loan programs have often been seen as the "lender of last resort," a resource to be utilized when all other possible financial institutions have already turned down a request for a loan. That is one valid perspective in understanding how the government as lender works. Government funds should not usually be considered the first alternative in seeking business financing. Several government loan programs *require* an applicant to have been turned down by a commercial lender before they can be considered.

Another perspective on government's role in providing loan funds can be seen in the "but for" test. Often government funds are loaned in order to make a project viable (i.e., "but for" this loan, a project would not be workable). Government financing can also be used to improve a financial package by improving the rate or the term of a loan. The Small Business Administration and other government agencies may be able to offer a better term or even a better interest rate to make a business loan easier for you to repay.

While there are a multitude of government agencies with the capacity to make loans, many are dependent upon appropriations or regulations in order to exercise their loan capacity. As noted earlier, that picture is constantly changing. One test that you can use before beginning the loan application process with a government agency is this: Ask about the number of applications submitted and the number of loans made in the last year. If there have been relatively few loans, considering the number of applicants, it may not be a good investment of time to seek these funds.

The business climate, and your situation, will dictate the necessary course of action. It is important for you to understand that government lenders operate with almost all of the same guidelines commercial creditors use, often with additional paperwork and reporting requirements. Increasingly, government lenders are applying many of the same rigorous tests of creditworthiness and collateral availability before considering a loan. Knowing what to expect from a government lender should give you some edge in successfully completing the loan process.

TYPES OF LOAN PROGRAMS

Government loan programs can be divided into two basic types— *direct loans* and *participation loans*. Some agencies offer loans of each type, and they will be discussed in detail on subsequent pages.

Direct Loans

Direct loans are just what they sound like—government giving the money directly to a business and expecting repayment directly to the agency. In this instance, government functions like a commercial lender—setting rates, terms, and establishing the mechanism for repayment. These types of loans are becoming increasingly scarce as a means of government financing and are often available only to specialized groups. Many experts, including some government loan officers, believe these loans will soon be phased out completely.

Participation Loans

There are two distinct ways that government may "participate" in a loan, "Immediate" or "Deferred," yet the process in each type of participation loan is similar. In all participation loans, the government and another organization, usually a commercial lender, jointly make the business loan.

An *Immediate Participation Loan* can be so termed because the government and commercial lender each put up a portion of the capital. In these loans, there may be two different interest rates, one set by the government, the other by the lender.

The second kind of participation loan, and the most common of all government loans, is called the *Deferred Participation Loan* or *Guaranteed Loan*. These loans are made by a commercial lender with *no advancement of government funds*. Government participation is in the form of a guarantee, and funds will be advanced only if the loan goes into default. The commercial lender will expect repayment of the loan from you and, therefore, applies standards which are comparable to their usual tests for repaying. These guaranteed loans are an advantage to both you and the bank. Your business may receive loan approval of a guaranteed loan more readily than a conventional arrangement with a lending institution. At the same time, the bank, while retaining first position on the loan, has its potential liability greatly diminished by the government guarantee and can show these loans in their portfolio, at only the "nonguaranteed" portion, thus improving their potential loan volume.

Summary

The type of loan, direct or participation, is important to your company for several reasons. First, it will affect the loan process (whom you deal with, i.e., government or financial institution) and the requirements involved in the loan approval. Second, the nature of the loan program will have a definite impact on the terms and rate applied to the loan. Third, the nature of the government involvement may have a direct impact on the criteria applied to determine creditworthiness and ability to repay the loan.

THE GOVERNMENT LOAN PROCESS

Direct Loans

In the case of a direct loan, you would deal with the government agency just as you would any other lending institution. The loan officer for the government entity will discuss with you the nature and purpose of the loan to see whether it fits the agency's requirements. In some instances, this initial contact may be handled over the telephone. After this initial contact, you should receive the proper forms which must be filled out *completely*. This is often the point of discouragement—when an entrepreneur faces the paperwork required for a government loan application. You may want to work closely with your accountant or other professional associates to be sure that the information is complete and accurate. Government agencies generally will not process any loan request until *all* required information is provided. The loan request is reviewed by the government agency's loan officer and, if complete, sent on to the agency's loan review committee.

Participation Loans

In the case of participation loans, generally you have minimal contact with the government entity, but deal mainly with the commercial lender. Typically, you would go to your bank to apply for a loan. If the banker determines that government "participation," such as a loan guarantee, is necessary for the bank to make a loan, he should discuss the requirements in detail, including why a guarantee is necessary, which federal agency might participate in the loan application, and the legal requirements of the agency for its participation. Many lenders are familiar with available government financing tools and can assist in completing the forms. Again, the information must be complete and accurate. The loan request is reviewed by the lending institution's committee and, if approved, forwarded to the government agency with a positive recommendation. The loan will then depend on the approval or denial of the government agency involved.

Although there may be variations of this pattern, these are the basic elements of the loan process. When dealing with nonfederal government loans, particularly those from state or local governments, or passed through from the federal government and administered locally, the requirements may vary.

The consistent factor in government loan applications is to provide complete and accurate information so that the loan review can proceed in an orderly fashion.

THE SMALL BUSINESS ADMINISTRATION

The largest single agency with responsibility for making business loans is the Small Business Administration (SBA). This organization, based in Washington with offices in most major American cities (see Exhibit 7-1), should be considered one of the primary resources for the entrepreneur interested in government financing. This section will describe several loan programs currently administered by the SBA.

First, a quick look into the background of the SBA.

Defining Small Business—Size, Eligibility, Need

One of the tasks given to SBA when it was created by Congress in 1953 was to decide what constitutes a small business. Since then, the definition has changed as inflation rose and manufacturing and distribution patterns changed. Unfortunately, there is still not a universal definition of small business. The following general guidelines may prove helpful, but the best course is for you to ask the SBA whether your company is eligible before proceeding with the loan process.

Generally, a small business must meet the following criteria:

1.   It cannot be dominant in its field.
2.   It must be independently owned and operated and not an affiliate of a larger business.

EXHIBIT 7-1. SBA FIELD OFFICES, ADDRESSES AND COMMERCIAL TELEPHONE NUMBERS

Region		City	State	Zip Code	Address	Commercial Telephone Numbers for Public Use Only
I	RO	Boston	MA	02110	60 Batterymarch Street, 10th Floor	(617) 223-3204
	DO	Boston	MA	02114	150 Causeway St., 10th Floor	(617) 223-3224
	BO	Springfield	MA	01103	1550 Main Street	(413) 785-0268
	DO	Augusta	ME	04330	40 Western Avenue, Room 512	(207) 622-8378
	DO	Concord	NH	03301	55 Pleasant Street, Room 211	(603) 224-4041
	DO	Hartford	CT	06106	One Hartford Square West	(203) 722-3600
	DO	Montpelier	VT	05602	87 State Street, Room 204	(802) 229-0538
	DO	Providence	RI	02903	380 Westminster Mall	(401) 351-7500
II	RO	New York	NY	10278	26 Federal Plaza, Room 29–118	(212) 264-7772
	DO	New York	NY	10278	26 Federal Plaza, Room 3100	(212) 264-4355
	BO	Melville	NY	11747	35 Pinelawn Road, Room 102E	(516) 454-0750
	DO	Hato Rey	PR	00919	Carlos Chardon Avenue, Room 691	(809) 753-4002
	POD	St. Croix	VI	00820	4A La Grande Princesse	(809) 773-3480
	POD	St. Thomas	VI	00801	Veterans Drive, Room 283	(809) 774-8530
	DO	Newark	NJ	07102	60 Park Place, 4th Floor	(201) 645-2434
	POD	Camden	NJ	08104	1800 East Davis Street, Room 110	(609) 757-5183
	DO	Syracuse	NY	13260	100 South Clinton Street, Room 1071	(315) 423-5383
	BO	Buffalo	NY	14202	111 West Huron Street, Room 1311	(716) 846-4301
	BO	Elmira	NY	14901	333 East Water Street	(607) 734-8130
	POD	Albany	NY	12207	445 Broadway-Room 236B	(518) 472-6300
	POD	Rochester	NY	14614	100 State Street, Room 601	(716) 263-6700

(Exhibit continues on next page.)

Regional Office (RO), District Office (DO), Branch Office (BO), Post-of-Duty (POD)

EXHIBIT 7-1 (SBA offices *continued*)

Region		City	State	Zip Code	Address	Commercial Telephone Numbers for Public Use Only
III	RO	Philadelphia	PA	19004	231 St. Asaphs Rd., Suite 640	(215) 596-5889
	DO	Philadelphia	PA	19004	231 St. Asaphs Rd., Suite 400	(215) 596-5889
	BO	Harrisburg	PA	17101	100 Chestnut Street, Suite 309	(717) 782-3840
	BO	Wilkes-Barre	PA	18701	20 North Pennsylvania Avenue	(717) 826-6497
	BO	Wilmington	DE	19801	844 King Street, Room 5207	(302) 573-6294
	DO	Clarksburg	WV	26301	109 North 3rd St., Room 302	(304) 623-5631
	BO	Charleston	WV	25301	628 Charleston National Plaza	(304) 347-5220
	DO	Pittsburgh	PA	15222	960 Penn Avenue, 5th Floor	(412) 644-2780
	DO	Richmond	VA	23240	400 North 8th Street, Room 3015	(804) 771-2617
	DO	Towson	MD	21204	8600 LaSalle Road, Room 630	(301) 962-4392
	DO	Washington	DC	20036	1111 18th Street, N. W. 6th Floor	(202) 634-4950
IV	RO	Atlanta	GA	30367	1375 Peachtree St., N.E., 5th Floor	(404) 881-4999
	DO	Atlanta	GA	30309	1720 Peachtree Road, N.W., 6th Floor	(404) 881-4749
	POD	Statesboro	GA	30458	52 North Main Street, Room 225	(912) 489-8719
	DO	Birmingham	AL	35203	2121 8th Avenue North, Suite 200	(205) 254-1344
	DO	Charlotte	NC	28202	230 S. Tryon Street, Room 700	(704) 371-6563
	POD	Greenville	NC	27834	215 South Evans Street, Room 102E	(919) 752-3798
	DO	Columbia	SC	29202	1835 Assembly, 3rd Floor	(803) 765-5376
	DO	Jackson	MS	39269	100 West Capitol Street, Suite 322	(601) 960-4378
	BO	Biloxi	MS	39530	111 Fred Haise Blvd., 2nd Floor	(601) 435-3676
	DO	Jacksonville	FL	32202	400 West Bay Street, Room 261	(904) 791-3782
	DO	Louisville	KY	40201	600 Federal Place, Room 188	(502) 582-5971
	DO	Miami	FL	33134	2222 Ponce De Leon Boulevard, 5th Floor	(305) 350-5521

		City	State	Zip	Address	Phone
POD		Tampa	FL	33602	700 Twiggs Street, Room 607	(813) 228-2594
POD		West Palm Beach	FL	33407	3550 45th Street, Suite 6	(305) 689-2223
DO		Nashville	TN	37219	404 James Robertson Parkway, Suite 1012	(615) 251-5881
RO	V	Chicago	IL	60604	230 South Dearborn Street, Room 510	(312) 353-0359
DO		Chicago	IL	60604	219 South Dearborn Street, Room 437	(312) 353-4528
DO		Cleveland	OH	44199	1240 East 9th Street, Room 317	(216) 552-4180
DO		Columbus	OH	43215	85 Marconi Boulevard	(614) 469-6860
BO		Cincinnati	OH	45202	550 Main Street, Room 5028	(513) 684-2814
DO		Detroit	MI	48226	477 Michigan Avenue, Room 515	(313) 226-6075
BO		Marquette	MI	49885	220 West Washington Street, Room 310	(906) 225-1108
DO		Indianapolis	IN	46204	575 North Pennsylvania Street, Room 578	(317) 269-7272
BO		South Bend	IN	46601	501 East Monroe Street, Room 160	(219) 232-8361
DO		Madison	WI	53703	212 East Washington Ave., Room 213	(608) 264-5261
POD		Eau Claire	WI	54701	500 South Barstow Street, Room 17	(715) 834-9012
BO		Milwaukee	WI	53203	310 West Wisconsin Ave., Room 400	(414) 291-3941
DO		Minneapolis	MN	55403	100 North 6th Street. Suite 610	(612) 349-3550
BO		Springfield	IL	62701	Four North, Old State Capital Plaza	(217) 492-4416
RO	VI	Dallas	TX	75235	8625 King George Drive, Bldg. C	(214) 767-7643
DO		Dallas	TX	75242	1100 Commerce Street, Room 3C36	(214) 767-0605
POD		Marshall	TX	75670	100 South Washington Street, Room G-12	(214) 935-5257
DO		El Paso	TX	79902	10737 Gateway West, Suite 320	(915) 541-7678
BO		Ft. Worth	TX	76102	221 West Lancaster Ave., Room 1007	(817) 334-5463
DO		Albuquerque	NM	87100	5000 Marble Avenue, N. E., Room 320	(505) 766-3430
DO		Harlingen	TX	78550	222 East Van Buren Street, Room 500	(512) 423-8934
BO		Corpus Christi	TX	78408	400 Mann Street, Suite 403	(512) 888-3331
DO		Houston	TX	77054	2525 Murworth, Room 112	(713) 660-4401
DO		Little Rock	AR	72201	320 West Capitol Avenue, Room 601	(501) 378-5871
DO		Lubbock	TX	79401	1611 Tenth Street, Suite 200	(806) 762-7466

(Exhibit continues on next page.)

149

EXHIBIT 7-1 (SBA offices continued)

Region	City	State	Zip Code	Address	Commercial Telephone Numbers for Public Use Only
DO	New Orleans	LA	70112	1661 Canal Street Suite 2000	(504) 589-6685
POD	Shreveport	LA	71101	500 Fannin Street, Room 6B14	(318) 226-5196
DO	Oklahoma City	OK	73102	200 N. W. 5th Street, Suite 670	(405) 231-4301
DO	San Antonio	TX	78206	727 East Durango Street, Room A-513	(512) 229-6250
POD	Austin	TX	78701	300 East 8th Street, Room 780	(512) 482-5288
VII RO	Kansas City	MO	64106	911 Walnut Street, 13th Floor	(816) 374-5288
DO	Kansas City	MO	64106	1103 Grande Avenue, Room 512	(816) 374-3419
BO	Springfield	MO	65803	309 North Jefferson, Room 150	(417) 864-7670
DO	Cedar Rapids	IA	52402	373 Collins Road N.E.	(319) 399-2571
DO	Des Moines	IA	50309	210 Walnut St., Room 749	(515) 284-4422
DO	Omaha	NB	68102	300 South 19th Street	(402) 221-4691
DO	St. Louis	MO	63101	815 Olive Street, Room 242	(314) 425-6600
POD	Cape Girardeau	MO	63701	339 Briadway, Room 140	(314) 335-6039
DO	Wichita	KS	67202	110 East Waterman Street	(316) 269-6571
VIII RO	Denver	CO	80202	1405 Curtis, Street, 22nd Floor	(303) 844-5441
DO	Denver	CO	80202	721 19th Street, Room 407	(303) 844-2607
DO	Casper	WY	82602	100 East B Street, Room 4001	(307) 261-5761
DO	Fargo	ND	58108	657 2nd Avenue, North, Room 218	(701) 237-5771
DO	Helena	MT	59626	301 South Park, Room 528	(406) 449-5381
POD	Billings	MT	59101	2601 First Avenue North, Room 216	(406) 657-6047
DO	Salt Lake City	UT	84138	125 South State Street, Room 2237	(314) 524-5800
DO	Sioux Falls	SD	57102	101 South Main Avenue, Suite 101	(605) 336-2980

	City	State	ZIP	Address	Phone
IX RO	San Francisco	CA	94102	450 Golden Gate Avenue, Room 15307	(415) 556-7487
DO	San Francisco	CA	94105	211 Main Street, 4th Floor	(415) 454-0642
DO	Fresno	CA	93721	2202 Monterey Street, Room 108	(209) 487-5189
BO	Sacramento	CA	95814	660 J Street, Room 215	(916) 440-4461
DO	Las Vegas	NV	89125	301 East Stewart Street	(702) 385-6611
POD	Reno	NV	89505	50 S. Virginia Street, Room 238	(702) 784-5268
DO	Honolulu	HI	96850	300 Ala Moana, Room 2213	(808) 546-8950
BO	Agana	Guam	96910	Pacific Daily News Bldg., Room 508	(671) 472-7277
DO	Los Angeles	CA	90071	350 S. Figueroa Street, 6th Floor	(213) 688-2956
BO	Santa Ana	CA	92701	2700 North Main Street, Room 400	(714) 836-2494
DO	Phoenix	AZ	85012	3030 North Central Avenue, Suite 1201	(602) 241-2200
POD	Tucson	AZ	85701	300 West Congress Street, Room 3V	(602) 629-6715
DO	San Diego	CA	85701	880 Front Street, Room 4-S-29	(619) 293-5540
POD	San Jose	CA	95113	111 West St. John Street, Room 424	(408) 275-7584
X RO	Seattle	WA	98121	2615 4th Avenue, Room 440	(206) 442-5676
DO	Seattle	WA	98174	915 Second Avenue, Room 1792	(206) 442-5534
DO	Anchorage	AK	99501	701 C Street, Room 1068	(907) 271-4022
BO	Fairbanks	AK	99701	101 12th Avenue	(907) 452-0211
DO	Boise	ID	83701	1005 Main St., 2nd Floor	(208) 334-1696
DO	Portland	OR	97204	1220 S. W. Third Avenue, Room 676	(503) 221-5221
DO	Spokane	WA	99210	W920 Riverside Avenue, Room 651	(509) 456-5310

Disaster Area Offices (DAO)

	City	State	ZIP	Address	Phone
DAO 1	Fair Lawn	NJ	07410	15-01 Broadway	(201) 794-8195
DAO 2	Atlanta	GA	30303	75 Spring Street, S.W., Suite 822	(404) 221-5822
DAO 3	Grande Prairie	TX	75051	2306 Oak Lane, Suite 110	(214) 767-7571
DAO 4	Sacramento	CA	95825	77 Cadillac Dr., Suite 158	(916) 440-3651

REGIONAL OFFICE (RO)   DISTRICT OFFICE (DO)   BRANCH OFFICE (BO)   POST-OF-DUTY (POD)

SBA Form 348 (06-85)   Previous Editions are Obsolete   Subject to Change

Regional Office (RO), District Office (DO), Branch Office (BO), Post-of-Duty (POD)

3. It must meet size standards based on the number of employees or annual receipts. These two standards vary for different industries.

SBA has prepared an exhaustive list of size requirements based on Standard Industrial Codes (SIC). A general rule of thumb, with many exceptions, defines a small business as one with fewer than 500 employees.

SBA also has rules against making loans or loan guarantees for uses such as these:

- Paying unsecured creditors, or principals
- Speculation, such as wildcatting in oil or dealing in commodity futures
- Non-profit institutions
- Newspapers, magazines, and similar enterprises
- Gambling
- Lending or investment
- Acquiring real property held primarily for sale or investment
- Monopoly
- Pyramid Sales Clubs
- Relocation of business under certain conditions such as movement to nullify a labor contract, or a move which would result in significant unemployment or a substantial loss from an existing lease

If a business meets the requirements of size and eligible activities, the next important test has to do with the appropriateness of an SBA loan. Generally, the SBA will not be the lender of first choice. No loan application will be considered if:

1. Financing is available from a commercial credit source at reasonable rates and terms; or
2. The business has assets which are not essential to growth or operations which could be liquidated for additional capital; or
3. Collateral is insufficient to meet the value of the loan, that is, an SBA loan cannot be used for what has been referred to as a "bail-out"; or

4. The loan proceeds will be used for payment to owners in the
business.

Increasingly the SBA is applying the same credit standards—adequate collateral and appropriate creditworthiness—as a commercial lender would use. The difference is that, in some instances, SBA is able to finance a business with different terms or rates or may be able to provide a loan or guarantee when a more cautious private sector lender would not make capital available.

Any entrepreneur planning to approach the SBA for a loan should be prepared to provide the last three years' historical financial statements, personal financial statements, and a complete description of the use of the funds being requested. The SBA usually requires business projections and pro forma financial statements before approving a loan or loan guarantee. While these requirements are not absolute, a loan request has a much better chance of success with this support information.

SBA LOAN PROGRAMS

The 7(a) Program

The largest of all SBA loan programs is the 7(a) program. Like most SBA loan programs, it takes its name from the section of the Small Business Act which has granted this authority and created the parameters for its operations. The 7(a) program has become almost exclusively a loan guarantee program. (The law does provide for *direct* loans, but only for the handicapped, veterans, and Minority Enterprise Small Business Investment Companies.)

Eligible activities under 7(a) loans include:

• Acquisition of borrower-occupied real estate
• Fixed assets such as machinery and equipment
• Working capital for items such as inventory or to meet cash-flow needs

The amount of the guaranteed portion of the loan cannot exceed $500,000. The SBA will guarantee up to 90 percent of the loan for the bank. Although 90 percent guarantees are the norm in some situations, the SBA may guarantee less than 90 percent of the loan.

The term for 7(a) loans is related to the life of the assets, the cash flow of the business or the use of the funds. Real estate loans, by statute, can be for a term up to 25 years and fixed assets may be financed for the effective life of the asset, typically three to seven years. Working capital terms are usually one to five years. In all cases the maturity of the loan is consistent with the time required by the applicant to make repayment; the term of the loan is in direct relation to the cash flow of the business.

The interest rate for all 7(a) loans is pegged to the prime rate. The law requires that the interest rate may not exceed 2.75 percent over prime, or 2.25 percent if the terms are under seven years. The rate may be floating or fixed as determined by the bank. If the rate is floating, it may be adjusted monthly, quarterly, semiannually, or annually.

These 7(a) loans can be used for financing up to 100 percent of the total capital needs for expansions of existing businesses. A typical start-up can expect to borrow 70 percent to 75 percent of the capital needed.

The credit and collateral criteria for these loans is usually stringent. As the potential borrower, you must be able to demonstrate that cash flow will be sufficient to repay the debt. Having passed this credit test, you should be prepared to offer as much collateral as possible to make this loan more attractive to the SBA and the commercial lender.

Typically, the collateral required includes a general security agreement and a lien on all assets of the business. Personal guarantees from the business principals will also be required. The SBA will expect to be named as beneficiaries for life insurance in an amount equivalent to the outstanding balance of the loan in case of the death of a principal in the business.

A 7(a) loan may be used in conjunction with other federal loan programs, but may not be used to guarantee a tax-exempt revenue bond. It is common to package a 7(a) loan with other federal loans in order to provide working capital for a business expansion. It is important to remember that the maximum amount the SBA may guarantee for any small business is one million dollars.

Overall, the 7(a) program is not designed to offer incentives to the borrower, such as a reduced rate or improved terms, but should be viewed instead as a financing tool in instances where the overriding issue is obtaining capital. To qualify for a 7(a) loan, you must demonstrate that you have been turned down by a commercial lender. The 7(a) loan guarantee will not necessarily improve the terms of your loan, but it may allow you to secure the capital you need that would otherwise be unavailable.

An example: Company A needed additional working capital after expanding their product line and machinery and equipment. In order to meet the demands of their heaviest season, they needed an additional $250,000 to purchase new inventory and finance existing receivables. After being turned down for a line of credit and a working capital loan by their bank because of the current level of debt, they approached the Small Business Administration in their hometown. They applied for the $250,000 loan under the 7(a) program and received approval in the form of a 90 percent loan guarantee. With the SBA guarantee, the bank was willing to make the loan. The small business gave the bank a lien on all available assets as well as a general security agreement and received the working capital they needed to make their inventory investment and fund their receivables. Under the loan agreement, the company paid 1.5 percent over prime for three years, in monthly installments. At the end of three years, having successfully satisfied all requirements of the loan, the bank established a revolving line of credit for the company to use in similar situations involving inventory and cash-flow cycles.

Frequently, it is unnecessary to approach the SBA directly. The bank will usually recognize situations where the SBA might be helpful and bring that to your attention.

The 502 Program

Another SBA loan program, also named for a section of law, is the 502 loan program. This program is designed to help the entrepreneur with the acquisition of fixed assets only and cannot be used for working capital or inventory.

While the previously described 7(a) program exists to serve the entrepreneur when the question of credit is the primary problem, the 502 program is designed to meet problems related to terms and collateral for a particular project. For example, you need to acquire a piece of equipment which will have a long life—of, say, 15 years— and wish to amortize the loan over the effective life of the equipment.

The commercial lender may *not* be willing to make the loan since loans from a commercial credit source are usually short-term—for periods such as five years. The 502 program, by providing longer terms for the acquisition of property, plant, and equipment, assists the entrepreneur in meeting his or her financing needs.

The acquisition of fixed assets under the 502 program, is accomplished through an arrangement between the SBA, a Local Development Company, a commercial lender, and your business concern. An unusual feature of a 502 loan is that your project must be in an area served by a Local Development Company (LDC). LDCs are usually formed by local governments or citizens whose aim is to improve the economy in their area. The SBA works through these organizations in the 502 program. Your local SBA office (see Exhibit 7-1) or commercial lender can advise you on this feature.

When utilizing a Local Development Company, the LDC acts as the legal borrower on behalf of your small business concern. The acquisition of fixed assets under the 502 program is actually a lease purchase agreement between a LDC and your firm, with the SBA acting as loan guarantor and a commercial lender acting as the funds originator. Loan procedures under this program can be somewhat complex, but valuable if you need long-term asset financing with minimum collateral.

Through 502 loans, the SBA and the LDC accomplish their goal of supporting local business. In addition, as with all government guaranteed loans, the commercial lender also benefits, by having their potential liability greatly reduced via the SBA guarantee.

In the 502 program, the maximum amount the government guarantees is $500,000. The SBA will generally make a 90 percent guarantee to the local lending institution through a LDC. The term for this loan, which is usually the key factor, is the life of the asset, not to exceed 25 years. Once again, interest rates are pegged to the prime rate, with a ceiling of 2.75 percent over prime. The loan can be at a fixed or floating rate.

In structuring all 502 loans, the SBA requires a minimum of 10 percent local capital investment be made in the project. This money can come from the entrepreneur, a local bank, the Local Development Company, or almost any other source. The remaining 90 percent of the project cost can then be financed through a commercial lender and a Local Development Company, with SBA guarantee. Usually, personal guarantees and life insurance will be required to cover the debt.

An example: Company B, a manufacturing concern moving into a new product line, needed to acquire machinery at a cost of $400,000. Although the equipment would have a useful life of ten years, the bank was unwilling to make a loan for a term of over five years. Management saw the need to lengthen the terms in order to meet the debt service requirements and match their funds to the effective life of the equipment purchase.

Working through a Local Development Corporation and their local bank, they obtained a $360,000 SBA 502 program loan for ten years at 1.25 percent over prime. Management made an additional equity investment of $40,000 to meet the requirements of the loan. They are presently making the monthly installment payments to retire the debt.

The 503 Program

In 1980, another section of the Small Business Act was passed, Section 503. This program is similar in many ways to the 502 program. However, the advantages of the 503 program include the increased total project size which may be accommodated.

The structure of a 503 loan involves a commitment of 50 percent of total project costs from a local lending institution, a 10 percent capital or equity investment, and 40 percent participation by the SBA, up to a maximum of $500,000. Under such arrangements, projects exceeding one million dollars could be financed using the 503 program.

Unlike other SBA loan programs, 503 loans must meet criteria which demonstrate a positive impact on the local economy. The normal guideline is the creation of at least one new job for every $15,000 worth of debt which is secured by their 40 percent share in the loan package. While these requirements are not rigid, the better the job creation ratio, the stronger the loan request.

The structure of the 503 program also requires the participation of a Certified Development Corporation (CDC) to act as agent for this loan. Any community served by an existing CDC is eligible for the 503 loan program. Many businesses outside a local CDC area have been able to secure financing through a statewide CDC. These exist now in many states. Contact the SBA office in your area or state (See Exhibit 7-1) to find out how your area is being served.

As in the 502 program, the proceeds from a 503 loan can be used for fixed assets only, including:

- Acquisition of land and buildings
- New construction or renovation
- Machinery and equipment
- Leasehold improvements, furniture, and fixtures

Working capital cannot be financed by a 503 loan.

Financing under the 503 program can have several different interest rates—one set by the bank for its portion, the other rate, the 503 portion, will be .25 to .75 percent above United States Treasury Bond rates of similar maturity at the time the debentures securing the loan are sold.

The test of credit and collateral are similar to the 502 program, with the primary criteria being cash flow to meet debt service requirements and adequate collateral to secure the loan. Personal guarantees and life insurance will usually be required, but individuals are normally not required to invest or secure their total net worth for collateral if the project has a substantial economic development impact on the community.

Lending institutions are usually interested in participating in this type of loan guarantee arrangement because they are in first position to acquire and liquidate all assets in case of default, even though their liability is only 50 percent. SBA usually holds second position in such an arrangement for their 40 percent share in case of a default.

The 503 loan program is a complex, but valuable tool for the entrepreneur. Not a good source of funds for business start-ups, refinancing or turnaround business ventures, this approach to government financing is most appropriate for the expansion of an existing business with strong credit and collateral, in search of better fixed-asset financing.

An example: Company C, a fish processing plant in New England, was ready to open an additional location nearer a port which served local fishermen. With a strong business history and a stable pattern of growth, this company could demonstrate its potential. They needed one million dollars for an expansion project which included the acquisition of an existing building, renovations to that building, and the cost of machinery and equipment for fish processing. The bank was unwilling to loan the entire amount, but working with the local Certified Development Corporation, the company put up capital of $100,000, the bank made a direct loan of $500,000, and the SBA guaranteed an additional $400,000. The new location was opened and 82 employees hired. Through this vehicle the company financed the real estate acquisition for 20 years and the remainder of the project for 15 years.

Other SBA Programs

There are a number of smaller and targeted programs which can provide both loans and loan guarantees to specific groups of small business people. The availability of these special funds can best be ascertained by contacting the SBA. Special loan programs have included but are not limited to:

- Handicapped Assistance Loans for physically handicapped small-business people
- Energy Loans to companies and firms involved in manufacturing and installing energy saving devices
- Disaster Assistance Loans
- Pollution Control Financing for small-business people
- Minority-Owned Business Loans for small-business people belonging to ethnic minorities, or who are women.

All government loan programs are designed to aid the entrepreneur in securing the financing necessary for business growth and expansion. The program requirements vary widely (see Exhibit 7-2, page 166, for a comparison of major programs) and are subject to change, but for the business executive willing to invest the time and energy, they may be a successful alternative when commercial credit is unavailable.

THE FARMER'S HOME ADMINISTRATION

Another federal agency which has aided business is the Farmer's Home Administration. An arm of the United States Department of

Agriculture, the Farmer's Home Administration focuses on providing assistance and loans to the nation's rural areas. Businesses in urban areas are ineligible to receive assistance under the Farmer's Home Administration program.

Recent changes in the federal budget have had a great impact on the loan and loan guarantee activities of this agency. You would be well advised to investigate the number of loan and loan guarantees made locally by the Farmer's Home Administration before pursuing the application process in any detail.

Defining Rural Areas

The Farmer's Home Administration works within closely defined parameters for rural areas in making loan decisions. A rural area may be defined as any area that is not a town or city with a population of 50,000 or more. Also excluded are those areas adjacent to urbanized areas with more than 100 persons per square mile. Priority is given to projects in rural communities and cities with a population of less than 25,000.

Types of Farmer's Home Administration Loans

The Farmer's Home Administration provides credit for a variety of uses in rural areas. It has participated in rural housing development lending as well as lending for public facilities in small towns and less populous counties. These programs would not generally be of interest to the small business executive although they may be used as a tool for housing or infrastructure development to enhance a business expansion.

The Farmer's Home Administration has provided two primary types of loans which could benefit the entrepreneur. The first are agriculture and agricultural production loans; the second, business and industry loans.

Agricultural Loan Programs. The agricultural loan programs provide credit assistance to applicants who are operating family-sized farms or cooperatives made up of family-sized farms. These loans include:

- Farm Ownership Loans
- Farm Operating Loans
- Loans to Limited Resource Farmers
- Specialized Loans, such as Aquaculture Loans
- Economic Emergency Loans
- Disaster Loans
- Grazing Association Loans
- Soil and Water Loans

The terms and conditions for these loans will vary from program to program, although generally they are loan guarantee programs which depend upon a local lending institution making the loan with a Farmer's Administration guarantee of up to 90 percent. These loans apply specifically to the business involved directly in agricultural production. For detailed information on these loans, you should contact the nearest state office for the Farmer's Home Administration.

Business and Industry Loans.   The Farmer's Home Administration is also active in guaranteeing loans, through commercial lenders, for the creation and expansion of industry in less populous areas. In recent years, however, allocations for these loan programs have been reduced. In some areas, loan activity has been severely restricted.

Having met the basic conditions of a rural area, the applicant must meet a number of other stipulations. These loans *may not be used* for any of the following purposes:

- To pay a creditor in excess of value
- To pay owners or shareholders or other equity owners
- For projects involving agricultural production
- For transfer of business ownership unless such transfer prevents a closing with subsequent loss of jobs
- For guarantee of lease payments
- For financing community antenna television services or facilities
- For guarantee of loans made by other federal agencies (such as the SBA)

• For projects of over one million dollars or over 50 employees where such projects will result in the transfer of operations with a significant impact on the labor or demand of existing markets.

If none of the preceding conditions exist, an entrepreneur can apply for a Farmer's Home Administration loan guarantee. The amount of the guarantee cannot exceed 90 percent. Loan guarantees are available for the following business activities:

• Acquisition of buildings and land
• Renovation of buildings or new construction
• Acquisition of machinery and equipment
• Working capital for inventory and cash-flow needs

The terms vary depending upon the nature of the loan, with maximums of 30 years for real estate, 15 years for machinery and equipment and seven years for working capital. The term of the loan is generally consistent with the use of the proceeds.

These Farmer's Home Administration loans generally require a commitment of at least 10 percent of total project cost in equity. The amount of equity required of a new business or start-up can be as high as 25 percent.

Credit and collateral are important considerations in the approval process. Your business must demonstrate a capacity to meet debt service requirements with cash flow, and the collateral must match the value of the capital used to acquire it.

The interest rate is determined by the local lending institution and the Farmer's Home Administration, and is usually set at an increment above the prevailing Treasury Bond rate of similar term. The rate may be either fixed or variable, depending upon the nature of the participation by the commercial lender.

The Farmer's Home Administration may require unconditional personal guarantees from owners and partners making the application. Life insurance may also be required of the applicant. In instances where the loan request exceeds one million dollars, a feasibility study is required.

The Farmer's Home Administration Business and Industry Loans do *not* include the precondition that an applicant has been turned down by a commercial lender before a loan guarantee can be granted by the agency.

In many rural areas, Business and Industry Loans have provided significant financial incentives to the creation of jobs and the investment of capital. It should be apparent, however, that the number of specific prerequisites may make this fund source unavailable to many entrepreneurs. See Exhibit 7-2, page 166, for a key terms and conditions comparison with other major federal loan guarantee programs.

THE ECONOMIC DEVELOPMENT ADMINISTRATION

The Economic Development Administration (EDA), an arm of the United States Department of Commerce, was created in 1965 to promote industrial and commercial development. Since its inception, this agency has supported business development with grants to communities, the creation and capitalization of local revolving loan funds, and direct assistance to businesses in the form of loans and loan guarantees.

Much of the infrastructure necessary for the development of new industrial parks and sites has been undertaken with the assistance of the EDA in underdeveloped areas in the country. In the last few years, the amount of money appropriated for EDA activities has steadily diminished. The agency has also decreased its lending activities. Refocusing of EDA energy into the capitalization of local revolving loan funds for business development marked a new direction for this agency.

Job Creation Loan Guarantee Program

Presently, the EDA is continuing to provide loan guarantees to businesses which will create new jobs in areas which have high unemployment, high percentages of families at or below the poverty level, and a net decline in per capita income between census periods.

As with the other government financing programs, EDA has its own particular requirements and standards. A unique feature is that a private lending institution is always the applicant for EDA loan guarantees. Loan guarantees may be up to 90 percent of the total loan value, although preference is given to those loan guarantee requests which are less.

The maximum amount of loan guarantee available is 10 million dollars, with a minimum amount of $550,000. These loan guarantees may be made for any of the following purposes:

- Acquisition and development of land and facilities for industrial or commercial use
- Construction or rehabilitation of buildings
- Acquisition of machinery and equipment
- Working capital

EDA is interested in job creation. At least one new job must be created for every $10,000 of government investment. Priority consideration is given to those applications with a job to cost ratio of $7,500 per job or less. The more jobs, the better the loan application.

Unlike the SBA, the EDA loan guarantees may require a higher equity ratio on the part of the entrepreneur. On any fixed asset loan, you must contribute at least 15 percent of the total project cost. In the case of a working capital loan, the equity position must be at least 20 percent.

The terms and conditions for the loan will be set by the bank, although the EDA will not provide a loan guarantee on any loan with an interest rate they consider excessive. Terms may be fixed or variable. As with most other government financing, the length of term must not exceed the weighted average useful life of the asset acquired with the loan proceeds. Twenty-five years is the maximum term for real estate with five years being the maximum term for working capital.

Credit and collateral conditions must be suitable to ensure repayment of the loan. In case of default, the value of the assets must be adequate to ensure loan repayment upon liquidation. The EDA will require (1) a minimum of three years' historical financial and operating statements, (2) a current financial statement (no more than 90 days old), (3) a projection detailing cash flow on a month-to-month basis for the first year and on a quarterly basis for the next two years, and (4) a current appraisal of the real property used as collateral for the loan.

A feasibility study is also required for any project with a total cost of one million dollars or more, or one which involves tourism, recreational projects or projects involving new and untried technologies.

A company interested in such a loan guarantee must certify to the following conditions.

- It has not relocated any or all of its facilities from one city to another within the last three years
- It will not use the proceeds of this loan to relocate operations with a consequent loss of jobs to the area
- It will not produce a product or service for which there is a prolonged or sustained excess of supply over demand

These requirements follow naturally from the EDA's position as an agency responsible for job creation, particularly in areas of high unemployment. For a key terms and conditions comparison with other major federal loan guarantee programs, see Exhibit 7-2.

The EDA has regional offices located in Philadelphia, Atlanta, Chicago, Austin, Denver, and Seattle. For further information, check with your nearest regional office or discuss the matter with your banker who will serve as the applicant for this loan guarantee program.

EXPORT-IMPORT BANK

The Export-Import Bank of the United States (Eximbank) was created in 1934 and established as an independent U.S. Government Agency in 1945 to assist American businesses in exporting. The Eximbank was designed to enhance the competitive position of U.S. exporters of all sizes, by offering financing competitive with financing provided by foreign export credit agencies to assist sales by their nation's exporters. The Eximbank is located in Washington, D.C.

This agency serves business and provides financing for export businesses in several different ways. There are programs which provide loan guarantees, programs which provide middle-term or interim credit to assist in the cash flow difficulties which sometimes affect receivables in export companies, and export credit insurance programs to safeguard investment in case of any political or economic disruption in the export market.

EXHIBIT 7-2. COMPARATIVE CHART OF MAJOR FEDERAL GOVERNMENT LOAN GUARANTEE PROGRAMS

Key Terms and Conditions	Small Business Administration (SBA)			Farmer's Home Administration (FHA) Business & Industry Program	Economic Development Administration (EDA) Job Creation Program
	7(a) Program	502 Program	503 Program		
Eligible Uses	Acquisition of borrower-occupied real estate Fixed assets Working capital Start-up or expansion	Acquisition of land, buildings, or new construction or renovation Fixed assets Start-up or expansion (Cannot be used for working capital)	Acquisition of land, buildings or new construction or renovation Fixed assets (Not good for start-ups) (Cannot be used for working capital)	Acquisition of land, buildings or new construction or renovation Fixed assets Working capital Start-up or expansion	Acquisition of land, buildings (for industrial or commercial use) or construction or renovation Fixed assets Working capital Start-up or expansion
Guarantee Maximums	90% of loan Up to $500,000	90% of loan Up to $500,000	40% of loan Up to $500,000	90% of loan Above $1 million a feasibility study is required	90% of loan Minimum $550,000, maximum $10 million. Above $1 million a feasibility study is required
Capital/Equity Requirements	Can be used for financing: Up to 100% of total expansion costs 70–75% of total start-up costs	10% local investment required, debt or equity	10% capital or equity investment 50% commitment from local lending institution	10% equity investment for expansions Up to 25% equity for start-ups	15% equity for fixed assets 20% equity for working capital
Terms	Real Estate: Up to 25 years Fixed Assets: Life of asset (typically 3–7 years)	Life of asset, not to exceed 25 years	Life of asset, not to exceed 25 years	Real Estate: Up to 30 years Fixed Assets: Up to 15 years	Real Estate: Up to 25 years Fixed Assets: Life of asset

	Column 1	Column 2	Column 3	Column 4	Column 5
Terms (*continued*)	Working Capital: 1–5 years			Working Capital: Up to 7 years	Working Capital: Up to 5 years
Interest Rate Maximums	Prime + 2.25% for terms under 7 years; Prime + 2.75% for terms 7 years or over; Fixed or floating	Prime + 2.75%; Fixed or floating	SBA Portion: .25 to .75% above U.S. Treasury Bond rates of similar maturity; Bank sets the rate for their portion of the loan; Fixed or floating	.25% or more above U.S. Treasury Bond rates of similar maturity; Fixed or floating	Interest rate is set by the bank, but must not be considered excessive by the EDA; Fixed or floating
Credit and Collateral	Stringent (offer as much as possible); General security agreement; Lien on all business assets; Personal guarantees; SBA as life insurance beneficiary	General security agreement; Personal guarantees; Life insurance	General security agreement; Personal guarantees; Life insurance	Collateral must match value of capital used to aquire it; Unconditional personal guarantees; Life insurance	Standard financial institution credit and collateral requirements. Value of assets *must* be adequate to ensure loan repayment.
Special Requirements	—	Your project must be in an area served by a Local Development Company. The SBA works through these organizations in the 502 program.	Your project must have a positive impact on the local economy—usually *at least* one new job per $15,000 of SBA investment. Must be located in an area served by a local or state Certified Development Corporation.	Project must be in an area that meets the FHA's definition of a rural area. Loans may *not* be used for a number of purposes including guarantee of lease payments or loans made by another federal agency, to pay owners or shareholders, etc.	Project must be located in an economically depressed area. Minimum of one new job for each $10,000 of EDA investment. Loan must be applied for by a private lending institution. No past (3 yrs.) or present move with loss of jobs.

Working Capital Guarantee Program

As a result of cash flow needs which often arise in export businesses, Eximbank offers a Working Capital Loan Guarantee program to meet the need for working capital. The program, established in 1982, provides a loan guarantee for any exporting project of a small or medium-sized business or minority-owned enterprise which is unable to secure credit from a commercial lender.

The guarantee is for 90 percent of the loan amount, both principal and interest, and is usually for a period of one month to one year. In some cases, the duration of the loan may be extended; however, this program is really designed to enable businesses to enter and sustain activities in the export market in the face of expanding receivables due to foreign exchange.

Since the purpose of the loan guarantee is to cover the potential risk of a commercial lender in making funds available to an exporter, the loan requires a heavy collateral commitment from the borrower. A manager should typically expect to secure this loan with assets of at least 110 percent of the outstanding balance of the loan.

You may find this program helpful in establishing or expanding your participation in the export market when commercial credit for such a venture is not available. These funds are *not* available to a business which is not using the proceeds directly to assist in the export of products to foreign markets.

Small Business Credit Program

Another activity of Eximbank is the Small Business Credit Program which provides middle-term *fixed rate* export loan assurances to encourage the expansion of export business. Recognizing that fixed rate financing is often needed to stabilize an order in a foreign market, this program provides assurances, to a commercial lender, of money available at a fixed rate to guarantee a loan for an export activity.

This program is designed for small businesses and uses the Small Business Administration's definitions for small business (discussed earlier in this chapter) to determine eligibility. Eximbank will issue an advance commitment for fixed rate financing to any eligible commercial lender if the lender is unwilling to offer fixed rate financing to the exporter without such a commitment.

The Eximbank commitment can be for up to 85 percent of the total contract price for the export shipment, and the financing terms are for one to five years. The stability of the fixed rate that this loan provides is intended to enhance the feasibility of the project for the exporter. The bank making the loan to the exporter is able to request disbursement of funds from the Eximbank when its alternative source of funds is more costly than the committed loan rate of Eximbank.

These loan commitments are for a maximum of $2.5 million per transaction with an aggregate total of $10 million per year for any one business. The rate of interest for these loans will vary according to the market served, with higher rates for richer countries and the lowest rates for the poorest countries. Generally, the Eximbank interest rate on these loans will be one percent below the minimum interest rates allowed by the Organization for Economic Cooperation and Development.

Medium-Term Credit Program

In some ways similar to the Small Business Credit Program, this Eximbank initiative also provides medium-term fixed rate interest support for export sales. The important difference is that to qualify for this loan support, you must offer evidence that your export competition is subsidized by a foreign country. This program's main purpose is to restore the competitive balance between American and foreign businesses.

Having demonstrated that foreign competition is subsidized, a U.S. business can secure a loan with terms and conditions similar to the Small Business Credit program.

Other Eximbank Programs

The Eximbank offers a number of other programs, generally through local lending institutions, that can provide incentives for the development of your export business, including Commercial Bank Guarantees and Export Credit Insurance to insure investments against sudden political or economic market disruption. The entrepreneur interested in the export market may find the Eximbank programs helpful in securing financing to make operations more profitable, although government budget pressures may make less funds available in the future.

SMALL BUSINESS INNOVATION RESEARCH PROGRAM

A different approach to providing government financial support to entrepreneurial activities is provided by the Small Business Innovation Development Act of 1982. This law is designed to include small private businesses in research and development activities supported by the government. It differs from other programs discussed in this chapter in that it is a hybrid between a loan or grant program and a new pattern of contracts for procurement of services. Recognizing that much of the private sector research and development (R&D) paid for by the government was done primarily by the nation's larger businesses, the Small Business Innovation Research program (SBIR) was created to insure participation by smaller businesses in these activities.

Rather than creating a new agency, the SBIR initiative spreads the responsibility among other agencies. Each is responsible for committing a certain amount of their research and development funds to small businesses through the SBIR program. The Small Business Administration oversees the program while each agency establishes its own programs and contract criteria.

The participating agencies include:

- The Department of Defense
- National Aeronautics and Space Administration
- Department of Health and Human Services
- Department of Energy
- National Science Foundation
- Department of Agriculture
- Department of Transportation
- Nuclear Regulatory Commission
- Environmental Protection Agency
- Department of the Interior
- Department of Education

Each of these agencies, with research and development budgets in excess of $100 million, directs some of its R&D work to small businesses.

Research Grants and Contracts

As previously stated, rather than a loan program, the SBIR program is designed to provide grant awards and contracts for research activities. Small businesses compete for the awards to develop and refine ideas over a period of years. The process includes:

Phase I. Research grants of up to $50,000 for projects which will evaluate the technical and scientific merits as well as feasibility of ideas (solicited or unsolicited, see below) which fall within the scope of the participating agency.

Phase II. Awards of up to $500,000 over a one- or two-year period to develop the most promising ideas.

Phase III. Public and private sector partnership to support and bring this new innovation to the marketplace. This will generally involve follow-up production contracts from the federal agency which supports the original research and development.

Any small business with 500 or fewer employees is eligible to participate in the SBIR program. Specific requirements vary somewhat from agency to agency, as each establishes priorities for research and development activities. Generally, the greatest problems for entrepreneurs is to identify the research and development needs of these various agencies and show that their company has the capacity to qualify for such research activities. To accommodate this problem, the SBIR program calls for two levels of response by small businesses.

First, there will be solicited proposals. In these instances, the entrepreneur responds to a request for a proposal (RFP) from a participating agency. (The Small Business Administration's Office of Innovation, Research and Technology periodically issues *presolicitation* announcements of general research and development topics of interest to specific federal departments.) By demonstrating the managerial and research competence to undertake such a task, the small business will be awarded the research grant.

The second type of proposal may be termed the unsolicited proposal. In this instance, the small business submits a proposal for research and development activities to an agency.

Before such a proposal is submitted, the small business should determine the following:

• Does the agency fund unsolicited proposals?
• Is the proposed research and development appropriate to this agency?
• Does the work duplicate previous research or research-in-progress?
• Is the proposal technically sound?
• Do the key investigators have the capacity to undertake the proposed research?
• Is the cost reasonable?
• Are the funds currently available?

Obviously, good information is a key in gaining access to the benefits of the SBIR program. The Small Business Administration is a valuable information resource. In addition, you should make full use of the National Technical Information Service (NTIS), a government clearinghouse of technical information and publications.

For the entrepreneur involved in research and development, the highly specialized Small Business Innovation Research program offers some new resources and potential business development, as well as additional funding opportunities. The terms and availability of resources under this program, however, vary greatly from agency to agency.

OTHER SPECIALIZED GOVERNMENT FINANCING OPPORTUNITIES

The funding programs discussed in this chapter provide the general picture of governmental financing tools presently available. There are also other, even more highly specialized fund sources, loan guarantee and incentive programs—which may apply only to one particular industry or activity—that are available from time to time from various agencies. These can include loan guarantees for businesses involved in defense production, special financing for international trade promotion, and even funds for American businesses planning on opening plants in foreign countries, providing, of course, such plants are not intended to reduce the level of employment opportunities in the

United States. Again, information sources are the key to your benefiting from these programs.

IN CONCLUSION: FINDING GOVERNMENT FINANCING RESOURCES

The process of raising capital from the best available source finally revolves around communication with all potential fund sources. It is the responsibility of the business person seeking funds, to stay in close contact with many different people in both the private and public sectors. The changes in financial availability in both sectors demands close attention. Just as you need to stay in touch with your banker, accountant, attorney, and business and financial analyst, communication with city hall, the state capital and the federal agencies can also be important when a financing need arises.

8

BUSINESS COMBINATIONS

Thousands of American companies, large and small, get together each year to discuss business combinations. The types of business combinations considered will include mergers, acquisitions, joint ventures, and licensing and franchising agreements. In many cases, the ultimate objective is to raise or enhance capital for future growth. The process allows companies to combine strengths to make the best of promising new business opportunities.

For the entrepreneur searching for a way to raise capital, some form of business combination may be an effective solution. In some cases, it may be the only solution.

Even though business combinations are quite common, it should be noted that the process is often the most complicated and time-consuming method of raising capital for growth. Finding the best company to deal with may be swift and easy in some instances—when you stay within your own industry or are approached by a suitable candidate—but more likely it will be a matter of eyeing prospects for a long time before you find a matching of circumstances that leads to a transaction. Once you locate a good prospect, there are the further tasks of evaluating each business, yours and theirs, and negotiating agreements satisfactory to both parties.

A common executive problem is the very length of the process. For an executive like yourself, busy running the day-to-day business, it is very easy to lose patience and neglect the pursuit or, conversely, for the pursuit to become all consuming, resulting in neglect of day-to-day business matters.

Fortunately, you can turn to outsiders who specialize in searching out and evaluating merger candidates. Although this approach may seem costly at first, it is often the best way to proceed in this highly sophisticated process. Choosing an effective and experienced specialist can result in benefits that far exceed the costs. Proper consideration of the various issues and obstacles to be encountered can mean the difference between success and failure of the project.

The variety of business combinations is nearly without limit. This discussion will concentrate on three broad categories:

1. Selling or Merging an Entire Company

2. Disposition of a Business Segment

3. Joint Ventures, Franchising and Licensing

SELLING OR MERGING AN ENTIRE COMPANY

Some executives will think of selling or merging as alternatives to consider after failing to raise capital from the more conventional sources. Asked why the company was sold, former owners are apt to say, "We could not find more equity capital and had to sell out." Instead of this somewhat negative view, we will focus below on the more positive aspects with regard to selling or merging a company.

Consider, for example, entrepreneurs who are usually good at starting businesses but sometimes poor at building them. (Some of the most brilliant in the start-up arena are lacking in the administrative skills and interest required to manage a maturing business. This has been especially true of recent start-ups in the emerging technologies.) If you are one of these entrepreneurs, merging or selling to a larger company can be a good strategy. The combination can provide capital for growth and may also include seasoned caretaker executives to take over for you. You might then use this new found freedom to develop new ideas and products for the business, or even start another business provided, of course, it does not compete with the old company.

For example, one of our recent engagements was to assist the owner of a computer software company to sell or merge with a larger software company. This individual was a very creative person with a successful company. However, he was unhappy with the day-to-day responsibilities of running the business which required his involvement in such activities as marketing, establishing new branches, and customer relations. Working for a new owner was acceptable to this individual so long as his new responsibilities were primarily in the area of developing new software products. Otherwise, he wanted to "cut and run" and start another software company based upon some new product ideas which he could not find time to pursue while running an established and growing company.

"Cut-and-Run" Situations

A "cut-and-run" (taking the sale proceeds and leaving the company) situation may be realistic only when the owner's presence is not a key factor with regard to the company's continuing success. Such situations might include: (1) a business which manufactures a product

protected by patents, (2) businesses with new products requiring large
front-end capital expenditures but little in production know-how, and
(3) a thoroughly developed and proven concept for which the know-
how can be transferred to new owners. The previous owner in many
cases is then free to pursue new interests so long as the new activities
do not involve competition with the previously owned business.

Noncompete Agreements

To prevent competition from previous owners, acquiring companies
will frequently require you to agree not to compete with them. Such
arrangements are usually referred to as noncompete agreements and
cover periods of from one to five years. A noncompete agreement is
not valid, however, unless the acquirer pays you, the seller, for this
privilege. The consideration paid for a noncompete agreement must
be separate from the amount paid for the business.

Lock-In Employment Provisions

If the owner's presence is deemed to be a key factor in the company's
continuing success, the surviving company will usually require a *strong*
commitment from the seller to stay on and run the business. (A seller's
promise to "stay around for awhile" is not enough.) Therefore, structuring a transaction of this nature is usually more complicated than
structuring the "cut and run." The surviving company will often insist
upon provisions in the agreements which attempt to lock in the previous
owner. One of the more frequently used lock-in provisions is the
"earn out" whereby a substantial portion of the purchase price is
contingent upon future results. You, therefore, have a vested interest
in staying on and making every effort to achieve the projections which
were represented during negotiations to sell the company.

Lock-In Example.   Sometimes the owner and/or existing personnel
are the *most* important factor in a business combination. For example,
many analysts have speculated that the 1984 acquisition of Electronic
Data Systems Corporation (EDS designs, installs and operates electronic
data processing systems) by General Motors was motivated by GM's
desire to have unlimited access to the EDS personnel organization
in building the GM of the future. It is also interesting to note the

key elements in structuring this transaction. One was specifically designed with former EDS shareholders in mind (in particular, Ross Perot, the founder and chief executive officer) as a built-in incentive for superior EDS operating results in the future. GM created a special issue of preferred stock which accounted for a substantial part of the total price paid for EDS. Special provisions were included which allow for this publicly traded issue of preferred stock to be sensitive to the future earnings of EDS. Thus, if Ross Perot stays with EDS and does an outstanding job, as measured by future EDS earnings, he has a chance to create additional value for himself and all other former EDS shareholders who accepted and held the GM preferred stock.

Locating Suitable Companies

Earlier in this chapter, we made reference to the difficulties in locating and evaluating suitable merger partners. With many thousands of companies spread over every state and beyond, it seems an impossible task to find those few acquirers who might have an interest in acquisitions as well as the specific attributes you are hoping to see in them.

There are two ways to carry out the search for suitable candidates. One is to do the job yourself. Some of the potential candidates are probably companies in your own industry or in closely related industries. You are drawn to them because it is where your own expertise lies. You keep close track of companies in your industry and are apt to know the ones most interested in growth through acquisitions. In addition, the U.S. Government Standard Industrial Classification (SIC) codes can be useful in sorting through the mountains of data to narrow the population of viable candidates to manageable proportions.

The second way is to place the search in the hands of an intermediary organization. These people will not pursue candidates who do not fit your criteria. In fact, they often bring with them extensive contacts and an intimate knowledge of the field. This can be extremely important if your timing does not allow for a drawn-out courtship. However, before engaging any intermediary, satisfy yourself as to their knowledge of your field and their experience and success rate in situations such as yours. An intermediary's services should include: (1) pulling together the relevant facts for presenting your company to qualified candidates on a discreet basis, (2) talking to competitors, suppliers, customers, and others to cut through superfluous data and move the project along on a timely basis, and (3) interpreting all the facts with an objectivity that only an outsider can apply. Note: grossly overstating the value of a company can seriously jeopardize the quantity and quality of good leads. And, although understating the value rarely happens, it does, and with equally disastrous results.

Another advantage of using a professional intermediary is that the search is the intermediary's principal job and it will be pursued relentlessly. If time is an important factor, you probably should not conduct the search yourself. The running of your company will most likely take precedence and a company seeking capital for a specific growth opportunity usually cannot afford the luxury of a slower paced search since opportunities last only so long.

DISPOSING OF A BUSINESS SEGMENT

Many companies are involved in more than one line of business. When faced with a need for growth capital, the diversified company will often have the option to divest of one or more business segments to raise funds. Divestitures of this nature might result when a company has the opportunity for rapid growth in one segment (subject to availability of funds) but is heavily in debt.

Deciding which segment to sell can be a real problem. It is usually easy to sell a segment which has a consistent record of earnings and cash flow—the so-called "cash cow." But what if you have strong personal or other attachments to this cash cow segment, maybe it was started years ago by your family and still bears your family name? The emotional factors involved in a transaction of this nature may well cause you to try other alternatives. Perhaps the answer is to sell the segment which needs growth capital. This approach may be especially apropos if time is of the essence in penetrating the market with a new product before stronger companies take advantage of the opening to enter the business. In other words, why not sell or merge with a company which has enough financial muscle to exploit the growth opportunity before it is too late?

Let us assume you are faced with the dilemma of having two good businesses—one is an early-stage, development company which has a very promising new product; the other is a mature business with several years of consistent earnings and cash flow. Projections for the development stage company indicate a substantial short-fall in working capital which cannot be funded with cash flow from the mature company. Your time is devoted entirely to the development stage company. The mature company has separate nonowner management. For one reason or another you do not wish to pursue the many other options available to you for funding the development stage company's working capital short-fall (you have never wanted the responsibility of running a public company, you do not want to go into debt to obtain risk capital, etc., etc.) so you decide to sell one of the businesses, but which one?

If you decide to sell the development-stage company, the process will likely involve many of the areas covered earlier in this chapter. Finding a qualified buyer will probably require a search. In addition, if your personal services are important to the continued success of the company, you may be required to stay on with the new owners for several years.

Management/Leveraged Buyouts

If you sell the mature company, a search for the most qualified buyer might still be appropriate. However, in addition, you may have the option of selling the mature business to its management. Management buyouts (MBOs) are usually leveraged buyouts (LBOs) and are quite common. But does this mean you will be selling at a lower price to a weaker buyer? Not at all. As with most LBOs, a substantial portion of the purchase price is borrowed by the buyer, in this case management, by pledging the acquired assets as collateral. In recent years, institutional lenders have also become more and more eager to provide buyout funds through investments in various forms of equity and/or quasi-equity, especially in those known as "mezzanine" capital investments. Mezzanine capital is a term referring to the high risk/high return investments which appear on the balance sheet between equity and collateralized debt. There are numerous examples such as preferred stock, convertible preferred stock, subordinated debentures with or without warrants, convertible subordinated debentures and many more. For one example of a leveraged management buyout financing, see Exhibit 8-1.

EXHIBIT 8-1. MANAGEMENT BUYOUT FINANCING EXAMPLE

"Buyco" (a fictitious name), consisting of five top management shareholders (Group A) and several outside investors (Group B), acquired their automotive parts manufacturing company, from the principal owner, through an assets purchase. Buyco's purchase included nearly all of the selling company's assets and the assumption of most current liabilities. Revenues and pretax profits, which had shown consistent growth in prior years, were $5.5 million and $1.4 million, respectively, in the year prior to the acquisition.

Financing Sources

Revolving credit line:	$ -0-
$750,000 credit line for working capital (not yet used)	
Term loan:	3,750,000
Bank term loan collateralized by fixed assets. Interest paid quarterly at prime + 2 percent, no principal payment for 18 months, followed by 22 equal quarterly payments. Compensating balance of $250,000 required.	
Note given to previous owner:	1,000,000
Payable annually over five years, interest at 11.5 percent.	
Subordinated debt:	1,000,000
Investor-shareholder note: provided by Group B (outside investor shareholders), no principal payments for five years, interest at 8.5 percent. Origination fee of $200,000 paid to Group B over two years. The company plans to refinance in five years and pay this loan off.	
Equity contributed by investors:	
Group A—Management shareholders	500,000
Group B—Outside investor shareholders	500,000
	$6,750,000

Employee Stock Ownership Plan (ESOP) Purchases

The MBO usually limits management ownership to the top four or five executives. But there is also a way, through employee stock ownership plans (ESOPs), for most all of the employees to participate in the purchase of their own company. An ESOP is a tax-qualified plan designed primarily to invest in employer stock. Under the Employee Retirement Income Security Act of 1974 (ERISA), an ESOP is a defined contribution plan and, accordingly, is not subject to minimum funding requirements or insurance regulations of the Pension Benefit Guaranty Corporation. ERISA specifically exempts ESOPs from the limitations placed on other employee benefit plans with respect to the percentage of the plan's assets which can be invested in an employer's securities. More importantly, however, ERISA allows ESOPs to borrow money in order to make such investments (the leveraged ESOP) and thereby provide a company with a potential source of low-cost capital.

The leveraged ESOP borrows money to purchase stock of the employer company. The stock may be newly issued, to raise new money for the company; or it may be previously outstanding stock where the present owners want to sell out, in which case the money raised is used to help purchase the business. Future employer contributions to the plan are tax deductible to the company and are used to repay principal on the purchase money indebtedness. Interest on the indebtedness is also deducted in determining the company's taxable income.

The Deficit Reduction Act of 1984 adopted an extensive package of additional tax incentives with respect to ESOPs. Some of the key changes which apply to leveraged ESOPs are as follows.

- To encourage banks and other commercial lenders to make loans to ESOPs, the Act allows these institutions to exclude 50 percent of the interest earned on ESOP loans from taxable income.
- Under certain circumstances, sponsor companies can now take a tax deduction for dividends paid on employer stock which is held in an ESOP.
- An individual or company who sells employer stock to an ESOP may be able to defer recognition of any gain on the sale if the sale proceeds are used to acquire securities of another company.

The above changes, coupled with the traditional tax benefits inherent in ESOPs, should lead to a significant rise in the use of these plans in mergers and acquisitions.

EXHIBIT 8-2.   ESOP PURCHASE STRUCTURING EXAMPLE

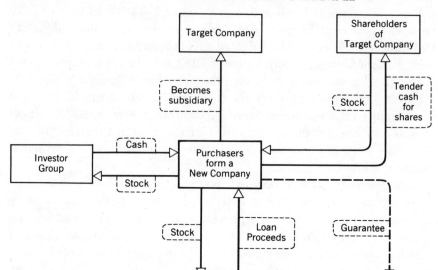

As ESOPs gain in popularity, the creative use of the plans to support LBOs and MBOs is certain to expand. Exhibit 8-2 illustrates one way an ESOP might be used in a buyout situation.

ESOP Purchase Example.   The transactions shown in Exhibit 8-2 are somewhat similar to those employed by larger companies such as the Dan River Inc. investor group, who took that company private. The investor group, comprised of Dan River's management and the investment banking firm Kelso & Company, established a new holding company and a tax-qualified ESOP. The total purchase price for Dan River (a *Fortune* 500 fabric manufacturer) was approximately $154 million. The investor group put up $5 million and the remainder of $149 million was a holding company bank loan. The holding company then issued $110 million of stock to the ESOP, principally for notes. The holding company used the $154 million to buy all the outstanding Dan River stock. Subsequently, Dan River became a subsidiary of the holding company. After the transaction, ownership of the company was split among Kelso (5 percent), Dan River management (25 percent), and the ESOP (70 percent).

On the negative side, if an ESOP is not already in existence, the formation of one can be costly and time consuming; therefore, in certain types of transactions, particularly those where timing is important, the creation of an ESOP may be inappropriate.

As you can see, the factors involved in disposing of a business segment are many and varied, and the opportunities for taking advantage of these techniques likewise are numerous for the well informed.

JOINT VENTURES

In situations where the objective for raising capital relates to a specific project, and the project serves the common or related interests of two or more companies, a joint venture may be the most appropriate business entity. Joint ventures are distinguished from other business entities in that they are generally intended to be of limited life, often of short duration, rather than a continuing business. Throughout the joint venture, each participant is usually in the same legal position as the general partner in a partnership. Despite the risk of unlimited liability, benefits to the joint venture participants can be quite compelling.

Benefits to Joint Venture Participants

The benefits to joint venture participants include the following.

1. *Synergism of the Participants.* This is a classic case of two companies joining forces because each has what the other needs. For example, imagine your company has substantial market penetration in a given industry or area, while the other party has a product or product idea that would fit well into the market where you are strong.

2. *Financing Vehicle.* A participant's investment in a joint venture consists of capital or services or probably some combination of both. The participants contributing primarily services are essentially having their project financed by the participants contributing primarily capital. For example: you contribute your market position and production

expertise and perhaps pay some of the start-up marketing costs, such as brochures and other promotional material. The other company finances the production of the product. The two companies share any profits or losses on a predetermined basis, relative to their respective investments, throughout the venture. At dissolution, the terms of the joint venture and the respective interests of you and your joint venture partner determines who retains the rights to the joint venture product, production facilities or other remaining assets.

3. *Limited and/or Transitional Affiliation.* Through joint ventures your growth objectives can be achieved without substantially or permanently changing your company's operations or ownership or that of the other participants. Once the life cycle has concluded and dissolution of the joint venture has taken place, the participants continue their separate existence.

This unique affiliation might also serve as a "trial marriage"—an initial phase in a transition leading to an ultimate business combination. The joint venture relationship allows participants to closely interact while working toward a common objective. Getting to know one another on this basis gives you the unique opportunity to better judge the merits of a more extensive, permanent combination, such as a merger.

"Trial Marriage" Example.   A "trial marriage" works as well for large companies as it does for small. A recent example: Schlumberger Ltd., an oil and gas services firm, and Dow Chemical's oil field services subsidiary, Dowell, were joint venture partners in Dowell-Schlumberger. Dowell retained exclusive rights to their current territory of the United States and Canada while the new joint venture provided oil field services, on a worldwide basis, in other hemispheres. More than satisfied with the Dowell-Schlumberger venture, the two participants agreed that Schlumberger would pay Dow $440 million for a one-half interest in Dowell and then subsequently merge Dowell and Dowell-Schlumberger into a jointly owned concern generating about $1.5 billion in annual revenues.

4. *Unique Effect on Risks and Rewards.*   Perception and evaluation of risks are different for each joint venture partner. And, while the risks of an undertaking may seem small relative to the rewards,

such risks might exceed the risk capacity of one or both the participants acting individually. Therefore, within the framework of a joint venture, the risks are shared, thus lessening an individual participant's exposure.

For the "right" participants in a joint venture, the rewards can be even greater than just the immediate profits. For example: your production "partner," as product originator and production financier, gains immediate distribution and recognition in the market through your existing marketing network and production expertise. Your company not only adds an item to its product line and reaches new customers with both the new product and your existing line, but achieves this with only a minimal promotion outlay since your marketing network is already in place. Therefore, the capital you would have used for new product development and financing production can be used to pursue other opportunities. Your joint venture partner likewise realizes available capital for opportunities other than for the marketing and promotional expenditures necessary to take a new product to market. Your production expertise and existing market position reduce the market-related risks and your partner's product knowledge and expertise reduce the risks of new product development and production.

Organizational and Structuring Considerations

The possible options for joint venture organization and structure are limited only by the imagination of the participants and their advisors. Your objectives and resources and those of the other joint venture participant(s) will influence such decisions as: (1) incorporation or partnership ownership, (2) the capital or equity interests vested to each participant relative to the nature, type, and amount of their investment, (3) centralized versus decentralized organization, (4) degree of direct or indirect operations involvement by participants, and (5) profit and loss allocation.

The joint venture, if properly conceived and executed, presents an opportunity to achieve growth without the necessity of permanently or substantially changing the capital structure of ownership of your business. Central to the success of a joint venture is the proper mix of participants and a clearly defined set of operating goals.

Joint Venture Example.   Illustrating this final point (the proper mix of participants and a clearly defined set of operating goals) is truly one of the boldest, most imaginative joint ventures of recent history, the joint research and development venture MCC (Microelectronics and Computer Technology Corp.). The venture includes more than a dozen U.S. manufacturers such as National Semiconductor, Motorola, Inc., Control Data Corp., and Digital Equipment Corp., and was formed to meet the foreign high-tech challenge, particularly that of Japan. The main projects planned will encompass researching and developing "fifth generation" technology: artificial intelligence, new computer designs, and database models and structures, as well as computer aided design and manufacturing techniques (CAD/CAM) and software and chip packaging. Each participant pays an initial fee of $200,000 and must agree to share the expenses—which will be in the hundreds of millions of dollars over the next eight to ten years— for at least three years. In some cases, participants will also contribute personnel to help fill the need for more than 250 researchers. Participants are then entitled to use the results for three years after a project is finished. After the three-year option period the technology will be open to licensing by any company, MCC member or not. So far reaching is the undertaking and the organization of the joint venture that the Justice Department, although not opposed to MCC's formation, had difficulty evaluating the possible antitrust implications. While there has been no lack of capital, resources, enthusiasm, or common interests, the key to MCC's success depends upon the continuance of its members' cooperation.

FRANCHISING AND LICENSING

When franchising or licensing concepts are discussed, one typically thinks of fast food restaurants, motels, auto rental agencies, employment agencies and so forth. While franchising is obviously well suited to these businesses, they represent only a small sample of the numerous opportunities where such a business entity is appropriate. Becoming most visible in the 1960s, franchising has provided a vehicle for the entrepreneur with limited capital to operate a business with the amenities of a large corporation. However, while joint ventures are generally as flexible as the participants agree to make them, licensing and franchises (two additional forms of joint ventures) are usually more formal.

Operational Requirements

The franchisor provides the intangible assets—product research, technology, formulas, patents, trade name, logo, customer and supplier lists, operational guidelines, marketing and advertising assistance. In some cases, tax, legal, insurance, accounting or managerial support services are also provided to the franchisee. The franchisee supplies the capital. Under the franchise or licensing contract, the franchisee receives the benefits of the aforementioned intangible assets and services in exchange for a commitment to conform to the franchisor's operating standards and procedures and payment of a periodic franchise fee.

Growth Opportunities

For smaller companies, franchising and licensing are suitable in situations where you as an individual or company develop a business concept (product or service) and desire growth, but have limited capital and/or resources with which to manage the growth. In some cases, you may not desire to be the executor of operations growth but rather seek only growth of the concept itself. However, at the same time, you will require some degree of control over the growth process and the resulting operations. The franchising process accommodates these objectives and provides for an immediate source of cash flow for you, the franchisor, thus permitting capital investment in company-owned operations or other growth opportunities.

As your business matures, the factors which compelled you to utilize franchising to facilitate growth generally abate. For example, the franchisor who in early years suffered from cash shortages might find itself seeking investments to use capital surpluses in later years. Coca Cola, probably one of the most renowned franchisors, will from time to time address its need to make sound strategic investments by acquiring the businesses it knows best, occasionally "buying-in" existing Coca Cola bottling franchises. In short, as with any business, the franchisor must have a strategy that anticipates the future and is flexible enough to meet changing needs.

Collaborative Ventures

Licensing combinations can also include ventures between you and a much larger company. In these instances, the larger company may license you to manufacture and/or distribute a product for them. If it is your product or product idea, you may license or sell the technology to the larger company, sometimes in return for the manufacturing and/or distribution rights or you may license them to manufacture and/or distribute your product. Such collaborative ventures can work in either direction, to the benefit of both participants, with the arrangements often including an infusion of equity investment in your company. However, these arrangements must be *very* carefully structured—as to the duration of the venture, the distribution of profits and losses, the degree of management involvement, and so forth—in order to protect the independence and viability of your company. In addition, you and your venture "partner" *must* have the ability to act and agree to act immediately on any such collaborative arrangement if the opportunity and the technology are not to be lost and the venture is to succeed.

9

RESEARCH AND DEVELOPMENT

As an entrepreneur yourself, you know first hand that nothing is more exciting, and nothing more potentially profitable, than an idea that can be developed into a major new product. Exciting is not the only word for it. It can also be costly and enormously risky.

Raising the money for research and development (R&D) often seems to require as much imagination as inventing the product. Promising as the new-product idea is to your expert eye, everybody knows there are unanswered questions that represent risks for investors—will the product be as good as you expect, will it fill a genuine market need, will it out perform the competition, will the costs of production and distribution allow you a fair profit, does your staff have the expertise to market this kind of product?

In this atmosphere (of exciting but unproven prospects) lie the risks that abound in the world of research and development.

As the manager of your business, with a new-product idea full of promise you would probably ask yourself these questions:

1. How can I raise the necessary R&D capital and still keep control of my product?

2. How can I protect the rest of my company's operations from the risks inherent in the costly process of researching and

developing this new product that may, or may not, prove successful?

3. Should my company finance and carry out the R&D ourselves? Or should I give up some of the control and rewards, and reduce our risks, by farming it out to an outside organization?

American business has been remarkably imaginative in creating R&D funding arrangements to fit virtually every set of circumstances, probably including yours. The business, accounting, legal, and tax aspects are described in this chapter, to help you find answers to the R&D questions that stand between your exciting idea and its success.

BUSINESS CONSIDERATIONS

R&D arrangements have been used to develop a wide variety of new products from the mundane to the exotic, from such high technology fields as genetic engineering, medicine, and computers to the long-established aircraft and small firearms industries. And, as might be expected, the terms of R&D arrangements vary as widely as the products, reflecting the trade-offs between the parties involved.

The types of R&D arrangements also vary widely. Some involve an established corporation or a new corporation that needs funds for one or more R&D projects, and investors who are willing to invest in the project(s). These R&D arrangements are usually formed as *limited partnerships** so that the investors can take tax deductions for substantially all of their investment in the partnership. As a result, they are able to reduce their financial risk since their net cash investment is reduced.

Other R&D arrangements may involve two corporations. In these arrangements, one corporation might perform the R&D under contract for the other, or the two corporations might form a joint venture to conduct their R&D on one or more projects with the intention of manufacturing and marketing the products they develop.

---

* Since R&D arrangements are so often structured as limited partnerships, we will frequently refer to "the partnership," even though other legal forms may be used.

While no two limited partnership arrangements are likely to be identical in all respects, there are some typical features that most possess and some typical steps taken in establishing most R&D arrangements.

Initial Steps

Generally, before a corporation establishes an R&D arrangement, it needs to complete certain basic steps:

- Your company should already possess the basic technology needed for development of the product that you expect will be successful in the marketplace. R&D arrangements generally are for the *development* of a product, not for basic research, because many investors believe that arrangements to finance basic research are too risky. R&D arrangements, to be attractive to investors, should "accentuate the 'D' and avoid the 'R.'"
- Your company should develop a strategic plan describing in detail the technical feasibility of the product to be developed, the R&D to be done, the anticipated demand and profitability of the product, the competition that the product will likely encounter, the time and costs of completing the R&D work, and the possible tax effects and cash flows to investors.

Raising Funds

Some companies, especially smaller companies, try to raise funds by themselves—generally from their owner-managers, friends, and relatives. These R&D arrangements usually have only a few investors and are relatively easy to establish: legal and tax advice is required, and advice from an investment banker on the financial terms of the R&D arrangement may be desirable.

Other companies try to interest one or more investment bankers in raising R&D funds for highly promising projects. Some of Wall Street's largest firms have assisted in the formation of R&D arrangements, including research and development limited partnership pooled funds, some of which have raised tens of millions of dollars. R&D funds under this method can be raised through either a public offering or a private placement. A public offering is registered with the SEC and one or more state securities commissions, while a private placement need not be registered with the SEC. Public offerings, which have been relatively infrequent, require the preparation of a prospectus, while private placements, which are far more common, are usually offered through a placement memorandum. The legal considerations of financing R&D arrangements through a public or private offering are discussed in the "Legal Aspects" section of this chapter.

Another source of R&D funds, although generally limited in amount, are governmental agencies. The Small Business Innovation Development Act of 1982 created the Small Business Innovation Research program (SBIR) to assist small businesses in the R&D arena through a federal grant program administered by the Small Business Administration. In addition, state and local governmental agencies are often interested in providing financial assistance. See Chapter 7, "Government Financing."

THE LIMITED PARTNERSHIP

R&D arrangements are usually limited partnerships because they offer numerous tax and business advantages over other forms of organization. The individual investors are the limited partners while your corporation, a subsidiary, or another affiliate is frequently the general partner. (However, in an increasing number of arrangements, the general partner is an independent entity, not related to your corporation. An advantage of this is that an independent general partner can often help the partnership oversee the development and/ or any contractor's activities. A disadvantage is that this outside partner can be an inhibiting factor on your corporation's activities.)

Exhibit 9-1 displays a typical R&D limited partnership structure, the elements and variations of which are explained in the following discussions.

Limited partners typically consist of a group of individual investors who are seeking an attractive investment together with tax benefits. In some cases, especially for small start-up companies, the limited partners may be affiliates of your company. As discussed in the "Accounting Treatment" section of this chapter, if affiliates own a significant portion of the limited partnership, your company may well have to account for the R&D arrangement as a borrowing. In some very large

EXHIBIT 9-1.   A ROAD MAP FOR A TYPICAL R&D LIMITED PARTNERSHIP STRUCTURE

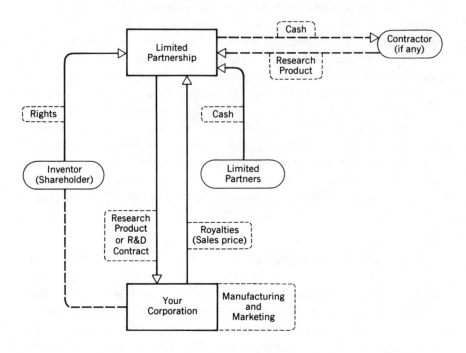

recent R&D arrangements there have been more than 100 limited partners.

Limited partners usually require a potentially significant after-tax annual rate of return (for example, 40 to 50 percent) from the project, commensurate with the high risks inherent in this type of investment.

Some R&D partnerships have been structured as "leveraged" partnerships to help the limited partners achieve the necessary rates of return by reducing their initial after-tax cash investments. In one form of leveraged partnership, part of a limited partners' initial investment consists of a recourse note, which, in certain circumstances, may permit the limited partners to take tax deductions in excess of their initial cash investment (see the "Tax Aspects" section of this chapter). The limited partners pay the note when your corporation needs the funds, or, if it does not need them, the note is paid by offsetting it against royalty payments due to the limited partners.

A leveraged R&D partnership may also be used when a corporation that is not affiliated with the inventor-corporation wants to hire the inventor-corporation to perform an R&D project for it. In such cases, the unaffiliated corporation lends funds to the partnership. These funds, along with those invested by the limited partners, are then used by your inventor-corporation for the R&D project. The limited partners also issue recourse notes to the *unaffiliated* corporation in an amount equal to the unaffiliated corporation's loan to the partnership. All the losses of the partnership are thereby allocated to the limited partners. If the R&D project fails, the limited partners pay off their notes to the *unaffiliated* corporation. If the project is successful, the notes are paid by offsetting them against some of the royalty payments that would otherwise be due the limited partners.

The Basic Technology

Your corporation normally makes available, as its investment in the R&D partnership, the basic technology for the product or process to be developed. You may either sell the technology or, more likely, license the rights to it to the partnership. In any event, you will want to retain access to the basic technology so that you will not have to buy the technology back in order to use it in products other than the ones being developed through the partnership.

One way for your corporation to retain access to the basic technology is to give the partnership a nonexclusive royalty-free license limited to the use of the technology in the R&D project. Another way for your corporation to retain access is to enter into a cross-licensing agreement with the partnership whereby you make the technology available to the partnership, royalty-free, for use in the R&D project in return for a royalty-free license from the partnership enabling you to use the technology in other applications. A third way for your corporation to retain access is to license the technology to the partnership for use in developing a specific product. Under this method, your corporation would retain all the other rights in the technology.

The R&D Contract

Your corporation (rather than a third party) ordinarily performs the R&D work for the partnership under a contract between you both.

One advantage of this is that the development work is then usually being performed by the people who developed the basic technology and who are therefore most familiar with the project. Another advantage is that it enables your corporation to manage and control the project. Frequently, the partnership's payments to your corporation for performing the development work are limited to reimbursement for the costs you have incurred. In other cases, the partnership may compensate your corporation on either a fixed-fee basis or a cost-plus basis.

An R&D partnership usually works best if its R&D project is clearly separated from your corporation's other R&D projects and if the R&D contract clearly defines exactly what is to be delivered at the conclusion of the contract work, if it is successful. This helps minimize the likelihood of disputes between the partnership and your corporation.

Development work is performed on a best efforts basis (i.e., the contract does not guarantee the project's success). Frequently, an R&D arrangement does not specify the course of action to be taken if the partnership's funds prove to be insufficient to complete the project. In some cases, the limited partners may be obligated, within limits, to invest additional funds to complete the project. In other cases, your corporation may or may not be obligated to complete the project. If you are not obligated, but wish to continue the project, you will have to raise the necessary funds or use funds on hand. Also, many R&D arrangements have been silent about the manner in which any royalties will be divided if additional funds have to be raised to complete the R&D project. Since this silence may turn out to be undesirable, potential investors may wish to question how royalties will be divided if additional funds have to be raised. One method of handling this matter is to provide that subsequent royalty payments will be adjusted pro rata to reflect the additional investments.

After the R&D Project Is Completed

The R&D partnership ordinarily has the rights to the basic technology (under the nonexclusive royalty-free license agreement or the cross-license agreement) and to the results of the R&D project when it is completed (see "Legal Aspects" section). If the project is not successful, the partnership will usually disband because it is not likely to be able to sell, or otherwise benefit from, the R&D work. However, the partnership's having the right to sell the results or to license them to someone else, if your corporation does not want to buy or license them, is desirable from the partnership's standpoint in case the partnership's opinion of their value differs from your corporation's opinion. Since you may not want the basic technology or the products developed to be sold to a competitor, you may retain the right of first refusal to purchase them if the partnership finds someone else willing to buy them.

Methods of Compensating Limited Partners.   If the R&D project is successful, the partnership may be compensated in one or more ways, depending upon the terms of the contract between it and your corporation. Some of the methods are:

- Your corporation may have an option to purchase, for a specified amount of cash or stock, the exclusive rights to the products developed.
- Your corporation and the partnership may enter into a joint venture to manufacture and market the products developed.
- Your corporation may have the right to purchase the exclusive rights to the basic technology and to the products developed after it has begun to pay royalties to the partnership, and it may have the right to offset some or all of the royalties against the purchase price.
- Your corporation may have an option to be the exclusive manufacturer/marketer of the new products. If you exercise the option, you would be obligated to pay royalties to the partnership. (In some R&D arrangements, the period during which your corporation has the exclusive rights to manufacture and market the new products may be limited if specified minimum royalty payments are not generated.) The royalty agreement may provide that:

  Royalties will be based on sales.

  Royalties will be based on any profits from sales of the new products.

  Royalties will be based on a certain percentage of sales until the limited partners have received a specified return on their investment, after which the percentage will decrease.

  Royalty payments are subject to a ceiling.

  Royalties are payable only if your corporation has a positive cash flow from manufacturing and selling the new products.

Your corporation will guarantee the limited partnership a minimum
amount of royalties.

Structuring Compensation Agreements.   The method of compensating the limited partners may have a significant effect on investors'
potential risks and rewards, and thus on the desirability of investing
in the R&D partnership. (It may also have a significant effect on the
costs of the R&D arrangement to your corporation.) For example,
investors' potential risks may be less if their royalties are to be based
on sales of the new products (rather than on the profits from the sales)
since their royalties would begin when sales begin rather than when
(and if) sales of the products become profitable. For the same reason,
investors may prefer royalties based on sales instead of a share of the
profits of a joint venture that manufactures and sells the new products.

As a result of this risk difference, R&D partnerships may have to
offer larger potential rewards to attract investors when investors' rewards
are to be based on a share of the profits than when their income is
to be based on percentage of the sales. In the former case, the long-
run costs of the R&D arrangement to your corporation will likely be
greater when the new products are highly successful, although the
costs will likely be less when the new products are not particularly
successful.

The method of compensating the limited partners may also determine
whether their compensation is taxable at ordinary income rates or at
capital gains rates. For example, royalty payments will likely be taxed
at ordinary income rates while any gain from selling the exclusive
rights to the products developed is likely to be taxed, in whole or in
part, at capital gains rates. The tax attributes of the limited partners'
compensation are discussed in more detail in the "Tax Aspects" section.

In some cases, an R&D arrangement may contain a provision that
the limited partners' compensation will be based not only on the
success of the products being developed under the R&D arrangement,
but also on the success of any "competing" products that may be
developed by your corporation at about the same time. An R&D
arrangement may contain such a compensation provision when your
corporation desires to continue performing R&D on other products
that may serve purposes similar to those served by the products being
developed under the partnership arrangement. Such a compensation
provision protects the limited partners in case your "competing" prod-

ucts displace the products developed under the R&D arrangement in the marketplace. If such displacement were to occur and the limited partners were not compensated, they would find that the company whose R&D they were helping to fund was competing with them. The possibility of such an occurrence might make an R&D arrangement too risky to attract investors.

In any case, all partnership compensation provisions should contain objective measures of:

1. Whether the products developed under the R&D arrangement are "successful,"

2. the purposes to be served by the products to be developed under the R&D arrangement and any competing products, and

3. the methods of determining the compensation to the limited partners.

Without these objective measures, your corporation likely could not account for the R&D arrangement as a contract for the performance of R&D (see the "Accounting Treatment" section). Contract accounting cannot be used if the limited partners do not bear the risks of loss if the products developed under the R&D arrangement are unsuccessful. They would not bear the risks if they were *assured* of payments on "competing" products.

In summary, R&D arrangements vary significantly from one arrangement to another—the structures of the arrangements are as diverse as the products being developed. Exhibit 9-2 shows the details of just one possible (and at this time popular) limited partnership R&D arrangement.

Trade-Offs

Many of the specific features of a particular R&D arrangement result from trade-offs between the potential risks and the rewards to both the investors and your corporation. For example, the greater the likelihood that a marketable product will be developed, the lower the potential returns need to be, and thus the lower the future costs of the successful R&D project would be to your corporation. Similarly,

EXHIBIT 9-2. AN EXAMPLE OF THE STRUCTURE OF A LIMITED PARTNERSHIP R&D ARRANGEMENT

The general partner (The corporation)
A wholly-owned subsidiary of a corporation.

The limited partners
Eleven investors investing a minimum of $100,000 each.

Type of offering
A private placement.

Use of proceeds (net of placement fees and expenses)
To develop the technology. A small percentage is reserved for the working capital needs of the partnership.

Allocation of profits and losses
Ninety-nine percent to the limited partners and one percent to the general partner unless the general partner makes additional capital contributions (see "The corporation's commitments" below), in which case there will be a corresponding increase in the general partner's percent.

The contractual arrangements
A cross-license agreement with the corporation under which the corporation will make available its know-how for the development of the technology in return for a royalty-free license of the technology for the corporation's use in other applications.

An R&D agreement with the corporation under which the corporation will perform the development work in return for reimbursement of its direct costs plus a specified percentage for overhead costs.

An agreement that grants to the corporation the option to enter into a joint venture with the partnership to manufacture and market the products developed in the project. (This option is exercisable for 30 days after the technology has been developed.) If the corporation enters into the joint venture, it will have:

- A right of first refusal to purchase the technology developed in the event the partnership decides to sell it. (The partnership cannot sell the technology until the joint venture has been in operation for at least 14 months and has manufactured and sold a specified number of units of the new product.)
- An option to purchase the technology developed. (This option is not exercisable until the joint venture has been in operation for at least two years and has manufactured and sold the number of units specified above.)

The corporation's commitments
To provide the partnership with additional capital to make up the shortfall if between 80 and 100 percent of the planned amount of funds is raised from limited partners. If less than 80 percent of the planned amount is raised, the corporation may, at its option, make up the difference.

To provide its technology base to the partnership.

To utilize personnel on the project who are already familiar with the basic technology and to hire additional professionals in the next two years to facilitate manufacturing and marketing the products developed as an outgrowth of the project.

To provide project personnel with incentive programs dependent on the success of the project.

The partners' expectations

To realize the benefits of deductible tax losses of approximately 90 percent of their initial investment during the development phase.

To realize ordinary income (from a joint venture) as a result of manufacturing and selling the products developed and, if certain options are exercised, to realize income from the sale of the technology to the corporation which may be taxed as long-term capital gains.

To realize a potential annual after-tax cash rate of return of up to 45 percent.

if the R&D arrangement can be structured so as to provide tax benefits (i.e., if investors can claim most of their initial investment as an ordinary loss and can treat some or all of their future income as capital gains) the gross returns to the investors can be less than if the arrangement were not a tax advantaged investment, and still provide them with the same after-tax rate of return on their investment.

Some investors try to reduce the risk of total failure by investing in an R&D arrangement that involves more than one R&D project. In return, they are willing to accept lower potential rewards. In addition, a proposed R&D arrangement involving a corporation with a history of R&D successes is likely to successfully attract investors while offering lower potential rewards than an equivalent arrangement involving an unproven corporation.

One of your investment banker's key functions is to help negotiate the specific features of the R&D arrangement so as to attract sufficient investors.

ADVANTAGES OF R&D ARRANGEMENTS

The advantages to corporations and investors in R&D arrangements, especially those that are limited partnerships, are many. A discussion of some of the major advantages follows.

1. *Control.* A major advantage to the management of your corporation is that it can retain significant influence over the R&D project as well as retain control over the corporation's other operations. If your corporation had to issue stock in order to finance the R&D work, your control might be diluted if the new owners purchase a sizable block of shares and decide they want to exercise a voice in the management of the corporation. The limited partners in an R&D arrangement do not have the right to exercise such a voice.

2. *Flexibility.* The limited partnership R&D arrangement can provide greater flexibility to your corporation than additional equity financing can. The limited partnership frequently can be terminated if the project is unsuccessful, if you exercise a buyout option, if a specified maximum payout has been reached, or if a specified period of time has elapsed. A corporation often has more difficulty in buying out a group of shareholders.

In addition, more flexibility may be available in establishing the terms of payment to the limited partnership. For example, the arrangement can be structured to establish an option price to buy out the results of the R&D project, to establish a maximum royalty payout, or to reduce the royalty percentage after the investors have received their initial investment back (or some multiple thereof).

Ordinarily, such flexibility cannot be achieved with equity financing. For instance, the same dividend rate must be paid on all shares of equity of the same class, and all the shareholders share in the profits of all your corporation's projects; new shareholders are not limited to sharing only in the proceeds from the particular R&D projects that their capital contributions financed. Furthermore, all shareholders—old and new—share in the enhanced value of the business resulting from a highly successful R&D project or from other causes, whereas the limited partners in the R&D arrangement do not share in the enhanced value of the business unless your corporation uses its stock to buy out the new technology.

3. *Tax Benefits.* The limited partnership, if it is properly structured, can be an effective tax advantaged investment for the limited partners (as described in more detail in the "Tax Aspects" section).

Although certain changes made by the Tax Reform Act of 1984 affect the timing of deductions, the limited partners can deduct most of their initial investment, and they may be able to treat some or all of their income in later years as capital gains. Deducting most of their initial investment reduces the limited partners' financial risks since their net cash investment is less, and it may enable them to take more risks than they could if they were only equity investors. Corporate shareholders ordinarily cannot deduct their investments when they make them, and their dividends are taxed as ordinary income.

These tax benefits of a limited partnership, if they can be realized, enable limited partners to earn a considerably higher rate of return than shareholders who make the same initial investment and receive the same paybacks but in the form of dividends from the corporation. As a consequence, investors who are looking for a specified rate of return may be satisfied with lower cash payments if they are limited partners in an R&D arrangement than if they are shareholders in a corporation. If your corporation is in a "tax loss" position, or if it is a start-up corporation without any taxable income, the R&D arrangement, in effect, enables you to transfer your R&D tax deductions to the limited partners. The transfer of tax benefits facilitates the financing of the R&D, as investors view their net investment as being 50 percent of their cash investment.

4.   Risk of Loss.   The corporation that employs an R&D arrangement may avoid the risk of a significant loss if the R&D project fails. The limited partners must assume the risk of loss if they are to realize the aforementioned tax benefits and if your corporation is to account for the arrangement as an R&D contract rather than as a borrowing.

This reduced risk of loss to your corporation may enable you to expand more rapidly than you otherwise could or to undertake major R&D projects without undue risk to the remainder of your business.

5.   Availability of Funds.   By employing an R&D arrangement, including R&D joint ventures with other companies, a corporation may have access to funds for R&D activities that otherwise would not be available. Thus, your corporation may be able to undertake more than one project at a time, or to increase the scope of a major project, or to undertake a major R&D project that it would not have been able to undertake. In some cases, the additional funds from an R&D arrangement have enabled a corporation to stay in business, to grow rapidly in its start-up years, or to become a viable competitor in its industry.

6. _Lower Initial Cost._ Your corporation's costs of funds from R&D arrangements may be less than the costs of borrowing during the R&D period, which often lasts from two to five years. The costs will also be less if the R&D project is a failure—unless your corporation is required to buy out the limited partners' interests—as there is no debt to repay and no interest payments to make. Your costs of funds from R&D arrangements may also be less than the "costs" of equity capital during the R&D period, and there is no dilution of equity or additional shareholders looking for dividends.

7. _Incentives for Key Employees._ A corporation may use an R&D arrangement to enhance its ability to compensate and retain certain key employees, such as its scientists and engineers, by permitting them to invest in the arrangement that is funding the R&D projects on which they are working. This should provide them with additional incentives to help assure the success of the projects and lessen the likelihood that they will leave the company to exploit their ideas elsewhere. If, however, the key employees' investment in the arrangement is significant, the corporation may be unable to account for the arrangement as a contract for the performance of R&D (see the "Accounting Treatment" section of this chapter).

8. _Balance Sheet Treatment._ If the R&D partnership bears the risk of loss in the event that the R&D project is unsuccessful, your corporation does not record the payments made by the R&D partnership under the R&D contract as a liability on its balance sheet or record R&D expense when the R&D work is performed. Thus, your corporation's debt-to-equity ratio will be lower than it would be if your corporation were to bear the risk of loss in the event that the project is unsuccessful. Further, your corporation's earnings will not be reduced when the R&D work is being performed, although they will be reduced in subsequent years if the R&D project is successful. (The accounting for R&D arrangements is discussed in detail in the "Accounting Treatment" section of this chapter).

DISADVANTAGES OF R&D ARRANGEMENTS

R&D arrangements are not without their disadvantages, especially to the limited partners. Some of the major disadvantages include the following.

1. *Risk of Loss.*   The most important disadvantage to investors is that R&D arrangements are generally high-risk investments—their success is by no means assured. The R&D project may not be a technological success or, even if it is, the product may not be saleable. For example, it may not meet the needs of the marketplace, or competitors may develop a better, cheaper product sooner. As a result, the anticipated royalty payments may not materialize for the limited partners, or your corporation may not exercise its buyout option.

The first page of a recent offering memorandum highlighted this disadvantage when it proclaimed in bold-faced type:

NO ONE SHOULD INVEST IN THE UNITS WHO IS NOT PREPARED TO LOSE HIS ENTIRE INVESTMENT.

2. *Higher Eventual Costs.*   The eventual costs to corporations of highly successful products that were originally developed through R&D arrangements may be higher than if the corporations had tapped

other sources of funds at the outset. This results because the limited partners in R&D arrangements will require ample potential and continuing rewards (in the form of royalties from your corporation) if they are to assume the significant initial risks that these arrangements generally entail.

3. *Time and Costs of Forming an R&D Arrangement.* R&D arrangements, especially those involving a number of independent investors, are often expensive and time-consuming for a corporation to establish. Legal and other fees may be significant; the public offering document or private placement memorandum requires substantial time to prepare, and additional time is required to locate the investors. During all this time, your corporation's competitors may be able to gain a significant head start in the race to the marketplace.

4. *Other Disadvantages for Limited Partners.* The limited partners in an R&D limited partnership are not entitled to a voice in the management of your corporation, and they do not share in the profits of all your corporation's projects or in the enhanced value of its business (stock) that may result from the R&D project or from other activities. Furthermore, with improperly structured arrangements, there is always the possibility that the IRS might attempt to disallow their tax benefits.

ADDITIONAL TYPES OF R&D ARRANGEMENTS

R&D arrangements may take other forms in order to better meet the needs and objectives of the parties. One form involves R&D limited partnerships that are structured differently from those we have been describing: these are "equity" limited partnerships and may be particularly suitable for start-up corporations that desire to maximize the amount of funds they can raise by obtaining funds from different groups of investors whose investment objectives differ significantly. Other types of R&D arrangements involve two or more corporations joining together to form very large "corporate" or "pooled" arrangements. These arrangements often involve complex accounting and tax issues.

Corporate R&D Arrangements

R&D arrangements involving two or more corporations can be structured quite differently depending upon whether one or both parties contribute funds, and upon whether one or both parties contribute technology and research capabilities. Some of the alternative structures for corporate R&D arrangements when *only one* of the parties contributes funds are:

- Both parties' returns are dependent solely upon the success of the venture as neither corporation makes an investment in the other.
- The corporation that contributes the funds receives debt or preferred stock in the corporate joint venture. Interest on the debt may be fixed or contingent; dividends on the preferred stock would almost always be noncumulative. The debt or preferred stock may be convertible into common stock of the joint venture corporation or of the corporation that contributes the technology and research capabilities. The conversion ratio may be dependent upon the success of the R&D projects when the party that contributes funds also contributes some of the technology and research capabilities—the greater the success, the more shares that are received on the conversion. There may also be a minimum conversion ratio.
- The party that contributes the technology may have to make certain payments to the other party if the R&D project fails.

Some of the alternative structures for corporate R&D arrangements when *both* parties contribute funds are:

- Both parties' returns are dependent solely upon the success of the venture as neither corporation makes an investment in the other.
- One of the companies also makes a significant investment (debt or equity) in the other.

• One of the corporations sells its technology to the joint venture in return for funds provided to the venture by the other corporation, and then the two corporations jointly perform and fund the additional R&D activities.

Equity Limited Partnership R&D Arrangements

A start-up corporation with some promising ideas and/or technology is likely to need funds both for R&D and for working capital, fixed assets, manufacturing start-up, market research, advertising, and so forth. An R&D arrangement that has to spend significant amounts of funds for non-R&D purposes may *not* be particularly attractive to potential investors interested in the limited partnership R&D tax benefits we have been describing. The reason (as explained in the "Tax Aspects" section) is that the limited partners may only be entitled to a tax deduction in the year they make their initial investment for that portion of their investment that is to be spent on R&D. In addition, the structures of the R&D limited partnerships that we have previously discussed may not be attractive to venture capitalists who might be willing to invest in a new corporation. They may not be particularly interested in the "tax-advantage" aspects of the partnership; rather, they may desire a significant, long-term "piece of the action" if the new business is successful. Furthermore, the venture capitalists may not be willing to invest all the capital a start-up company needs.

Operating Procedures.   In situations like that described in the preceding paragraph, an "R&D equity partnership" may be attractive. This type of partnership arrangement operates as follows (there can be many variations to fit particular circumstances).

• A start-up corporation is formed. Your new corporation issues convertible preferred stock to the venture capital investors and common stock to the founders/key employees.
• An R&D limited partnership is formed. Your new corporation transfers cash and the rights to use its basic technology to the partnership and thus your new corporation becomes the general partner. Your new corporation/general partner usually has more than a 50 percent interest in the capital and profits of the limited partnership, unlike

those limited partnerships described previously where its percentage interest would normally be very small. The limited partners—individuals interested in investing cash in an R&D arrangement—contribute the remaining capital and receive the remaining profit interest.

- The partnership agreement specifies that virtually all the partnership's initial losses (resulting from the initial R&D efforts) will be allocated to the limited partners (so they can deduct them as ordinary losses for tax purposes) until the losses are approximately equal to the limited partners' capital contributions and the bases of their investments in the limited partnership have been reduced to nominal amounts. Thereafter, virtually all the losses will be allocated to the general partner (your new corporation).

- The limited partnership is incorporated in a tax-free transaction if the R&D projects are successful but before the partnership becomes profitable. The limited partners receive a series of convertible preferred stock (with a very low basis) in this new company. Their interest in this newly incorporated company equals their former interest in the profits of the limited partnership. As the general partner, you receive another series of preferred stock in the newly incorporated company (which is distributed to your original start-up corporation's venture capitalists) and some common stock (which is distributed to your original start-up corporation's common stockholders, i.e., founders/key employees).

Investor and Corporate Advantages. This type of R&D arrangement offers certain advantages to investors and to start-up corporations over the types of R&D arrangements described previously and over a traditional new corporation. The advantages include the following.

- More funds may be obtained because two different groups of investors with different investment objectives can be tapped (venture capitalists and individuals looking for tax-advantaged investments).
- The cost of funds is reduced because of the initial tax write-offs available to the limited partners.
- The founders/key employees may suffer less dilution of their holdings because of the tax benefits available to the limited partners.

- The venture capitalists' financing is supplemented by the limited partners' investment thereby encouraging venture capital involvement.
- The venture capitalists may obtain a greater equity interest in the corporation per dollar of investment.
- The venture capitalists can be helpful to the founders/key employees in managing your company since the latter may lack managerial expertise and experience.
- Your newly incorporated company may not have to pay royalties on the new products if the R&D project is successful since all the parties to the R&D arrangement will be shareholders.
- The limited partners may have fewer difficulties in obtaining capital gain tax treatment since their income is likely to arise from selling their low-basis shares in the newly incorporated company rather than from royalties or from selling their rights to the results of the limited partnership's R&D activities.

The R&D equity partnership has some significant disadvantages in that (1) It involves numerous legal complexities, (2) management control issues can be difficult to resolve, (3) the limited partners can block the tax-free incorporation, and (4) the IRS is likely to scrutinize these R&D arrangements quite closely.

Pooled R&D Arrangements

Another variation of the R&D limited partnership involves two or more companies seeking funds for their own R&D projects through a single limited partnership. This multicompany pool offers investors the opportunity to invest in the development of a diversified group of products and may thus enable them to reduce the risk of total failure, even more so than if they had invested in a single-company R&D arrangement involving more than one R&D project.

These pooled arrangements are complex and usually involve unrelated companies. As a result, an investment banker ordinarily is required to bring the parties together and to market the partnership interests. This feature of pooled R&D arrangements often provides another advantage to investors: the presence of sophisticated management to represent them in evaluating and monitoring the R&D activities.

ACCOUNTING TREATMENT

Some corporations use R&D limited partnerships because they do not have other means of financing their R&D. But most corporations that choose to use an R&D limited partnership are able to finance at least some of their R&D from internal cash flows, borrowings, and equity offerings. Further, they may transfer some R&D projects to partnerships like those described in the preceding section to preserve other means of financing for additional R&D projects, to avoid risking too much of the company's capital on a single project, or because they perceive that the funds from a partnership have a lower initial cost.

The dollar volume of R&D arrangements has steadily increased in the 1980s as has the involvement of public companies as inventor-corporations. Some of the arrangements early in this period appeared to be loans, or infusions of additional equity, particularly when investors' returns were guaranteed or when insiders were involved in the arrangements as limited partners. But other deals appeared to represent the transfer of the risk of loss to the limited partnership in return for the potential of significant rewards if the projects were commercially successful.

Accordingly, some transactions were accounted for as financings; that is, the cash received by the corporation was recorded as a loan or as additional equity, and the R&D costs were expensed by the corporation as incurred. Other transactions were treated as sales of R&D under contract.

Given a choice, your corporation is likely to prefer the latter accounting method for the following reasons.

- It keeps the R&D expense out of current net income (especially for a young company, this could mean the difference between a loss and a profit) and
- It keeps the financing off the balance sheet (thereby presenting a better debt-to-equity ratio).

Net income and debt-to-equity ratios are traditionally important indicators in lenders' and investors' analyses of a company's financial health. Thus, if two corporations account for similar transactions differently, the accounting may make a difference in the companies' abilities to borrow or obtain equity financing, no matter how comprehensively the transactions are disclosed. Further, if two companies account for very different transactions as if they were the same, one of the companies may be gaining an advantage in the capital and debt markets.

Accounting Alternatives

The basis for determining the accounting treatment for R&D arrangements generally depends on which of the parties has an investment at risk if the project should fail. Structuring R&D arrangements when the investors stand the risk of loss and yet giving the investors satisfactory returns for that risk is sometimes difficult.

Because of perceived abuses between form and substance—reality and accounting treatment—during mid-1981, the SEC staff took the position that virtually every R&D arrangement represented a borrowing. Their key concern was the widespread practice of the corporate general partner bailing out the investors even when agreements did not require it.

In late October 1982, the Financial Accounting Standards Board (the accounting rule-making authority in the United States) issued an authoritative pronouncement, Financial Accounting Standard No. 68, "Research and Development Arrangements" (FAS 68). FAS 68 reiterated the historic premise related to "risk of loss" with much elaboration on how to determine the real substance of an arrangement. Under FAS 68 there are two key questions: (1) Are the limited partners looking to the success of the R&D for their investment returns? and (2) To what extent is the corporate general partner obligated to repay other parties?

Determining the answers to these two questions is frequently not easy—FAS 68 elaborates on the many facets to be studied in making the determination. In some cases, both accounting alternatives may be applied to the transaction (i.e., part of the arrangement is accounted for as a loan and part as a contract for performance of R&D).

While a detailed explanation of the many and varied elements of R&D arrangements that must be considered in determining the proper accounting treatment is beyond the scope of this chapter, there are two matters that deserve your attention. First, whenever the limited partner investors in the R&D arrangement include parties related to your corporation, the likelihood of the arrangement being accounted for as a loan is increased substantially. There are exceptions, but such exceptions must be carefully structured and usually prohibit material investment by any related parties.

Second, FAS 68 does prescribe the following disclosure requirements for R&D arrangements accounted for as R&D contracts.

• The terms of significant agreements under the arrangements (including royalty arrangements, purchase provisions, license agreements, and commitments to provide additional funding) as of the date of each balance sheet presented.

• The amount of compensation earned and costs incurred under such contracts for each period for which an income statement is presented.

Elsewhere in your reports to shareholders, you may wish to present detailed analyses of all your major R&D projects by describing them and setting forth their progress and outlook. Such analyses should delineate between R&D financed by your corporation and R&D performed under contract for others.

FAS 68 only covers disclosures in your corporation's general purpose financial statements. However, your corporation or the limited partnership will also need to report to the limited partners. We believe that, in addition to receiving accounting and tax information, the partners will expect to receive a detailed analysis of the R&D project. This could be accomplished by periodically updating the "proposed activities" section of the original offering document and disseminating it to the limited partners.

LEGAL ASPECTS

Structuring, financing, and implementing R&D arrangements involve a careful analysis of the myriad legal ramifications in addition to business, tax, and accounting considerations. Although a detailed analysis of the legal ramifications associated with R&D arrangements is beyond the scope of this chapter, the following discussion highlights some of the basic considerations.

Federal Securities Laws

Limited partnership interests, if offered for sale, are considered to be securities under the Securities Act of 1933 (Act) and, unless eligible for a statutory exemption, must be registered with the SEC. For a more comprehensive discussion of public and exempt securities offerings see Chapter 2, "The Going Public Decision" and Chapter 3, "Private Placements," respectively.

Blue Sky Laws

In order to protect investors, all fifty states have enacted some type of securities legislation commonly referred to as "Blue Sky Laws." Generally, securities which fall under the federal securities laws will also be subject to the Blue Sky Laws.

There are some exemptions from registration under the Blue Sky Laws. The categories of exempt transactions are similar to those provided under federal law, but keep in mind these rules vary from state to state. Most state Blue Sky Laws provide an exemption for an offering where the total number of offerees is less than a specified number. Additionally, most states provide an exemption for isolated transactions which are dependent upon: (1) the type of offer, (2) the number of units offered, (3) the manner of the offering, (4) the relationship of the seller to the offerees. Unless the offering of the securities fits within a Blue Sky Law exemption, state registration of securities will be required.

Prospectus and Private Placement Memorandum

Whether the offering is public or private, the antifraud provisions of the federal securities laws are applicable. Therefore, in order to avoid liability, full-disclosure should be achieved through the proper documents.

A well-prepared and complete prospectus or placement memorandum may also indicate to potential investors that considerable care and expertise were exercised in the formulation of the R&D arrangement. The prospectus or placement memorandum should answer the types of questions potential investors are likely to have, such as the following:

- What is the potential market for the products to be developed?
- How quickly can the new products be brought to market (e.g., is government approval required)? Are the products patentable? How vulnerable are they to rapid obsolescence?
- Is your corporation capable of manufacturing the new products in commercial quantities? Does it have the necessary facilities?
- What technological advances must be made to develop the products?
- Has an independent feasibility study been performed?
- How successful has the researcher been with similar products in the past?
- How successful have the investment bankers' prior R&D arrangements been?
- Will the corporation's fees for performing the R&D include an element of profit?
- What happens if the money runs out before the project is finished?
- What are the major risks involved?
- Is the projected rate of return reasonable in relation to the risks involved?
- What will my rate of return be if the R&D project takes twice as long to complete as planned?
- What will my rate of return be if sales of the new products are only half of those anticipated?
- What happens if your corporation decides not to manufacture and market the new products after they have been developed?
- What happens if the project fails?
- What will my tax consequences be if I decide to invest in the arrangement?

In order to answer most of these types of questions, the prospectus or placement memorandum will need to be fairly detailed. The most important sections to the potential investor normally include the following.

- The summary of the limited partnership or other entity.
- The significant risk factors.

- Information about your corporation, including financial and other information about its business and management, and its track record in developing other, often related, products.
- The description of the R&D activities to be performed and the products to be developed.
- The use of the proceeds to be raised. (In addition to funding the R&D, funds will be required for the underwriters, commissions, organizational expenses, and working capital.) A potential investor should reasonably expect that at least 85 percent of the proceeds will go to the R&D.
- The anticipated market for the product to be developed, the marketing methods to be used, and the anticipated competition.
- The percentage of the limited partnership's profits and losses to be allocated to the limited partners.
- The contract between the limited partnership and your corporation setting forth the potential payments if a marketable product is developed.
- The potential cash flows and taxable income to the limited partners if the project is successful.
- The limited partnership agreement itself.
- The tax opinion that sets forth the probable tax consequences to the limited partnership and to the limited partners, for example, the deductibility of costs and the tax treatment (capital gains or ordinary income) of the proceeds if the project is successful.

Proprietary Rights

In putting together the R&D arrangement, there are necessary legal documents which need to be drafted in order to protect the proprietary rights of the respective parties. One of the most important rights to be protected is the right to the contracted-for technology.

In the case of an R&D limited partnership, all the proprietary rights to the developed technology including any patents, patent applications, trademarks, and copyrights generally rest in the partnership. Furthermore, the contracting party and the partnership need to agree upon the party responsible for making any requisite patent filings. Usually the procedure is either to have the developer obtain a patent in the partnership's name or have the partnership assume primary responsibility for filing with any necessary assistance from the developer.

The rights to the resultant technology should also be clearly delineated. It is common practice for an R&D agreement to provide that the products which result from the R&D work—including any inventories, improvements, designs, patents, technologies, know-how, including any subsequent invention, discovery, or improvement made by your corporation (purchaser of the results) with respect to the resulting products—are deemed to be the purchase of technology from the partnership. This is to prevent the purchaser corporation from using the resulting technology in direct competition with the partnership at no cost.

Determining the proprietary rights of the parties in an R&D arrangement is affected by numerous considerations not the least of which is the marketplace. Suffice it to say that care must be taken to address all the issues when structuring the arrangement.

TAX ASPECTS

The potential tax benefits or detriments of R&D arrangements are key factors, both to potential investors and to corporations that are considering entering into such arrangements. R&D arrangements can be particularly effective as tax-advantaged investments. An effective tax-advantaged investment should achieve one or both of the following goals.

• Provide current deductions to the investors, while permitting them to defer income; and/or
• Allow ordinary loss treatment for the deductions, while permitting capital gain treatment of the income.

Most tax-advantaged investments are organized as limited partnerships because, unlike a corporation, a partnership is not a taxable entity; items of partnership income and loss flow directly to the partners and are included in their income tax returns. The following discussion assumes the R&D arrangement is a limited partnership. As stated previously, other forms of organization are, of course, possible and sometimes are used.

The taxation of R&D arrangements is a complex subject. This section describes the most important tax concerns from the perspective of investors and then your corporation. However, it does not discuss all the details that potential investors and corporations should consider before undertaking an R&D arrangement. Furthermore, the section does not consider the effects of state and local tax laws, which may be quite different from the federal income tax law and which may differ substantially from one state to another.

Investor Tax Goals—How to Structure an R&D Arrangement

Potential limited partners will want to address the following tax issues when considering an investment in an R&D arrangement.

Will the Partnership Generate Deductions (and Credits) for the Investor and Will the Partner's Investment Be Recovered Currently Through Ordinary Deductions, or Will Some of the Investment Result in Capital Expenditures That Are not Deductible Currently?   Generally a partnership's expenditures are not deductible until the partnership begins "carrying on" a trade or business. However, there is an important exception to this general "carrying on" rule for R&D expenditures, which may enable the limited partners to deduct these expenditures at the time they are made. R&D expenditures may be currently deductible as long as they were incurred "in connection with" a trade or business, a less strenuous test than "carrying on" a trade or business.* Expenditures that are not currently deductible should be capitalized. Some of the capitalized expenditures may be recovered at ordinary income rates, through amortization, while others are only recoverable at the capital gain rate. Even if the partnership has deductible expenses, the limited partners will not be entitled to deduct the expenses if the expenses exceed their basis in the partnership or if the partners are not "at risk."†

If the partnership is "carrying on" a trade or business, *which is not the usual case in an R&D arrangement*, the limited partners may also be able to claim an R&D tax credit. This credit equals 25 percent of

---

* See the sixth question, "Will the Research and Development Expenditures Be Deductible?"
† See the fifth question, "Will the Partners' Deductions Be Limited?"

a taxpayer's qualifying R&D expenditures in excess of a base-period amount. Qualifying expenditures include 100 percent of the cost of research undertaken directly by the taxpayer and 65 percent of that undertaken by others on his behalf. A taxpayer that incurs R&D expenditures while performing R&D on behalf of others, such as under an R&D contract in an R&D arrangement, *cannot* include those expenditures when computing its credit.

In order to be eligible for the credit, a taxpayer must have incurred the R&D expenditures while "carrying on" a trade or business. Although the taxpayer may deduct the *expenditures*, provided they were incurred "in connection with" a trade or business, the credit is available only if the "carrying on" test is met. One of the reasons Congress imposed the stricter "carrying on" test in order to qualify for the R&D credit was to bar the credit from R&D tax shelter arrangements. However, the partners in an R&D arrangement may be entitled to claim the credit if the arrangement uses the product of the research in producing or providing a product or service (possibly in addition to licensing the product of the research to others). Even when the credit can be claimed, it can only be used to offset tax attributable to the activity or business that generated the credit. In other words, the investor partner in an R&D arrangement cannot use the credit to offset taxes on income not related to the R&D project.

The only exception to the "carrying on" test arises in the case of a research joint venture. In this case, the venturers may be able to claim the credit for the venture's R&D expenditures, even if the venture itself is not carrying on a trade or business, provided the venturers (such as two established corporations) are carrying on a trade or business to which the research applies and which is entitled to the results of the research.

Obviously, the rules related to the deductibility of R&D expenditures and the tax credit are quite complex, and you will need professional assistance to enable you to take advantage of them.

Will the Partnership Generate Taxable Income and, if So, Will the Income Be Taxable at Ordinary Income Rates or at the Capital Gain Rate?

The answer to this question depends largely on the partnership's role in developing the new products and its role after they have been developed, and on each individual partner's actions. For example:

- If the partnership has a royalty interest in the new products, through a licensing or similar agreement, the royalties will be taxed at ordinary income rates.

- If the partnership manufactures and sells the new products or services, it will have sales and cost of sales which are taxed at ordinary income rates.

- If the partnership develops a patent that it uses in its business, the capitalized costs, if any, of the patent may be depreciated over its useful life and deducted at ordinary income rates.

- If the partnership sells the patent or all of its rights to the technology for which a patent has been applied, any gain on the sale may qualify for capital gain treatment (although some or all of any depreciation deductions taken previously would be recaptured as ordinary income).*

- If a partner sells his partnership interest, the gain or loss on the sale would generally be a capital gain or loss, except that the partner would have to recapture as ordinary income some or all of his share of any depreciation deductions.

When Will the Limited Partner's Investment Be Deductible? The Tax Reform Act of 1984 (TRA) significantly changed the requirements for determining the proper timing of certain deductions by both cash

---

* Section 1235 of the Internal Revenue Code provides long-term capital gain treatment for the gain on certain dispositions of certain patents, regardless of the seller's actual holding period, and regardless of whether the patent qualified for capital gain treatment in the seller's hands under other Code Sections.

Code Section 1235 treatment is only available for sales by a "holder" of the patent to an unrelated buyer. A "holder" is defined as an individual who created the patent or who purchased the patent from its creator before the patent was usable. Treasury Regulations make it clear that a partnership *cannot* qualify as a holder, but that the individual partners can qualify.

If Section 1235 treatment is unavailable, the partnership may wish to assert that the patent is a capital asset or is an asset used in a trade or business. In order to receive long-term capital gain treatment in these cases, the patent must have been property held by the partnership—other than as an inventory item—for more than six months, or the patent must have been depreciable property held in the partnership's trade or business for more than six months and in either case must have been disposed of in a sale or exchange. If the partnership has held and depreciated the patent, then upon its sale (or upon a partner's sale of his interest in the partnership), the depreciation deductions will be recaptured as ordinary income.

Case law holds that in some circumstances Section 1235 is the only section under which capital gain treatment is available for the sale of a patent. Therefore, it is possible that if Section 1235 is unavailable, a partnership's sale of a patent will not be treated as a capital gain.

and accrual basis taxpayers. The new economic performance standard provides that otherwise deductible expenses can now be claimed only when the services to which they relate are performed or, in the case of property, when the property is delivered. In the case of a cash-basis tax shelter partnership, however, deductions can be claimed at the time of payment as long as performance occurs within 90 days after the end of the partnership's year.

The timing of deductions may also be affected by the "related party" provisions of the Internal Revenue Code which require the matching of deductions claimed by the payer with the income recognized by the payee. Among the related parties subject to these rules are corporations and partnerships where the same persons own more than 50 percent of the corporation's outstanding stock and more than a 50 percent interest in the partnership's capital or profits. As previously discussed, R&D limited partnerships are often structured with a contracting corporation to perform R&D and serve as general partner so that the related party rules may be applicable.

Although the new economic performance requirements and related party rules will generally lengthen the period over which a limited partner's investment will be recovered, the new provisions do not adversely affect the ability to claim deductions for R&D activities. Of course any portion of the limited partner's investment that is not spent on R&D or other deductible or amortizable items will be recovered at the time the partner sells or otherwise disposes of his partnership interest.

Will the Investment Entity Qualify as a Partnership?   In order for the R&D arrangement to achieve the benefits of being a limited partnership (i.e., the items of partnership income and loss flow directly to the partners and are included on their income tax returns), it must qualify as a partnership for tax purposes. To do so, the entity must *lack* at least two of the following corporate characteristics:

• Indefinite life
• Free transferability of ownership interests
• Centralized management
• Limited liability

If the entity has more than two of these characteristics, it will be taxed as if it were a corporation, rather than as a partnership. If that happens, the entity will usually be subject to tax, and the taxable income and losses will not be passed through to the shareholders (investors). As a result, the investors will not receive any tax deductions when the R&D expenses are incurred, and they will only be entitled to take a deduction if they terminate their interest in the R&D arrangement at a loss. Therefore, from the investor's standpoint, it is essential that the arrangement be recognized as a partnership for federal income taxes, rather than as an association taxable as a corporation.

If the arrangement qualifies as a partnership, the IRS will honor the partnership's method of allocating profits and losses to the general and limited partners provided the method has "substantial economic effect" (i.e., the tax and economic effects are consistent).

Will the Partners' Deductions Be Limited?   Even though an entity qualifies as a partnership, there are limits on the tax benefits it can pass through to its partners. In general, a partner's deductions from a partnership may not exceed his basis in the partnership. In addition, individuals, Subchapter S corporations, and closely held corporations that are partners in an R&D limited partnership must be "at risk" and cannot deduct more than the amount they have "at risk." A partner's basis in a partnership (1) includes his contributions of money and other property to the partnership, (2) is increased by his share of the partnership's income, (3) is decreased by his share of the partnership's losses, and (4) is decreased by the distributions he receives from the partnership. A general partner's basis in the partnership also includes his share of the partnership's "recourse liabilities" (liabilities to which the partner would be subject in the event of a partnership default). All partners (including limited partners) may generally include their share of the partnership's nonrecourse liabilities as part of their basis.

However, even if a partner has a basis in an R&D limited partnership, he must be "at risk" in order to deduct his share of the partnership's R&D expenses, if he is subject to the "at risk" rules. Furthermore, he may not deduct more than the amount he has "at risk" in the R&D partnership. The meaning of "at risk" for tax purposes is similar to its meaning for accounting purposes, as discussed previously in the accounting section. Thus, in order for a partner to be "at risk," the

R&D contract must make clear that the partners bear the risk of loss if the R&D is unsuccessful. Guarantees that the research will be successful or will have any particular economic utility, guaranteed minimum royalty payments, or guarantees that the partnership will be "bailed out" through a buyout arrangement if the R&D project is unsuccessful could result in the IRS denying a partner a deduction for some or all of his share of the R&D expenses.

A partner is considered to be "at risk" for the amount of cash and the tax basis of other property he has contributed to the activity as well as for his recourse borrowings with respect to the activity. Any tax losses incurred in an activity and any withdrawals from the activity will reduce a taxpayer's "at risk" amount while any income earned in the activity will increase his "at risk" amount. Generally, a partner is not considered to be "at risk" for his share of the partnership's nonrecourse liabilities.

Will the Research and Development Expenditures Be Deductible?

In order to be deductible as R&D expenses, expenditures must meet the following Treasury Department definition of research and experimental expenditures:

> Costs incident to the development of an experimental or pilot model, a plant process, a product, a formula, an invention, or similar property and the improvement of already existing property of the type mentioned.

Research and experimental expenditures do not include expenditures for the acquisition or improvement of land or depreciable or depletable property that is to be used in connection with an R&D project, if the R&D partnership acquires ownership rights in the property. Similarly, research and experimental expenditures do not include expenditures for acquiring another's patent, model, production, or process. Thus, the R&D contract should provide that your corporation, not the partnership, will acquire any assets of these types that are required for use in the R&D project, and that the ownership rights in them will not be transferred to the R&D partnership. (If, however, the partnership does acquire assets of these types, depreciation relating to them may qualify as deductible R&D expenses. In addition, if the property qualifies for the investment tax credit, the partners may be entitled to claim it.) The costs of producing, marketing, or quality control testing of the products developed do not qualify as R&D expenses.

Furthermore, proposed Treasury regulations, if adopted in their present form, could substantially curtail R&D deductions for the development of computer software.

In addition to meeting the definition of an R&D expenditure under Section 174 of the Internal Revenue Code, an R&D expenditure must be paid or incurred "in connection with the taxpayer's trade or business" in order to be deductible currently. As a result of the Tax Equity and Fiscal Responsibility Act of 1982, deductions under Section 174 may give rise to tax preferences, which in turn may cause one to be subject to the alternative minimum tax.

While the types of expenditures that will qualify for the R&D deduction are usually reasonably easy to identify, the point at which a trade or business begins is not. The existence of a trade or business is a question of fact, as it depends largely on the actual intention of the taxpayer. If the taxpayer genuinely holds itself out as selling goods or services, it is generally considered to have a trade or business, but its motive does not appear to be to make a profit, a trade or business generally will not be considered to exist.

The presence of gross receipts from an activity that are significant when compared to the activity's expenses is one indication that a trade or business exists. However, the landmark Supreme Court case, *Snow et ux. v. Commissioner*, held that the absence of gross receipts did not prevent the deduction of R&D expenditures when expectations of profits were high and the general partner was putting about one-third of his time into the research project. The question of whether a specific R&D limited partnership has incurred R&D expenditures "in connection with a trade or business" will continue to be decided on a case-by-case basis.

Corporate Tax Concerns

Your corporation will be interested in many of the preceding tax issues in order to make the R&D arrangement attractive to investors. If your corporation is one of the limited or general partners in the limited partnership, it will be taxed on its allocable share of the partnership's income or loss, and it will receive its allocable share of any tax credits, just as the other partners do. In addition, it may have taxable revenues and deductible expenses from an R&D contract with the limited partnership.

If your corporation is in a tax loss position or if it is a start-up corporation without any taxable income, the R&D arrangement, in effect, may enable you to transfer the R&D tax deductions to the limited partners. This may enable your corporation to achieve a lower after-tax cost of funding its R&D program. However, if the R&D program is highly successful, the costs to the corporation may be greater than if it had obtained other sources of funds at the outset.

One tax disadvantage to your corporation of a R&D arrangement is that the R&D expenses it incurs under the R&D contract with the limited partnership will generally not be eligible for the R&D tax credit. These expenses would likely be eligible for the credit if the R&D were funded internally or from debt or equity financing. This factor may slow the growth of R&D arrangements as some corporations may decide to employ more traditional means of raising funds for their R&D so that they do not lose a substantial R&D tax credit.

10

CASH MANAGEMENT

In recent years, more and more attention has been focused on what might be called the very best way to raise capital—by doing a better job of managing your company's cash.

As obvious as that concept may be, it is often neglected. Entrepreneurs underestimate how productive it can be. They tell themselves the company has been getting along quite well with a rather easy-going attitude toward cash disbursements and receipts, and it would be hard to impose stricter discipline. And management, busy at producing and selling a line of products, does not find it easy to keep up-to-date on all the new thinking in the art of cash management.

There is another reason for neglect. Management suspects that while large corporations might realize substantial savings, the benefits for small to midsize companies are probably too insignificant to bother with. The facts suggest just the opposite.

Better cash management may be even more important for a growth company in its early stages than for the large, mature organization. The young, emerging company—bursting with ideas and energy, though it may be—nevertheless has a limited track record. Therefore, the sources of outside funds available may be limited and expensive. What aggressive management of the company's cash flow means is that savings are there for the taking, you can accumulate capital in this way and thus reduce reliance on outside funds. In effect, it provides capital that you would otherwise have to borrow.

An extra benefit, as you will see in the detail of this chapter, is that sound cash management practices will earn respect from suppliers and customers that will pay off in countless ways. No matter what the size of your company, managing your cash more effectively may be one of the keys to your growth, even your survival. The first step is to examine the cash flow cycle which holds the secrets to good cash management.

THE CASH FLOW CYCLE

Most business managers are familiar with the revenue and cost cycles of their businesses. This information is typically presented in the income statement, which describes the economic performance/profitability of the business during the reporting period. While important to the long-term health of the business, profitability is not the primary determinant of current liquidity. The key ingredient in managing business liquidity is the cash flow cycle.

Simply stated, the cash flow cycle is: (1) the investment of cash in inventory or product, (2) the sale of the product, and (3) the receipt of cash payment for sale. Because of the order in which these business activities must occur, the liquidity of the firm is directly affected by the timing differences in cash transactions for each activity. Cash disbursements (for inventory, raw materials, labor, etc.) and inventory overhead expenses (such as warehousing and plant premises) and cash receipts all occur at disconcertingly different times, thus the need for greater cash flow to support liquidity.

The relationship between your income statement (profitability) and your actual cyclical flow of cash is accounted for on the balance sheet in the various elements of working capital. Increases in working capital must be financed by your business and, if not properly controlled, may result in serious liquidity problems. It is unfortunate that business managers cannot arrange to pay raw material suppliers, personnel, premises lessors or mortgagors, and service vendors when they collect funds for the products they sell. This arrangement could significantly reduce the need for sound cash management practices. Most business managers, however, do not have the luxury of such arrangements and, therefore, must focus on the control of the cash flow cycle. Much of this chapter will focus on controlling that cycle.

Cash Flow Cycle Example.   Exhibit 10-1 presents a typical business's cash flow cycle segregated by the asset cycle and the liability cycle. The business purchases raw materials which are held for an average

EXHIBIT 10-1.   "BEFORE" CONTROLLING CASH FLOW

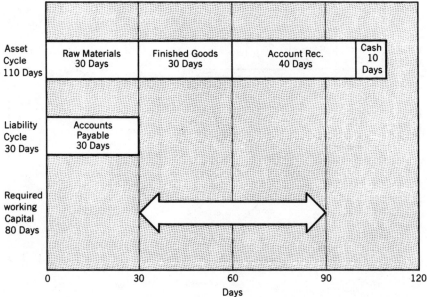

of *30* days before converting those materials to finished goods. In this example, finished goods are considered held in inventory for *30* days prior to shipment to customers and conversion into accounts receivable. The company's customers typically pay *40* days after the product shipment. The company also keeps a minimum cash balance, equalling approximately *10* days of sales, for operating purposes. In the liability cycle, accounts payable are deferred for *30* days. As a result, this business has 80 days (30 + 30 + 40 + 10 − 30) of sales value invested in net working capital. Therefore, 80 days worth of sales must be financed through loans, infusions of capital or the retention of earnings.

Controlling the Cash Flow Cycle

Exhibit 10-2 presents the desired effects of controlling the cash flow cycle. Raw material and finished good inventories have been reduced

EXHIBIT 10-2.   "AFTER" CONTROLLING CASH FLOW

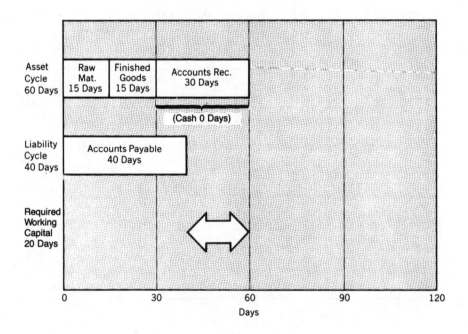

to 15 days each, and accounts receivable have been reduced to 30 days. Cash is controlled to eliminate idle balances. Accounts payable are deferred for an average of 40 days. Net working capital is reduced from a total of 80 days to 20 days—a 75 percent reduction in the working capital requirements.

Consider the actual financial effect of a working capital restructuring (such as shown in Exhibit 10-2) on a firm with annual sales of $5 million. Before restructuring, the required net working capital of 80 days of sales value would equal approximately $1,096,000 ([$5,000,000 ÷ 365] × 80). Through restructuring, the working capital required is reduced to 20 days of sales or approximately $274,000 ([$5,000,000 ÷ 365] × 20). Where has the remaining $822,000 gone? The improvement does not typically show up in the balance of cash. Instead, good business people will take this opportunity to reduce expensive debt or reinvest in assets that support increased sales levels.

The economic benefit of a reduction in net working capital may be most dramatically seen in the example of debt reduction. To the entrepreneur or the manager of a high-growth company, external financing may be very expensive. An entrepreneur, whose only alternative funding source is venture capital, may in fact have an annual financing cost of 30 to 50 percent. When this is applied to our example, the $822,000 reduction in working capital would reduce annual interest expense by between $246,600 to $411,000 per year. Examined more directly, at $5 million in annual sales, and 30 to 50 percent financing rates, each day's sale value squeezed out of net working capital is worth from $4110 to $6850. ([$5,000,000 ÷ 365] × [.3 or .5]). Therefore, a reduction of 60 working capital days reduces annual interest expense by between $246,600 to $411,000 ([60 × $4110] to [60 × $6850]). This quantification methodology can help the business manager determine whether changes in operating methods or procedures are beneficial when compared to the cost of making those changes.

Fluctuating Sales: Cash Flow Effects

This cash flow approach to cash management is particularly important in understanding the effects on your business of rapid expansion or contraction of the sales level. For example, Exhibit 10-3 presents the effects on a company with rapidly increasing sales for five months followed by three months of significant contraction. Despite continuous

EXHIBIT 10-3. INCOME STATEMENT—CASH FLOW EXAMPLE

	Monthly Statements							
	1	2	3	4	5	6	7	8
Income Statement								
Sales	100	150	200	250	350	250	200	150
Cost and expenses (80%)	(80)	(120)	(160)	(200)	(280)	(200)	(160)	(120)
Net	20	30	40	50	70	50	40	30
Cash Requirements								
Working assets:								
Minimum cash (15 days)	50	75	100	125	175	125	100	75
Inventory (60 days)	200	300	400	500	700	500	400	300
Accounts receivable (45 days)	150	225	300	375	525	375	300	225
Subtotal (120 days)	400	600	800	1,000	1,400	1,000	800	600
Working liabilities:								
Accounts payable (30 days)	100	150	200	250	350	250	200	150
Net working capital	300	450	600	750	1,050	750	600	450
Cash (required) throw-off	—	(150)	(150)	(150)	(300)	300	150	150

234

profits through the entire period of time, this company has experienced significant demands for additional working capital during the expansion cycle but generated significant extra, unallocated cash ("throw-off") during the contraction cycle. As Exhibit 10-3 demonstrates, a business may require large injections of additional capital to fuel rapid growth. Conversely, cash throw-off during sales decreases can be illusory, because cash will be required later during the next expansion in business. These cash flow effects are particularly important for companies in seasonal markets, such as toys or construction. Reducing the net number of days of working capital can significantly reduce the size of your cash requirements or cash throw-offs in fluctuating sales situations. However, it cannot change the fact that additional working capital will still be required for growth and that cash throw-off will frequently occur during the contraction of a business.

APPROACHES TO CONTROLLING WORKING CAPITAL

The key to cash management is in controlling the flow of cash through working capital accounts and thereby reducing your investment in working capital. In order to effectively control working capital accounts, the business manager must focus on the individual elements of working capital: inventory, accounts receivable, accounts payable, and cash. This section presents approaches to each.

Inventory

To adequately control inventory, consideration should be given to reducing the *lead times* required for materials and services. Without good production and purchasing planning, overly long lead times can result, frequently causing significant overstocks of one or more products. Therefore, planning is the real key to the control of raw material, work-in-process, and finished goods inventory levels. It should be noted that inventory can generally be defined as those costs which have been incurred but which have not yet been sold to customers. In service companies, this would include labor or materials which have been expended but not billed. Sound "inventory" control in service businesses is critical to the liquidity of those companies.

The greatest single requirement for planning inventory levels, and thus production and purchasing lead times, is reasonable sales forecasts. Sales forecasting requires adequate anticipation of customer requirements. If close working relationships exist between your marketing personnel and your customers, it may be feasible to request long-term forecasts of orders from major customers. The availability of this information from customers may save a great deal of additional interest and obsolescence costs. If this requirement is presented to customers in terms of better service and cost control, customers will frequently be willing to assist you in planning your production.

In planning lead times from your company's suppliers, the converse may be true. If you can supply vendors with your anticipated purchases over an extended period of time, it may be easier for those suppliers to assure shorter lead times on your orders from them. A continuing dialogue with suppliers can also be a significant source of information on future problems in your supply channel. Thus, changes in vendor lead times and the availability of their products can more frequently be included in your company's planning process.

Improved management information systems in sales forecasting, production planning, and purchasing can often convert good sales forecast data into timely, meaningful information on departmental production loading, material requirements and labor requirements. With good management information systems, changes in any variable can quickly be reflected in inventory and production plans.

Business managers frequently analyze the number of inventory turns per year or the average number of days of inventory. This information assists in controlling the overall level of inventory. However, additional improvement in inventory levels may be realized if individual products or raw materials are evaluated in relation to their usages or customer shipments. This can frequently assist you in identifying slow-moving or obsolete inventories and areas in which purchasing or production planning could be improved.

Accounts Receivable

The investment in accounts receivable and related risk of customer default is typically minimized in those companies that maintain close working relationships with their customers. Payment terms, credit limits, and collection programs are useful only if used to reinforce the basic agreements which have already been negotiated with the customer. If your expectations regarding customer collections and terms are presented to the customer during the initial selling process and at the same time pricing and service levels are considered, then your organization will be better positioned to collect those receivable balances. Candid discussions with customers regarding the mutually beneficial nature of your relationship with them can help assure that interest expenses can be minimized and potential liquidity problems avoided. By projecting an image of being firm about collections, most companies will be successful at controlling accounts receivable.

Payment terms can be used to make earlier customer payment beneficial to your customer. For example, offering customers a one percent discount to pay in 10 days as opposed to net payment in 30 days is the equivalent of offering that customer 18 percent on his money (effectively offering one percent to pay 20 days earlier). Frequently, companies that offer discounts are dissatisfied with the results, claiming that customers continue to pay late but also take the discount. This problem means the customer does not grasp the relationship that must exist for a discount program to work. Within that relationship it must be understood, during the sales negotiation, that the firm intends to enforce the 10 day maximum and that the payment must be in your office by the 10th day to be eligible for discount. If the customer understands, he rarely will try to take an unearned discount.

Collection programs must also be used to reinforce terms which were agreed to in the original negotiation. Collection programs which represent "hounding" will typically have the effect of generating animosity and reducing the likelihood of early payment. If, however, the original negotiations explained your collection program and your expectations pertaining to credit, a collection call could simply reiterate the interrelationship between pricing, service, and payments. Frequently, a collection call can serve not only to collect bills on time but also to build a better, mutually-rewarding relationship with the customer.

Your collection procedures should be designed to alert customers to an *escalating* concern on the part of your company. Three consecutive telephone calls from your collection manager to the customer's accounts payable clerk will not be as productive as one call from your collection manager, a second call from your controller to the customer's controller, and finally a call from the president of your company to the president of the customer's company. This approach can serve to emphasize that the relationship is becoming strained as invoice payments are delayed, and that your entire organization is becoming increasingly concerned about the status of that customer's account.

Credit limits can also be used as a method of creating awareness of credit problems at successively higher management levels in your company at a relatively early point. If a customer purchases goods every 10 days and your payment terms are "due in 30 days," then credit limits which are equal to 45 days of sales will effectively limit shipments to the customer by specifying that no invoice can achieve 45 days without approval from upper management. This will elevate a collection problem in your company as an account reaches "critical" levels.

Another critical element in a sound accounts receivable collection program is the invoicing process. If invoices are prepared in a timely manner and forwarded to the customer at the earliest possible date, then customer complaints that invoices were too late to take the discount or to process through their accounts payable system can be minimized. In situations where large volumes of invoices are required, improvements to the invoicing process may require automated systems to speed up the processing of invoice-related data or invoice preparation. The invoicing process should be evaluated to ensure that invoices are properly prepared with all terms and conditions and that necessary documentation is forwarded with the invoice. In evaluating information which is required for invoice preparation, data requirements may include information typically associated with your accounts payable system (out-of-pocket costs that comprise an invoice). For example, professional service companies that invoice based on time and expenses may need your accounts payable detail in order to properly bill their expenses. Some types of construction companies, which bill on a cost-plus basis, also require a significant amount of accounts payable data on which to base invoices to their customers. A complete range of financial and operational information required for invoice preparation should be considered in determining the enhancements to your company's information system that may be required for improved invoicing.

One final note on payment terms: for those companies that work on large contracts or that have a few very major customers, negotiating specific terms of payment and methods of payment can be critical to the liquidity of the business. If large amounts are to be received from a limited number of customers, it may be advantageous to negotiate with those customers for wire transfer payments and possibly trade-offs in prices in order to gain earlier availability of those funds. Again, a candid relationship with the customer regarding the full range of issues for a mutually beneficial relationship is critical to maintaining sound control of accounts receivable.

Accounts Payable

As indicated earlier, it would be ideal if working liabilities were always equal to working assets. Since that is not the case, accounts payable can be used to bring them more into balance. In a practical sense, you can take certain actions that have the effect of giving you noninterest-bearing loans from your suppliers.

When you negotiate terms of your relationship, try to extend your payment period to the maximum. This is simply a matter of keeping your money as long as possible before paying it out. This will cut down on the amount you might have to borrow (and pay interest on) in order to keep faith with your suppliers. Many of the negotiated payment terms used to enhance your accounts receivable can be reversed and applied for your benefit in accounts payable. Negotiated payment terms with your vendors should include the exploration of benefits that can be accrued from cash discounts, convenient timing of payments to coincide with your cash flow cycle, or even more specialized arrangements such as lines of credit, bartering and equity investments. Any saving could be important in reaching your goals of profit and growth. Most suppliers and vendors would appreciate your spelling out these goals, knowing that they will benefit in the long run as you prosper and become a bigger customer. This is another example of how a close, candid relationship can benefit both customer and supplier.

Cash

In our introduction, we focused on the management of the balance of cash. To organize the numerous activities associated with this single working capital account, this section has been separated into three subsections: cash forecasting and daily cash reporting, banking services, and short-term investments.

Cash Forecasting and Daily Cash Positioning

1. *For Planning.*   The management of cash or near-cash balances for most early-stage, high-growth companies can be significantly enhanced by simply forecasting receivable collections in relation to accounts payable and payroll disbursements. Automated accounts payable and receivable systems can provide very timely information for use in generating at least weekly projections of required cash outlays in relation to anticipated cash collections. This information considered with scheduled cash transactions, such as debt service payments and short-term investment maturities, can alert management to critical cash balance shortages or cash balance excesses. Early knowledge of these circumstances will provide greater flexibility in planning alternative courses of action.

2. *For Investment.*   In addition to forecasting cash for planning purposes, business managers often create internal systems and procedures that gather sufficient information to daily convert cash in the bank into an *earning asset* (see "Short-Term Investments" section following). These information systems and procedures are collectively referred to as daily cash positioning or daily cash worksheet preparation. Cash positioning procedures are performed daily because the actual cash balance in the bank will vary considerably from day to day, even though cash transactions on the company books may occur at less frequent intervals. The timing of these procedures is usually in the morning so that investment decisions can be made prior to daily financial institution transaction deadlines. Typical sources for gathering cash positioning information are listed in the following table.

DAILY CASH POSITIONING SOURCES OF INFORMATION CHECKLIST

Required Data	Source of Data
Opening balances	Financial institutions
Current-day deposits	Cashier's department

Required Data	Source of Data
Checks issued	Accounts payable dept.
	Remote operations
	Payroll dept.
Maturing investments	Financial files
Debt service	Financial files
Transfers in	Remote operations
	Financial institutions
Target balance (if any)	Financial files

Banking Services. Financial institutions offer an array of services for managing cash. The following table provides a listing of the most common cash management services, and a description of the purpose of each. Overview descriptions of the services are also provided in this section.

In most cases, financial institutions require some form of compensation for providing these services. For example, compensation is requested in the form of demand noninterest-bearing cash balances. To ensure the selected form of compensation is best for the company, the business manager should request that the services be priced in the form of cash fees and in cash balances. By comparing the methods of compensation, the most economical form can be selected.

CASH MANAGEMENT SERVICES

Service	Purpose
Lockbox	Accelerate incoming receipts and reduce your cash receipts clerical effort
Zero-balance accounts	Consolidation of excess funds in bank accounts into a single master account
Depository transfer checks	Transfer of funds from other banks to the operating bank by check
Wire transfers	Transfer of funds for immediate use
Balance reporting	Provide information about actual cash balances at the bank

Lockboxes at your bank may prove to be beneficial in a number of ways. In addition to accelerating the availability of funds in your account, lockboxes may also be utilized to relieve your personnel of cash processing requirements and to improve the efficiency of that process. Bank lockboxes are frequently equipped with state-of-the-art check processing equipment which can both minimize the cost and increase the rate at which items are processed (particularly useful for companies that receive large volumes of small transactions). Frequently, these systems can also supply your company with information which is valuable in applying cash receipts to your accounts receivable system. For companies with small volumes of large receipts, lockboxes can assist you in removing those large payments from the mail one to two days earlier and collect those monies from your customer's bank on a more timely basis.

Consolidating excess funds from disbursement and payroll bank accounts is typically accomplished through zero-balance services which automatically fund checks as though they were paid from a single master or concentration account. The benefit of using zero-balance accounts can be calculated by determining the *average* bank account balances maintained in disbursement accounts and payroll accounts and then applying the marginal investment rate to the total average balance. For example, an entrepreneur may have three business operations, each with a separate operating disbursement account and payroll account. Assuming that each of the six accounts has an average balance of $6000, then $36,000 could be consolidated into a single account for investment or other purposes. Assuming a marginal investment rate of 10 percent, the gross income attributable to consolidating these funds and investing the $36,000 would be $3770 per year assuming monthly compounding. Assuming the bank charged $25 per account, per month, to provide the zero-balancing capability, the annual banking service charge would be $1800 (2 accounts × 3 operations × 12 months × $25) leaving $1970 of incremental interest income for your firm.

Services provided for transferring funds from other banks include Depository Transfer Checks (DTCs) and wire transfers. DTCs are typically employed for regular daily transfers of funds deposited into banks by remote operating entities. Because wire transfers are expensive, they are usually employed in circumstances of large dollar-amount transfers, or where the transfer amount is nonroutine and an immediate need for the money exists. A general guideline for wire transferring funds is that unless the funds are needed for liquidity purposes, wires should not be executed in amounts less than $25,000.

Many banks in the United States offer customers daily balance reporting as of the close of business on the prior day. This balance information can be extremely useful in controlling cash balances in bank accounts as described in the "Cash Forecasting and Daily Cash Positioning" section of this chapter. These daily balance reports can be received on microcomputers, via terminal printers and via telephone communication.

Short-Term Investments.   Investing in short-term money market instruments requires certain control procedures because the investments are transacted by telephone. This means that substantial amounts may be daily charged to your bank account on a telephone request basis. To control this environment, several procedures are available.

• Employees authorized to execute investments should be identified in official company documents filed with the bank.
• Identification codes, known only to the bank and to authorized employees, should be used when making investments.
• Only certain types of investments with low risk/high liquidity characteristics should be authorized. These types of investments should be identified in official company documents filed with the bank. Usually, these investments include securities of the U.S. Treasury, major bank certificates of deposit, high-grade commercial paper, major bank acceptances, and securities of government agencies.
• Each investment should be entered in the company records and the internal documents supporting the transactions should be matched to investment purchase confirmations—received from the financial institution—on a timely basis.

PHASES OF CASH MANAGEMENT DEVELOPMENT

As a company grows in size, the planning and control procedures and methods must change to accommodate growth. Procedures and methods should be evaluated based on costs and benefits to ensure that the timing of the improvements is correct.

Sales vs. Availability and Cost of Capital

Typically, a growth company's financial strength will improve dramatically as cash flow increases. With improved financial strength, external financing alternatives change dramatically. The availability of alternative sources increases because banks and other financial institutions will more readily advance cash based on strong financial positions and performance. (Actually, a highly successful growth company will frequently find that working capital can be financed from internal sources after some period of time.) In addition, the cost of capital will decline dramatically with increased financial strength (see Exhibit 10-4). Because financial institutions will finance working capital for the successful growth company, raising capital through costly venture placements will be avoided and bank credit lines at prime or slightly higher interest rates will be available.

Timing Cash Management Improvements

The typical growth company will move through three distinguishable phases of cash management development as cash flows grow from zero to approximately $40 to 50 million per year. The transition from one phase to the next will vary by industry and company, but the transition points will occur based on the cost/availability of working capital and on the total dollar cash flow through the company.

EXHIBIT 10-4. PHASES OF CASH MANAGEMENT DEVELOPMENT

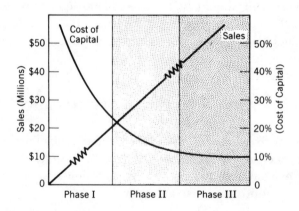

Phase 1 can be characterized by a company with sales between $1 million and $10 million per year. These companies are experiencing high growth, high costs of capital and frequently unavailable sources of working capital. During this phase, management should focus heavily on short-term cash planning procedures/systems, vendor and customer relations and policies, and improved planning and control of purchases and inventory. The desired effect is to minimize the net working capital requirements of the business and thereby reduce both the cost of working capital and the pressures for additional external financing sources.

As the company's sales grows to around $10 million per year, the profitability and financial strength typically will improve to the point where working capital is more available and the cost of capital is dramatically reduced. These are characteristics of a company which is entering Phase 2 of cash management development. Phase 2 will often continue until the company's sales reach approximately $30 million per year. In this $10 to $30 million range of sales, cash flows will run from $40,000 to $120,000 per business day. In addition to enhancing management information systems to control and plan receivables, payables and inventory (to minimize net working capital), the company should begin to focus on the management of banking relations and cash investment balances. Bank relations should be redefined to include more favorable terms on credit and the expansion of bank services to assist in managing cash at these greater levels. Bank services which may be of assistance include balance reporting of "current day" collected and uncollected balances, and controlled disbursing to enhance management's ability to plan daily cash and investment (or loan reduction) activities.

As the company's sales reach approximately $30 million per year, important working capital financing alternatives are usually available and the cost of such financing declines. These are characteristics of the company entering Phase 3 of cash management development. Above this level of sales, due to the magnitude of cash that flows through the company on a daily basis, even small improvements in the number of days required in working capital or, in other words, the flow of cash, can have a dramatic effect on the benefits derived. You may find that cash management "studies" will prove beneficial in identifying bottlenecks in the cash-flow cycle that result from interdepartmental differences in priorities, policies, or procedures. These interdepartmental conflicts frequently can be resolved when the differing priorities are compared to the priority for sound working capital management. At this level of development, you may also find that evaluations of alternative short-term investments may be useful in improving your investment yield. Often, significant enhancements to management information systems or increased sophistication of the banking and cash processing relations will result from evaluations of the company's total working capital planning and control systems.

11

TAX PLANNING

The very idea that a company's tax program can be an important contributor in raising capital for growth is probably a pleasant surprise for many entrepreneurs.

Nobody loves taxes. But at least there is a bright side to this inescapable drain on your cash: a tax program that takes advantage of every possibility the law allows can save substantial sums, and money thus saved can significantly reduce your dependence on outside financing.

The logic is disarmingly simple:

• Pay only the minimum amount of taxes due
• Pay them on the latest date permissible

Simple as the strategy is, carrying it out is one of the most complex challenges in the life of a company, starting even before the company comes into existence. It begins with deciding what kind of organization to create in the first place in order to realize the best tax break for the owners. From that moment on, tax considerations enter into virtually every major decision you make.

This chapter tells you how a professional tax program is constructed, how taxes affect your decisions, the benefits that can be realized, and how careful management of your tax program can produce capital for growth.

It begins with a general discussion of how to minimize the effect of taxes on cash flow.

MINIMIZING THE EFFECT OF INCOME TAXES ON CASH FLOW

For a growing business, income taxes can represent one of its most significant, continuing obligations. Managing this obligation requires advance planning and an effective maintenance system so that only the minimum amount of taxes due are paid and that these taxes are paid no earlier than they are actually due. Properly managed, this system can significantly reduce the adverse effect of taxes on your cash flow. The start-up phase of a business is not too early to start planning.

The major elements of an effective tax management system are:

• Comprehensive tax calendar
• Tax minimization strategy plans
• Competent compliance function
• Good accounting records

Each business should maintain a complete tax calendar to plan for all required tax filings and payments. In doing so, filing requirements and payments can be anticipated, giving you time to identify tax planning opportunities and minimize the tax burden and its effect on your cash flow. Penalties can also be avoided. Often, the penalties associated with not filing or late filing are quite high, much higher than the cost of borrowing funds, so care should be taken to identify all of the forms and payments which are necessary.

Your tax advisor can generally help you to set up a comprehensive tax calendar. If you construct your own, the Internal Revenue Service can help by supplying small-business guides which describe the types of federal taxes and requirements for compliance. Information about state or local taxes may be available by calling the appropriate agency (generally the Secretary of State's office).

As soon as all of your tax filings and payments have been identified and their timing noted, then the planning process can begin. Planning means studying the tax law so you can develop a strategy to minimize your tax liability.

Very rarely do the federal income tax laws permit business income to be excluded from taxation. Therefore, almost all tax strategies relate to three areas:

1. the timing of income and deductions;
2. character of income (e.g., capital gains versus ordinary income; capital gains are generally taxed at a lower rate); and
3. avoidance of double taxation of income.

The results of tax planning must be seen not only in terms of advantages and tax savings, but also possible disadvantages and costs. Hence, your tax strategy should also take into account how decisions made primarily for tax purposes might affect future opportunities. For example, the use of an S corporation in order to pass losses through to investors may restrict your possibilities for issuing stock in the event more capital is needed (see subsection "When to Use What Entity" under "Selection of Entity" section following).

Good tax planning involves reviewing all proposed corporate transactions for their potential tax impact, both federal and state. Planning before the fact is important because there are generally few, if any, options available after the transaction has taken place. The saying "it's easier to prevent a problem than it is to correct one" applies.

Planning for taxes at the state and local levels is often overlooked. Generally, state and local taxes are not carefully examined because they are erroneously considered insignificant when compared to federal taxes. However, state and local taxes can be quite costly in certain situations. It is usually beneficial to examine how they would be affected by any major or unusual corporate transaction. For example, whether a new business segment operates as a division or a branch versus a separate corporation in a particular state may have a significant impact on how much state tax is paid. Restructuring such a transaction may be an appropriate strategy if state or local tax savings result in a benefit overall.

Proper tax planning requires the use of professionals. Your outside tax advisor or qualified tax personnel should possess the skills necessary to map out your business tax strategies and to inform you of any potential tax developments which may affect your tax planning. Your tax advisor or tax personnel should be identifying your tax planning needs and volunteering ideas instead of reacting only to your periodic inquiries. Your obligation is to keep your advisors informed of changes in the business or proposed transactions so that they may evaluate the tax ramifications and planning opportunities, if any. If you are not pleased with your outside tax advisor, then change and do not be discouraged. Sometimes it takes going through several tax advisors before you find one who is right for your needs.

Note: Tax compliance (filings and payments) can be delegated to your outside tax advisor. Just be sure that you discuss in advance how your in-house clerical personnel can be used to the maximum extent in performing routine tasks and providing assistance to the advisor. In this manner, you can use your advisor for the more important aspects of proper tax compliance and pay only for the skill level required.

In the tax planning process, the need for good accounting records should be obvious. Accounting records are the basis upon which many tax planning strategies are conceived and evaluated; for example, selection of tax accounting methods, selection of a tax year-end, the amount of estimated tax payment required, and so forth. Accounting records are also used as supporting documentation in the event of a tax audit. Maintain good accounting records and you are certain to reduce the chance of making decisions based on poor information.

SELECTION OF ENTITY (LEGAL BUSINESS FORM)

Each business must have a legal form. Although the tax aspects are important, the selection of legal entity should not be based on tax considerations alone. Some of the concerns which affect entity selection include limitation on liability, ability to finance expansion, management form, and ability to transfer ownership or control. The choice of entity may depend on the compatibility of the form with the stage of development your business or a segment of your business is in. (See "When to Use What Entity" which follows.)

The most common business forms are sole proprietorship, partnership, S corporation, and regular corporation (C corporation). Each of these forms has advantages and disadvantages. It is important to understand the differences, because the manner in which they are taxed and the circumstances in which a particular form should be used can have a significant effect on your business's cash flow.

Sole Proprietorship

A sole proprietorship is the easiest business form to begin and operate. In general, all items of business income, deduction, loss, and credit are reported directly on an individual's tax returns and taxed at personal rates. Liability is not limited to the assets of the business because the owner and the business are considered to be one and the same. The owner can be held liable for all debts, so a creditor will evaluate all of the owner's personal assets and liabilities, and earnings potential before lending funds. Other factors important to sole proprietorships include, on the minus side, the nonavailability of lower cost employee benefit plans and the higher self-employed social security rate; on the plus side, the availability of Keogh and IRA plans.

Partnership (Exclusive of Limited Partnership)

The partnership form of business is often used to bring together people who have different talents and financial resources. A partnership is not subject to federal income tax. Rather, the items of business income, gain, deduction, loss, and credit flow through the partnership and are taxed at an individual rate to each of the individual partners. The partnership can be easily formed, but its dissolution or transfer of ownership can be difficult. Transferring ownership may be easier, however, if a well-drafted buy-sell agreement is executed. As with the sole proprietorship, partnership liability is not limited to business assets, so the partners' individual assets can be at risk. To prevent misunderstandings and spell out the rights of individual partners, a detailed partnership agreement should be prepared at the beginning. Additional partnership factors are estate planning difficulties, the technical tax laws regarding contributions and distributions of property, and the limitation of tax losses to a partner's share of contributed property and liabilities.

S Corporation

An S corporation's tax requirements are similar to those of a partnership, although there are certain major differences (e.g., basis for loss). Except under unusual circumstances, the S corporation is not taxed as a corporation. Accordingly, income, deductions, gains, credits, and losses are reported directly by the shareholders on their personal tax returns. The S corporation form can be used only where there are *less* than 36 shareholders and one class of stock. The S corporation retains the limited liability feature of a regular corporation, so shareholders' personal assets are generally not at risk.

Corporation

Each state has certain requirements for forming a corporation. After formation, there are further requirements for operation that must be followed to maintain corporate existence. The corporation is taxed as an entity, using a corporate rate structure. The current (1985) maximum rate is 46 percent on taxable income in excess of $100,000. A corporation is a "double tax" entity. Its income is first taxed at the corporate level and then a second time when it is distributed to its shareholders. Other factors of consideration when contemplating corporate formation include possible additional taxation on any accumulated, undistributed corporate income and the costs of administering the many legal and accounting requirements.

When to Use What Entity

Nontax issues aside, each business form will have certain tax advantages and disadvantages in relation to the stage of development of your company or of a segment of your company which you may wish to spinoff for tax advantage or other purposes.

1. The start-up phase of a business generally requires capital and produces tax losses. These tax losses can often be best utilized if they are passed directly to the investors or owners who provided the initial funding for the business and used to offset tax liability on their personal tax returns.

Both partnerships and S corporations are "pass-through" entities which permit investors to utilize the tax losses on their individual tax returns. Losses may be limited, however, to the amount of the investor's contribution, plus undistributed earnings and, in the case of a partnership, allocable portions of debt. Losses of an S corporation are limited to the shareholders' capital contribution, plus undistributed earnings and the S corporation's indebtedness to the shareholder. If losses go unutilized because an investor has insufficient basis in the entity, they may be carried forward and utilized in years when the investor's basis in the entity increases (either through additional capital contributions, loans, or an increase due to profit in excess of distribution to the investor). A drawback posed by both partnerships and S corporations is that these forms may restrict certain ways of raising additional amounts of capital (e.g., the issuing of stock to additional investors is limited by the maximum number (35) of investors allowed in an S corporation, and there may be little market for partnership investors due to potential liabilities).

2.   The growth phase of a business is associated with expansion and the need for more capital. The business will most likely be producing taxable income if it has reached this stage. In this period, the regular corporate form usually meets the objectives of investor/owners. A corporation can accumulate earnings to finance growth without tax penalties. With this corporate form, the owners can also issue additional shares for further financing. These shares may also be issued to provide compensation to the management group.

3.   Once past the growth stage, a corporation generating consistent taxable income and cash flow should consider adopting S corporation status. This, of course, depends on whether it meets the qualifications (e.g., no more than 35 *individual* shareholders). Higher profits make double taxation a more critical problem if owners desire regular dividend distributions. The S corporation eliminates the double tax problem since earnings are taxed only once, at the shareholder level.

In summary, it should be remembered that it is possible to change the form of the entity as the business matures. A sole proprietorship could be incorporated or changed into a partnership. A partnership could be incorporated. Since tax rules covering the conversion of entities can be complex and restrictive, consultation with a tax advisor is recommended whenever a change is being contemplated.

SELECTION OF ACCOUNTING PERIOD AND METHOD

The determination of taxable income depends upon the taxpayer's selection of what accounting methods to use, as well as which accounting period. By a close examination of each, a taxpayer can maximize the deferral of tax payments.

Accounting Period

For tax purposes, the annual accounting period is the annual period regularly used by the taxpayer to compute income in keeping its books. If this is a calendar year or fiscal year, it will become the taxpayer's taxable year. If any of the following three conditions are satisfied, the taxpayer's taxable year will be a calendar year:

1. The taxpayer keeps no books.
2. The taxpayer does not have an annual accounting period.
3. The taxpayer's annual accounting period (other than a calendar year) does not qualify as a fiscal year.

In general, a taxable year may not exceed 12 months. However, a taxpayer may elect to compute his taxable income on the basis of a tax fiscal year which varies from 52 to 53 weeks.

A new taxpayer may adopt a taxable year in its first tax return without securing prior approval from the IRS if the requirements discussed above are satisfied. The taxpayer must adopt this tax year on or before the time prescribed for filing its initial tax return (without regard to extensions).

Partnerships and S corporations are subject to special rules regarding their choice of a tax year. A newly formed partnership may adopt a taxable year which is either the same as all the principal partners, or a calendar year if all the principal partners do not have the same tax year. In most other instances, the partnership must obtain approval for its adoption of a taxable year from the Internal Revenue Service. To secure such approval, the partnership must be able to establish a business purpose for selecting that particular accounting period. In general, a newly formed S corporation must adopt a calendar year unless a business purpose for a fiscal year can be established to the satisfaction of the Internal Revenue Service.

Tax Considerations. Initially, a new corporation may be able to achieve income tax deferral and thereby maximize its cash flow by a judicious choice of its taxable year. For example, if a new corporation begins business on January 1, 1986, and it is anticipated that by August 31, 1986, it will generate taxable income of $100,000 and by December 31, 1986, it will generate taxable income of $200,000 for the 12 months, it may be beneficial to adopt an August 31 year-end. The result of adopting the August 31 year-end is the ability to take immediate advantage of the lower tax rates applicable to taxable income under $100,000 for the initial short taxable year. The payment of tax at the higher rate of 46 percent on the $100,000 earned from September 1, 1986, to December 31, 1986, will be deferred by being reported along with 1987 fiscal income in the tax year ending August 31, 1987.

If a business has a natural end of business year, for example immediately after a peak sales period, this natural year-end should usually be adopted at some point as the taxable year-end, for ease of accounting and record keeping. Frequently, a company will select a year-end which minimizes tax payments initially and later switch to a natural business year when the company is more mature.

Changing Accounting Periods. Once you have adopted a taxable year, with few exceptions it cannot be changed without prior approval of the IRS unless permitted by tax statute or tax regulations. To secure approval, a taxpayer must file Form 1128 with the Commissioner of Internal Revenue, Washington, D.C., on or before the 15th day of the second calendar month following the close of the short period caused by the change in year-end.

Approval will generally not be granted unless you and the IRS agree to the terms, conditions, and adjustments under which the change will be effected. Approval will usually be granted where you establish a substantial business purpose for making the change. A change to the natural business year of your company, for example, will usually be accepted as a substantial business purpose for making the change if such natural business year is established.

It is possible for a corporation to qualify for an automatic taxable year change* if the following conditions are satisfied.

---

* There are also special rules which apply to S corporations and partnerships for changing their taxable years.

- Your company cannot have changed its accounting period in the ten years prior to the beginning of the short period that will result from this change.
- There is no net operating loss in such short period.
- If annualized, the taxable income for the short period will be at least 80 percent of the corporation's taxable income for the previous year.
- Any special tax status of your company must be kept for the short year and the tax year immediately preceding the short year.
- Your company does not elect S corporation status for the tax year following the short period.

Accounting Method

The accounting method selected can significantly affect the tax liability of your company. The election of an accounting method occurs with the first filing of your tax return. Thus, your initial return takes on great importance.

In general, you may use one of the following overall methods:

1. The cash receipts and disbursements method;
2. the accrual method; or
3. a hybrid method.

Cash Receipts and Disbursements Method.   The cash method is used by most individuals and many businesses primarily due to its simplicity and flexibility. It also can help you defer recognition of taxable income by accelerating expense payments or deferring collections at year-end. In general, under this method, items which constitute income are recognized only when actually received by you. Expenditures are deducted for the tax year in which actually paid. As you can see, this permits great flexibility in monitoring your taxable income.

However, if an expenditure results in the creation of an asset which has a useful life that extends substantially beyond the close of the tax year, such expenditures must be capitalized and then depreciated over their useful life. If inventories are material to the business, a taxpayer must use the accrual method to measure sales and cost of goods sold.

Accrual Method.   Under the accrual method of accounting, income is included in gross income when it is earned, whether or not the cash has actually been received. Income is considered to be earned when all the events have occurred which fix the right to receive such income and the amount of such income can be determined with reasonable accuracy.

Accrual basis taxpayers may deduct an expense in the year the liability becomes fixed and the amount can be reasonably determined. In addition, economic performance must have occurred for an expense to be deductible. The point at which economic performance occurs depends upon the underlying transaction:

1. For liabilities arising from receipt or use of property and services—when the property or service is received or used.

2. For liabilities requiring the taxpayer to provide property or services—when the taxpayer performs the service or provides the property

3. For liabilities requiring a payment to another person resulting under a worker's compensation act or arising out of any tort— as the payments are made to the person

An exception to the economic performance rule is provided, for certain recurring items in which economic performance occurs within eight and one-half months following the end of the taxable year.

Hybrid Method.   A hybrid method of accounting involves the use of elements of both the cash and accrual method. This method can be used if the method clearly reflects income and is consistently used. An example of a hybrid method is where the taxpayer uses the accrual method to report sales and cost of goods sold and uses the cash basis to report other items of income and expense. A small retailer may choose to use this method.

Deferring Taxes.   It is possible to defer taxes and thereby maximize cash flow by choosing the appropriate method of accounting. The *cash method* of accounting offers the advantage of being able to time receipts and expenditures. For example, a cash-basis taxpayer can control the inclusion of income by accelerating or slowing up its collections from customers or can control deductions to some extent by accelerating or deferring payments for such items as repairs, supplies, or taxes.

The *accrual method* of accounting provides less control over income recognition and deductions. Income is generally recognized when earned, which is usually before receipt of payment. Deductions may be permitted before payments are made, but this has been modified to some extent by the economic performance requirement. An accrual-basis taxpayer may be able to defer income by reducing shipping and invoicing near year-end. Likewise, deductions could be accelerated by requesting the delivery and billing of supplies or repairs before the end of the year. It may be preferable for a business, which is required to use the accrual method for sales and its cost of sales, to use a hybrid method and report its other income and expense items on the cash basis.

Changing Accounting Method. In general, you officially choose your overall method of accounting by the method used on your first income tax return. Thereafter, you must use the same method unless permission is obtained from the IRS to change. A taxpayer is allowed to use different methods of accounting for each trade or business. However, to be considered separate and distinct, a complete and separate set of books and records must be kept for each trade or business.

To obtain permission to change your method of accounting, an application for permission must be filed on Form 3115 within the first 180 days of the tax year in which it is desired to make the change. A request for a change will usually be approved if the taxpayer agrees to make certain adjustments to income, beginning with the year of change, over a one- to ten-year period. These adjustments are required to prevent items of income and expense from being duplicated or omitted as a result of the change in accounting method.

TAX ACCOUNTING FOR INVENTORIES

Taxpayers are required to maintain inventory records in order to clearly reflect income. Tax accounting for inventories* involves the

---

* Inventories must include all finished goods, goods in process, and raw materials and supplies which will become part of the product or will be offered for sale.

method of inventorying goods (quantities) and the method of inventory costing. The value of an inventory is determined by these two methods. Since inventories significantly affect the amount of taxable income, there exists an enormous tax savings potential by inventory planning.

Valuation of Inventory

Inventory may be valued at either (1) cost, or (2) the lower of cost versus market value. The cost of merchandise purchased during the year is usually the invoice price less trade or other discounts, plus freight and other handling charges. The cost of goods produced or manufactured during the year usually includes:

1.   Cost of raw materials and supplies used;
2.   cost of direct labor; and
3.   indirect production costs for the item.

Most taxpayers (except those on LIFO, discussed below) will adopt the lower of cost versus market method of valuation. Under this method, each item in the inventory is valued at both cost and market value, and the value at which it is included in inventory is the lower of the two calculations for that item. This method allows for the tax deduction of an *unrealized* loss (when market value of inventory is lower than cost, the difference is deductible). As a result, this will effectively defer taxes until the market value is higher than your cost, at which time you lose the deduction, thus increasing taxable income and, therefore, your taxes.

Determining Inventory/Cost-Flow

There are four available methods for determining inventory that a taxpayer may use.

1.   Specific identification
2.   FIFO
3.   Average costing
4.   LIFO

In the specific identification method, a cost-flow assumption is not used. Instead, each unit is priced at its cost. This method is generally used by jewelry retailers or custom equipment manufacturers.

Under the FIFO (first in, first out) method, the cost-flow assumption used is that the first goods purchased or produced are the first goods sold. This method will generally be used by a taxpayer that cannot identify its goods with specific invoices and wants to be able to use the lower of cost versus market method of valuation.

Average costing is a method in which inventory is determined by the use of a weighted average of beginning inventory and purchases during the year. This method is generally used by a taxpayer whose inventory consists of commodities which are intermixed and stored for long periods of time prior to sale.

LIFO (last in, first out) is a method of sequencing the flow of *costs* through the inventory so that the most recent costs incurred to acquire or produce inventory is charged to the cost of sales. Consequently, current costs are matched against current revenue. This is particularly effective in reducing the impact of inflation upon profits. As a result, the single most important reason for taxpayers to adopt LIFO is the tax savings and increased cash flow which result.

Theoretically, the use of the LIFO method results only in deferring taxes (see next paragraph) which can be considered as an interest-free loan from the government. The LIFO reserve on the balance sheet, after applying the taxpayer's effective tax rate, provides an estimate of the magnitude of this interest-free loan. As long as inflation continues and a taxpayer's LIFO inventories remain relatively constant or increase in size, the tax deferral tends to become permanent.

There are several factors you should consider in determining the potential tax savings to be generated by LIFO. For example, if anticipated future purchase or production costs of inventory are expected to decline, LIFO would not be beneficial. If inventory levels are expected to decline significantly in the near future, the tax deferral will be decreased or eliminated. LIFO could increase your taxes in future years if the market value of your company's inventory were below its LIFO cost, since a taxpayer on LIFO is not allowed to write down its inventories to market when market is lower than cost. Also, LIFO may cause a company's taxes to increase initially, since the opening inventory in the year LIFO is adopted must be at cost. If the previous year's closing inventory was stated at a lower amount because of a write-down to market, or because of inventory reserves, these write-downs must be restored to income over a three-year period that begins in the tax year when LIFO is elected. Other considerations are the taxpayer's effective tax rate and the interest rate.

There are financial and administrative aspects to adopting LIFO that you must consider. Once the LIFO election is made for tax purposes, the LIFO method must also be used for credit purposes and for the purpose of reports to shareholders, partners, proprietors, and beneficiaries. A corporate taxpayer should consider what impact LIFO will have on its creditors, financing agreements, profit-sharing plans, and shareholder agreements. In addition, there generally is an added cost burden in calculating the LIFO costs. The LIFO election is made by filing Form 970 with your tax return for the year of adoption of LIFO. Once a company adopts its inventory methods, it may not change without the consent of the IRS.

MINIMIZING TAX LIABILITIES

There are various other elections, in addition to inventory methods, a company can make which will minimize its tax liability (see below). It is important that a taxpayer get help from qualified tax personnel, since, in some cases, if these elections are not properly made, the benefits may be *permanently* lost. In many cases, these elections may produce results different from those results obtained for financial accounting purposes. These differences between tax accounting and financial accounting are usually represented by the lower—but only deferred—tax liability on a taxpayer's balance sheet. A reminder: any deferred tax liability is in essence an interest-free loan from the U.S. government.

Long-Term Contracts

A company that derives income from long-term contracts may elect to report income under the percentage-of-completion method, or the completed-contract method. For this purpose, a long-term contract is a building, installation, construction, or manufacturing contract which is not completed within the tax year in which it was entered into.

Under the completed-contract method, the taxpayer reports the income and deductions allocable to a specific contract in the tax year in which the contract is completed. A taxpayer may not delay the completion of a contract for tax purposes. Under the percentage-of-completion method, a taxpayer includes in income during a tax year a portion of the contract price based upon the percentage of the contract completed during the year. Expenditures made during the tax year which are allocable to the contract are deducted.

The completed-contract method will generally provide more tax deferral than the percentage-of-completion method and will avoid disputes with the IRS regarding the yearly estimates of the percentage of completion. However, this method can result in a bunching of income.

Installment Sales

The installment method of reporting certain sales income provides for tax deferral, can minimize the bunching of income, and may minimize alternative minimum tax with respect to a sale of a capital asset. The installment method is applied differently to those who sell personal property as their business than it is to taxpayers who sell real estate or a casual sale of personal property. These are the only three types of sales that qualify for installment reporting.

Any taxpayer who sells, as their business, inventoriable personal property, requiring two or more payments, may choose to use the installment method. Under this method, only a percentage of each payment received is taken into income. The percentage applied is the ratio of your gross profit from the sale to the total sale price. Once the installment method of reporting sales income is chosen, all transactions are included. Permission is not required from the IRS to change from the accrual or any other accounting method to the installment method.

For other taxpayers, it is assumed you will use the installment method of reporting income with respect to sales of real estate and casual sales of personal property. At least one payment must be received *after* the close of the taxable year in which the disposition occurs for the sale to qualify for the installment method. The amount of the gain reported on a sale for each period is computed by applying the ratio of total gain to the contract price to the payments received for the tax reporting period. A taxpayer can elect not to use the installment method by reporting on a timely filed tax return the entire gain for the tax year in which the sale is made. You may desire to "elect out of" (not use) the installment method if it is anticipated that your tax bracket will be higher in the years the payments are to be collected than in the year of sale.

Bad Debts

There are two methods available for determining bad-debt deductions— the specific charge-off method and the reserve method. Under the specific charge-off method, the taxpayer can claim a bad-debt deduction when a specific business debt becomes either partially or wholly worthless. To be entitled to a deduction for a debt that is partially worthless, the taxpayer must be able to satisfy the IRS that the debt is partially worthless and the amount of the worthlessness.

The other method a taxpayer may choose is the reserve method (the establishment of a bad-debt reserve account). Under this method you take a tax deduction for debts that are *expected* to become bad, in an amount based upon a reasonable addition to the reserve. The reasonable addition to the reserve is usually determined by a formula based upon the bad-debt history of your business.

A taxpayer chooses its bad-debt deduction method in its first return in which it is entitled to such a deduction. The method is subject to IRS approval upon examination of the tax return. The method chosen must be used in all future years unless permission is obtained from the IRS to change. Most taxpayers prefer to use the reserve method, since it generally accelerates the timing of a bad-debt deduction and will usually generate the largest deductions in the higher income years when deductions are needed the most.

Research and Development

Research and development expenditures are the costs of developing an experimental or pilot model, a plant process, a product, a formula, an invention, or similar property improvements. R&D expenditures do not include the costs for ordinary testing or inspection of materials or products for quality control, efficiency surveys, management studies, consumer surveys, advertising, or promotions. A taxpayer has three alternatives for the treatment of R&D expenses. The expenditures may be expensed in the year paid or incurred, or they may be deferred and amortized. If neither of these two methods is used, the expenditures must be capitalized and a deduction will not be allowed until the project is abandoned or deemed worthless. It is generally preferable to expense the R&D expenditures. At this time, but subject to repeal, there are also tax *credits* for increased R&D expenses, equal to 25 percent of the excess of the qualified research expenses for the taxable year over the average of these expenses of the previous three years (base period research expenses). The credit applies to qualifying amounts paid or incurred after June 30, 1981 and before January 1, 1986. Special transitional rules on the base period apply to the first two years of credit. To compute the credit, base period research expenses cannot be less than 50 percent of the expenses for the current year. The term "qualified research" refers to research and development conducted in the experimental or laboratory sense. Any unused credit may be carried back three years (as if the credit were in effect for earlier years) and forward 15 years.

Start-Ups Costs

A taxpayer that pays or incurs start-up or investigatory expenditures for a trade or business that subsequently begins operations can elect to amortize the expenditures over a period of not less than 60 months commencing with the month the business begins. Business start-up costs are those incurred after the decision to start the business but before operations begin. Investigatory costs are those expenditures incurred in reviewing a potential business in order to reach a decision to acquire or enter the business. To amortize these expenditures, a statement must be attached to a timely filed tax return. The statement must contain a description of the expenditure, the amounts, the dates incurred, the month the business began or was acquired, and the number of months in the amortization period.

For taxable years beginning after June 30, 1984, all start-up costs must be capitalized and, at the taxpayer's election, be amortized over a period of not less than 60 months. If the election to amortize is *not* made, the expenditures are capitalized and a deduction is not allowed for such expenditures until the business is sold or liquidated. Expenses incurred in the expansion of an existing business could generally be deducted or capitalized and amortized if the taxpayer so elected.

Depreciation and Investment Tax Credit

A taxpayer has been provided with many alternatives regarding depreciation and investment tax credit (ITC).

A taxpayer may elect to expense (rather than capitalize and subsequently depreciate) a limited amount (up to $5,000) of *eligible* tangible property in the year of acquisition. No ITC will be allowed on the property that the taxpayer elects to expense.

With respect to ITC, a taxpayer has two alternatives. The taxpayer may take the full ITC and reduce the asset's depreciable basis by 50 percent of the ITC taken or reduce the ITC percentage taken and not reduce the depreciable basis of the asset.

For a taxpayer to determine which alternative will save the most in taxes, you must consider your marginal tax rate, required rate of return, and when you will actually be able to use the deductions and credits. Accounting costs must also be considered.

Real property is generally not eligible for the credit. However, at this time, but subject to repeal, the investment tax credit is allowable for expenditures to rehabilitate qualified buildings to be used for nonresidential purposes and certified historic structures. The credit is equal to 15 percent of qualified expenditures for buildings 30 to 39 years old, 20 percent for buildings 40 years or older, and 25 percent for certified historic structures.

There must be substantial rehabilitation, which means that the expenditures for the current and preceding year must exceed the greater of the adjusted basis of the property or $5,000 (a five-year period is provided for certain phased rehabilitation). At least 75 percent of the existing external walls must be retained, with certain additional requirements applying if they are not retained as external walls. Also, once the building is placed in service, an accelerated method of depreciation may not be used.

OPTIMIZING OF ESTIMATED TAX PAYMENTS

The strategy in making any kind of estimated tax payment is to pay the minimum required amount, on the required due date, and no more. Because the amount paid is an estimate of the tax liability, keeping the payment to the absolute minimum requires maintaining accurate accounting records and knowing the filing requirements and exceptions thereto.

Estimated Tax Requirements

Form 1120-W is available to assist in estimating corporate tax and determining deposits. Payments are due on the 15th day of the 4th, 6th, 9th, and 12th months of the corporation's taxable year.

Taxpayers may be penalized for not paying enough tax for an *installment period*. The amount of underpayment subject to the penalty is the excess of (1) 90 percent of the tax shown on the return for the year (after certain adjustments), allocated evenly to the quarterly periods, over (2) the amount paid for the quarterly period. If (2) is greater than (1), the excess is applied first against prior underpayments to limit the penalty incurred. Any remaining overpayment can be applied against subsequent underpayments. The penalty is assessed from the installment due date to the earlier of: the date penalty is paid by subsequent overpayments, or the original due date of the return. The rate is determined by reference to the prime rate.

A corporation that has made estimated tax payments that *exceed* 80 percent of the tax, but not 90 percent, will be assessed an underpayment penalty of 75 percent of the regular penalty.

However, if your taxable income is less than $1 million, generally no penalty is imposed for a quarter if the cumulative amount paid by the installment date equals or exceeds the lesser of:

1. The prior year's tax, allocated evenly and cumulatively to the quarterly periods, if the prior year comprised 12 months and a tax liability was shown on the filed return.
2. A tax, allocated evenly and cumulatively to the quarterly periods, computed on total prior year's income (annualized for a short taxable year) using current rates and exemptions, but otherwise using the prior year's tax law.
3. 90 percent of the tax, allocated evenly and cumulatively to the quarterly periods, computed on annualized income from the beginning of the current year to various dates preceding the installment due date.

An annualization penalty exception is also available. The penalty exception is intended to benefit those corporations that have wide seasonal variations in income. The factor used to annualize the income of the months prior to the installment date is the ratio of the average preceding three years' income to the average income of the corresponding months in those years.

The tax computed under each exception includes all taxes except the minimum tax, less any allowable credits.

Special rules apply to "large corporations"—those corporations or controlled groups having $1 million or more of taxable income in any of the three preceding taxable years. Large corporations are not able to use exceptions (1) or (2). This means a large corporation will have to pay 90 percent of the actual tax due, pay 90 percent of the tax on annualized taxable income, or pay the penalty.

Quick Refund of Overpaid Estimated Tax

If a corporation overpays its total tax liability by making estimated tax payments higher than necessary, it may make an application on Form 4466 for a quick refund. The refund request must be made within 2.5 months after the close of the corporation's taxable year, and before the date on which the corporation files its tax return. However, the overpayment must be equal to at least 10 percent of its expected tax liability and, in any case, not less than $500.

Refund Claims

A refund which is related to a carry-back of benefits (such as a net operating loss or carry-backs of certain tax credits) may be claimed using Form 1139. The Form 1139 generally must be acted upon within 90 days by the IRS. The corporation must file the Form 1139 within one year after the year in which the loss or credit arises because, after this time period, only an amended return Form 1120X may be filed to claim the refund. The IRS has no requirement to respond within a certain time on an 1120X, so the 1139 should be filed whenever possible.

If you incur a net operating loss in the current year, but reported taxable income in the preceding year, the taxes payable on the income of the preceding year may be postponed by filing a Form 1138. The

Form 1138 allows you to extend the time for payment of taxes due to the expectation of a net operating loss which can be carried back. Although you will be charged interest on the postponed tax payment, the payment of taxes followed by a refund, due to a net operating loss, is avoided.

USE OF FOREIGN ENTITIES

When U.S. taxpayers decide to conduct business outside the United States, tax planning is essential. The form in which the foreign business is structured will influence its tax consequences. Likewise, the tax rules of the foreign countries in which the business will operate are a critical consideration.

Foreign operations can operate as a branch of a U.S. company, as a partnership, as a foreign corporate subsidiary, or by using a special entity called a Foreign Sales Corporation. The entity chosen can affect the foreign taxes you pay as well as the U.S. taxes on your foreign operations.

The issues involved are quite complex, both from the U.S. federal tax standpoint and the numerous foreign tax jurisdictions. Generally speaking, using a branch of a U.S. company in a foreign country can be beneficial if losses are incurred, but may be detrimental when the branch becomes profitable. The same is generally true of partnerships, although there are exceptions in both cases.

The use of a foreign corporation to conduct your business abroad will usually maximize your tax deferral. While a thorough discussion of the many tax ramifications of doing business in foreign countries is beyond the scope of this book, there follows an explanation of some of the rules and regulations for a specific type of foreign company, the Foreign Sales Corporation.

Foreign Sales Corporation

For several years the U.S. government has had tax laws designed to encourage exporting and doing business abroad. The continuing U.S. trade deficit is responsible for this favorable legislation. Until 1984 the legislation provided for a special type of company called a Domestic International Sales Corporation (DISC). There were substantial tax benefits to selling abroad through a DISC. As with most favorable tax legislation, some began to view what once was considered an incentive to stimulate exports as a tax loophole. Therefore, the Deficit Reduction Act of 1984 generally replaced DISCs with a new type of export vehicle called a Foreign Sales Corporation (FSC).

Qualification Requirements of a FSC.   To qualify as a FSC, a corporation must satisfy the following requirements.

1.   A FSC must be organized under the laws of a foreign country or a U.S. possession. The foreign country must be a party to an exchange of information agreement with the U.S., or be an income tax treaty partner which the Treasury certifies as having an acceptable exchange of information program under the treaty.

2.   A FSC may not have more than 25 shareholders.

3.   A FSC may not have preferred stock.

4.   A FSC must maintain an office outside the U.S. and must maintain a set of permanent books and records at such office.

5.   A FSC must have one nonresident director.

6.   A FSC may not be a member of a controlled group of which a DISC is a member.

7.   The corporation must elect to be a FSC.

8.   A FSC's tax year must conform to the taxable year of its majority shareholder.

FSC Tax Exemption Rules.   A FSC will be exempt from U.S. tax on any portion of its income which is attributable to foreign trading gross receipts. Foreign trading gross receipts include gross receipts from the following:

1.   Sale or lease of export property for use outside the United States;

2.   services related or subsidiary to the sale or lease of export property;

3.   certain engineering or architectural services for projects located outside the United States; and

4. export management services provided for an unrelated DISC or FSC if at least 50 percent of the FSC's gross receipts are from #1 and #2 above.

Export property is property manufactured, produced, grown, or extracted in the United States by a non-FSC and is held primarily for sale, lease, or rental in the ordinary course of business by or to a FSC for direct use, consumption, or disposition outside the United States. Oil and gas will not quality for FSC benefits.

In order for an export sale to qualify as a foreign trading gross receipt, the FSC must satisfy the "foreign managed" and "foreign economic process" requirements.

The FSC will meet the foreign-managed test if:

1. All directors' and all shareholders' meetings are held outside the United States;
2. the principal bank account is maintained outside the United States; and
3. all dividends, legal and accounting fees, and officers' and directors' salaries are disbursed from foreign bank accounts.

To satisfy the foreign economic process requirement, certain export selling activities must be conducted outside the United States. Specifically, the FSC or an agent of the FSC must participate in the solicitation, negotiation, or the making of the export transaction contract outside the United States.

Finally, and equally important, the FSC or its agent must incur outside the United States either 50 percent of the direct costs of all or 85 percent of the direct costs of each of two of the five following types of activities: advertising, processing of customer orders, transportation, billing and collections, and the assumption of credit risk.

Transfer pricing rules are used to allocate income between a FSC and its related supplier. Income may be allocated to the FSC based upon arm's-length pricing. Alternatively, the taxpayer may use the greater of one of the following two administrative pricing rules for allocating income to the FSC:

1. 23 percent of the combined taxable income earned by the FSC and its related supplier attributable to foreign trade gross receipts, or

2. 1.83 percent of the FSC's foreign trading gross receipts, but not more than 46 percent of combined taxable income.

The amount of the FSC exemption depends on the transfer pricing rules used to allocate income between the FSC and its related supplier. If the shareholder is a U.S. corporation and the arm's-length pricing method is used, or if the supplier is unrelated, the exemption will be 32 percent of the FSC's foreign trade income. The exemption under the administrative pricing rules is 15/23 of the amount determined under the administrative pricing rule used.

There is no exemption allowed for nonexport profits, investment income (such as dividends, interest, royalties, rents, and certain other passive income) or carrying charges (unstated interest and amounts in excess of the sale price for an immediate cash sale).

FSC Taxation.   A FSC will file a U.S. income tax return and be liable for U.S. tax on its nonexempt income under the normal U.S. tax rules.

Shareholder Taxation.   A FSC dividend received by a nonresident alien or foreign corporation will be subject to U.S. tax. A domestic corporation will generally be allowed a 100 percent dividends-received deduction for amounts distributed from a FSC out of earnings and profits attributable to export income.

Small Exporters.   Because of the problems inherent in the foreign activities requirement of the FSC, the Deficit Reduction Act of 1984 provided two alternatives for small export business: (1) the small FSC, and (2) the interest charge DISC.

1.   *The Small FSC.*   A small FSC is a foreign corporation that meets the requirements to be a FSC. However, a small FSC is not required to satisfy the foreign management and foreign economic process tests. The FSC benefits are available for export income up to $5 million of export gross receipts. A FSC may not elect to be a small FSC if it is a member of a controlled group that includes a FSC or a DISC.

2. The Interest Charge DISC. The interest charge DISC is a DISC which, in general, has a 94 percent deferral of DISC taxable income. The shareholder of the interest charge DISC must, however, pay interest yearly on the tax deferred post-1984 accumulated DISC income. The interest will be pegged to the Treasury bill rate and will be deductible by the shareholder. The interest charge DISC deferral is limited to the income on $10 million of gross receipts. Taxable income attributable to gross receipts in excess of $10 million will be taxed currently to the shareholder. For small exporters who find the foreign economic activity requirements too burdensome, a small FSC or interest charge DISC may be more desirable.

Tax Havens

One of the most important decisions a taxpayer must make in operating its business overseas is the selection of the country or countries in which the business will be conducted. Many taxpayers will set up a base company in a tax haven country. The base company will direct business activities in other countries through foreign subsidiaries, branches, or agents.

A tax haven country will be used because it imposes a low tax or no tax on income earned outside of it. Also, in many cases, there will not be withholding imposed on dividends and interest. This low level of tax allows the base company to use its funds for further business expansion. The U.S. shareholders of a base company will generally pay no tax on its income until the payments are repatriated via dividends, interest, royalties, or upon sale or liquidation of the base company.

It should be pointed out that the deferral of U.S. tax on the foreign corporation's earnings will be limited if the corporation is determined to be a controlled foreign corporation, a foreign personal holding company, or if other penalty provisions in the U.S. tax law are applicable. A technical discussion of controlled foreign corporations or foreign personal holding companies is beyond the scope of this chapter, but be aware that foreign operations need to be carefully structured by experienced professionals.

APPENDIX—OUTLINE FOR A NEW VENTURE BUSINESS PLAN

INTRODUCTION

New business ventures today are particularly attractive to many entrepreneurs. Potential rewards and growth opportunities are often outstanding, and innovators are eager to see their ideas become useful products. Too often, however, the entrepreneur focuses the most attention on the technical or developmental aspects of the product and stops short of some critically important business considerations in starting a new company or launching a new product.

One of the first steps in any new business venture should be the development of a business plan. As professional accountants and advisors, we have provided assistance to many new business ventures, and have found that the planning stage is an essential part of launching a successful enterprise. After a detailed review of numerous business plans, we have developed the outline presented here. This plan is the result of many years of service to entrepreneurs, company managements, and investors.

The plan and accompanying analyses serve several purposes. They:

• Help you determine the feasibility of pursuing the difficult steps necessary to start a new venture
• Tell you the kind of information you will need to present in raising capital from outside investors
• Give you a firm basis for developing a more detailed operating plan

In the following pages you will find a generalized approach to writing a plan for a new business venture. In some situations, only part of this outline may be appropriate for your purposes; in others, the full outline should be used. In either case, however, you should always tailor the plan to your specific situation and objective.

An effective plan should emphasize the strengths of the proposed venture, but it should also anticipate and deal with any potential problems or challenges to be faced. Your consideration of each point in the outline will provide the basis for answering many questions that arise in your relations with potential investors or during the early operational phases of the venture.

THE BUSINESS PLAN

I. EXECUTIVE SUMMARY

This section should not be a mere listing of topics but should emphasize the high points of your proposal, including: (1) the purpose of the plan (e.g., to attract investment by professional venture capitalists), (2) a characterization of the market potential, (3) significant product features, (4) product development milestones, (5) target financial results such as "achieving $1 million in sales in 1987, breaking even in second quarter 1988, and growing to $35 million in sales and $3.5 million in after-tax profits by 1989." The major technical, operational, and financial milestones represent "risk step-down" points. Achieving these milestones lends substantial credibility that the company will succeed. The executive summary should be a succinct overview of the entire new venture business plan.

II. TABLE OF CONTENTS

This section of a business plan should be designed to assist readers in locating specific sections and points in the plan. Excessive detail should be avoided here, however.

III. COMPANY DESCRIPTION

    A. What business are you in?

    B. What are your principal:

        1. Products or services?
        2. Markets?
        3. Applications?

    C. What is your *distinctive competence*? (What are the chief factors that will account for your success?)

    This section should provide potential investors with a specific picture of your objectives and give them good reasons for believing you will succeed. Since all professional investors have excellent alternative opportunities, you must show that your chances for success are better than these alternatives. If you are entering a competitive field (and most entrepreneurs are), this *distinctive competence* description is very important. It is important that your distinctive competence be related to a need. Examples (stated informally) include the following:

    • Our software technology makes it easy for a customer to convert from his existing obsolete system to new hardware. This will meet an important need because conversion has been one of the industry's major problems.

- Due to a technological and manufacturing breakthrough, we will be the lowest cost entry in a market that is very price sensitive.

- We have very strong business relationships with design engineers for customers that order $50 million a year, and our product (or service) solves numerous problems inherent in developing their new product lines.

IV. MARKET ANALYSIS AND MARKETING

A. Industry description and outlook

1. What industry are you in?
2. How big is it now? How big will it be in five years? Ten years?
3. What are its chief characteristics?
4. Who are or will be the major customers? Specifically, are they *Fortune* 500 Industrial or Service companies; companies with $75 million in sales or more, etc.; or are they small proprietorships?
5. What are or will be the major applications (industry, type of operation, etc.) of your product or service?
6. What are the major trends in the industry?

B. Target markets

1. What are the major market *segments* you will penetrate?

Analysis of market segmentation may be one of the most critical parts of the plan.

Major mistakes have been made in this area. Some common ones include:

a. Assuming the size of customers is normally distributed and that the median equals the mean. If the distribution is not normal, 50 percent of the customers may not be above the average. If an "average-sized" customer can afford the product, this may only be 10 percent of the total customer base.
b. In many markets, 20 percent of the customers may represent 80 percent of the demand. Ignoring factors which prohibit penetration of this 20 percent may cripple the entire marketing effort.

    c. Even very successful companies often have surprisingly low market shares. Consequently, market share assumptions should be realistic. Even a realistic market share assumption of 10 percent could really represent 50 percent if careful market definition and segmentation showed that only 20 percent of the assumed market "qualified" as potential customers. For instance, given that any business above the average size was a prime target, this situation could occur if careful analysis showed that only 10 percent, not 50 percent, of customers were above the mean.

    d. Lack of clear definition of the products or services to be sold.

    e. No accurate estimate of the profitability of each product or service.

2. For each major application, what are the following:

    a. Requirements by the customer or regulatory agencies?
    b. Current ways of filling these requirements?
    c. Buying habits of the customer?
    d. Impact on the customer of using your product or service?
       • User economics. (How much will it save them per year? What return on investment will they get?)
       • Other impacts. (Will they have to change their way of doing things? Buy other equipment? Change work habits? Modify organizational structure?)
    e. How will these segments and applications change over the next three to five years?

C. Competition

1. What companies will you compete with (including those like you who are not yet in the market)?
2. How do you compare with these competitor companies?
3. What competition will you meet in each product or service line?
4. How does your product or service compare with others (especially through the eyes of the customer)?
5. What is the market share of each existing competitor?

6. Do you threaten the major strategic objectives or self-image of competition or just financial results (e.g., will competition seek to destroy you at any cost)?

7. Do you interface with important, noncompetitive equipment whose manufacturer might still be reluctant to support your product due to warranty, liability or image considerations?

D. Reaction from specific prospective customers

1. What prospective customers have you talked to?
2. What was their reaction?
3. Have they seen or tested a realistic prototype of the product or service?
4. If so, what was their reaction?

E. Marketing activities

1. What are your plans for:

   a. Marketing strategy ("one-stop shopping," specialization, market share objectives, image)?
   b. Distribution (direct, retail)?
   c. Promotion (advertising, conventions, etc.)?
   d. Pricing (demand pricing or cost-based pricing, volume discount—how will pricing change over time)?
   e. Sales appeals?
   f. Geographical penetration (domestic, Europe, Far East, etc.)?
   g. Field service or product support?
   h. Setting priorities among segments, applications, marketing activities? The limited human resources in a new venture cannot be all things to all people, regardless of the opportunities.

F. Selling activities

1. How will you identify prospective customers? Consider not just the companies, but the relevant decision-makers who can spend money on your product, either discretionary or budgeted funds.

2. How will you decide whom to contact and in what order?
3. What level of selling effort will you have (for example, the number of salespeople)?
4. What efficiency will you have (for example, how many calls per salesperson)?
5. What conversion rates will you be able to obtain (for example, how many calls per demonstration; how many demonstrations per sale)?
6. How long will each of the above activities take in person-days? In elapsed time?
7. What will your initial order size be? What is the likelihood and size of repeat orders?
8. Based on the above assumptions, what is the sales productivity of each salesperson?
9. What is the commission structure for the salespeople? Does it have increasing or decreasing rates for exceeding quota? What will the average salesperson earn per year and how long will he/she have to wait to receive commissions (e.g., sales cycle milestones)?
10. What evidence do you have to back up your answers to the estimates above?

This section on marketing and marketing analysis is often of critical importance. Probably the most common single error is to assume you can validly predict what you can sell by gathering some general numbers on the size of the market, then project a market share for yourself. The argument usually goes like this: "We will be selling a new microcomputer. The total market for these computers is about $100 million a year and growing 10 percent a year. Of this, 25 percent is automatic typewriters. Thus, the portion available to us is $25 million the first year, $27.5 million the second year, $30.3 million the third, $33.3 million the fourth, and $36.6 million the fifth year. We project capturing ½ of 1 percent the first year, or $125,000; and growing to 10 percent of the market, or $3.67 million by the fifth year." Unless this kind of reasoning is backed up with detailed answers to the kinds of questions asked above, it is unconvincing and probably wrong.

V. TECHNOLOGY: RESEARCH AND DEVELOPMENT

A. What is the essence and status of your current technology (idea, prototype, small production runs, etc.)?

B. What is your patent or copyright position?

   1. How much is patented or copyrighted?
   2. How much can be patented or copyrighted?
   3. How comprehensive and how effective will the patents or copyrights be?
   4. Which companies have technology that is superior or equal to yours?
   5. Are there additional means of protecting your technology (such as secrecy or speed in putting out the product or service)?

C. What new technologies or scientific approaches exist that may become practical in the next five years? What factors limit their development or acceptance?

   One common pitfall here is to compare the technology you are working on now and will have on the market in a year or two with that which competition has now. Instead, you should compare what you will have by the time you are in the market with what others will have then.

D. What are the key research and development activities and related milestones and risks?

E. What new products, hopefully derived directly from first generation products, do you plan to develop to meet changing market needs?

F. Are there any regulatory or approval requirements (U/L, EPA, FCC, etc.)?

VI. MANUFACTURING/OPERATIONS

A. How will you accomplish production or conduct service operations?

   1. How much will you do internally and by what methods?

    2. How much through subcontracts, both initially and after one or two years?

B. What production or operating advantages do you have?

C. What is your present capacity for level of production or operations? How can this be expanded?

D. What are the critical parts? Are any of these parts "single- or sole-sourced" or do you have backup vendors? What are the lead times of these parts?

E. What are the standard costs for production at different volume levels?

VII. MANAGEMENT AND OWNERSHIP

A. Who are your key managers?

B. How do you intend to attract and compensate key people (i.e., stock, incentive bonus, etc.)?

C. What are their skills and, particularly, their experience, and how does this relate to the success requirement of your venture?

You should think carefully about these issues for two reasons. First, it is *extremely* important to differentiate between ownership and management roles, even when assumed by the same individuals. Second, it may be better to defer hiring an individual rather than have the job outgrow him/her in a year.

D. What has their track record been, and how does this relate to your requirements?

The most common problem here is failing to relate your team's capability to the success requirement of your business. As an example, the chief engineer might be described as having a fine M.I.T. education and important-sounding job titles with sophisticated companies, but with no mention of work he has actually done. This information does not directly substantiate that he really could design the complex product necessary for the company.

E. What staff additions do you plan, when, and with what required qualifications?

For example, you may not now have a candidate for the Vice President of Finance position—or even need one immediately—but it is important to state your plans to support this function when required.

F. Do any managers have outstanding "noncompete" agreements with previous employers? If so, get opinion of counsel regarding the validity or applicability of these agreements.

G. Who is on your board of directors?

It is important to think ahead about the role of your board when you become operational. It may be inappropriate to have certain early investors serve on the board if their potential for nonmonetary contributions is not substantial.

H. Who are your current stockholders, and how many shares does each own? (Include comments about options and related prices.)

While it may be necessary or expedient to permit investment by many small and/or unsophisticated investors, their presence may cause concern among professional investors or headaches or diversion of management effort during the evolution of the company.

I. What is the amount of stock currently authorized and issued?

VIII. ORGANIZATION AND PERSONNEL

A. How many people will you need by type?
B. What compensation method will be used by type (salary, stock, profit-sharing, etc.)?
C. Show sample organizational structures for formative years and thereafter.

IX. FUNDS REQUIRED AND THEIR USES

A. How much money do you require now?
B. How much will you require over the next five years, and when will it be required?
C. How will these funds be used?

D. What portion of the funds are expected to be raised from debt rather than equity? Use two debt assumptions for your capital requirements after the break-even point.
E. What terms?

If this is a first request for outside investment, you should prepare a scenario for the attraction of required capital, approximate price per share and timing, and show the dilution or percentage ownership of the initial and subsequent investors.

F. When do you plan to "go public"?

A major concern of professional investors is both the future value and liquidity of their investments. A company that is not profitable enough or large enough (e.g., less than $20+ million sales) within five years might not be of interest. This is also true if management indicates an unwillingness to go public for fear of losing control.

X. FINANCIAL DATA

A. Present historical financial statements and projections for the next three to five years, including:

1. Profit-and-loss or income statements by month or quarter, at least until break-even, and then annually to cover a five-year period. (It is common to present monthly statements for the first year, quarterly statements for the next two years, and then for two or three annual periods). This analysis should show the results based on two different debt vs. equity assumptions with resultant interest expense. The break-even point should be clearly identified. Show market value of the company based on a price/earnings ratio of similar companies.
2. Balance sheets at the end of each year.
3. Cash budgets.
4. Capital budgets for equipment, etc.
5. Manufacturing/shipping plan.

B. What key assumptions have been made in your pro formas, and how good are these assumptions?

This section is especially important. These assumptions should most often reflect industry performance and, if not, specific justification should be given. Key considerations are whether these are "best-case" numbers, "worst-case," or something in the middle, which is preferred. The data should be based on several different assumptions to determine the reasonableness of the information. It is important to note, however, that too much financial information can be worse than too little. Each company must project those points it believes are most appropriate. An aid to listing major assumptions has been included in Exhibit 1.

XI. ADMINISTRATIVE CONSIDERATIONS

A. Careful thought should be given to naming the new business. The name, especially for a new business, should reflect the major thrust of the business or be distinctive in some way, such as the APPLE computer. In addition, possible trademarks and service marks should be identified. For example, TANDEM, a company that manufactures "fail-safe" computers through use of linked processors, has the following distinctive, descriptive trademarks:

- "NON-STOP" GUARDIAN operating system
- ENTRY screen for matter
- ENVOY data communications manager
- EXPAND networking capability
- XRAY system performance monitor

A subsequent search by an attorney to see if the name or trademarks you have chosen are available for use, should be undertaken early and, if available, they should be reserved.

B. The plan should be printed and bound.
C. Copies of the plan should be controlled and distribution recorded.
D. Private placement disclaimers should be included, if the plan is being used to raise capital, especially through the issuing

EXHIBIT 1.   SOURCES OF PLANNING PARAMETERS FOR A NEW BUSINESS VENTURE

Business ratios must be used cautiously. Every company's financial ratios and performance will be different. Industry, size, growth rate, product line, degree of labor intensiveness, degree of vertical integration, distribution methods, and other factors will influence the financial structure and performance of the venture.

Information on industry averages for virtually all forms of businesses is readily available at major public libraries and from industry trade associations. A few of these sources are listed below.

Sources of Information
- *Almanac of Business and Industrial Financial Ratios*; Troy, Leo, Ph.D.; Englewood Cliffs, N.J.; Prentice-Hall, Inc.

- *Annual Statement Studies*; Robert Morris Associates; Philadelphia, Pa.; RMA.

- *Industry Norms and Key Business Ratios*; Dun and Bradstreet; New York, N.Y.; D&B.

Key Ratios
In addition to comparing your projections to industry norms, for balance sheet and income statement items certain key ratios should be calculated and compared. A few of these ratios and calculation formulas are included below.

Current ratio:	$\dfrac{\text{Current assets}}{\text{Current liabilities}}$
Days sales in receivables:	$\dfrac{\text{Receivables}}{\text{Annual sales}} \times 365$
Inventory turnover:	$\dfrac{\text{Annual cost of sales}}{\text{Average inventory}}$
Debt equity:	$\dfrac{\text{Total liabilities}}{\text{Net worth}}$
Return on equity:	$\dfrac{\text{Net income}}{\text{Net worth}}$

of exempt (unregistered) securities. These disclaimers have been included in Exhibit 2.

XII. APPENDICES OR EXHIBITS (as required)

A. Resumes of key managers.
B. Pictures of the product/prototype.
C. Professional references.
D. Market studies, articles from trade journals.
E. Patents.

EXHIBIT 2.   EXAMPLES OF PRIVATE PLACEMENT DISCLAIMERS

–The information contained in this private placement memorandum is confidential and is intended only for the persons to whom it is transmitted by the company. Any reproduction of this memorandum, in whole or in part, or the divulgence of any of its contents, without the prior written consent of the company, is prohibited.

–The offering of the securities discussed in this private placement memorandum has not been registered with the Securities and Exchange Commission in reliance upon an exemption from registration contained in Section 4(2) and Rule 146 of the Securities Act of 1933, as amended.

–No person has been authorized to give any information or to make any representations other than those contained in this private placement memorandum in connection with the offering hereby, and, if given or made, such other information or representations must not be relied upon as having been authorized by the company.

–This private placement memorandum does not constitute an offer to sell or solicitation of an offer to buy any securities other than the securities offered hereby, nor does it constitute an offer to sell or solicitation of an offer to buy from any person in any state or other jurisdiction in which such an offer would be unlawful.

–Resale of the securities discussed in this private placement memorandum may not be made unless the securities are registered under the Securities Act of 1933, as amended, or unless the resale is exempt from the registration requirements of the Securities Act of 1933, as amended.

–Neither the delivery of this private placement memorandum at any time, nor any sale hereunder, shall under any circumstances create an implication that the information contained herein is correct as of any time subsequent to its date.

–Offers and sales will only be made to persons who have the knowledge and experience to evaluate the merits and risks of the investment and who have the economic means to afford the illiquidity of the securities offered hereby.

–The information set forth herein is believed by the company to be reliable. It must be recognized, however, that predictions and projections as to the company's future performance are necessarily subject to a high degree of uncertainty and no warranty of such projections is expressed or implied hereby.

–All corporate documents relating to this investment will be made available to an offeree and/or his offeree representative upon request to the company.

–The company shall be under no obligation whatsoever to sell or issue any securities referred to in this memorandum except pursuant to a duly executed stock purchase agreement between the company and the purchaser thereof.

INDEX